T0121364

✳ CELEBRATION FOR – JOURNEY OF *THE GREAT CIRCLE* ✳

This unique, heartfelt, and visionary book penetrates to the deepest questions of the human journey, and offers touching and inspiring poetic images to guide us. Oman Ken brings the wealth of his experience and deep insights as a welcome roadmap to awakening. I recommend Journey of *The Great Circle* to anyone dedicated to fathom the mysteries of life and advance on your own healing journey.

--- *Alan Cohen, bestselling author of* **A Course in Miracles Made Easy**

In his book, **Journey of *The Great Circle***, Oman brings forth "pearls" of wisdom - and has strung those pearls together in a compelling narrative and practice. Bottom line: If you find yourself going around in circles in life, go around THIS circle, and you will spiral to a higher and brighter view.

--- *Steve Bhaerman, aka Swami Beyondananda "cosmic comic" and co-author with Bruce Lipton of* **Spontaneous Evolution: Our Positive Future and a Way to Get There From Here.**

Oman's book inspires us to embark on a sacred journey and exploration of what life is truly about - and what really matters. Here is a book that can be utilized every day to polish the Diamond of our Souls.

--- *Rama Jyoti Vernon, co-founder of* **The Yoga Journal** *and author of* **Yoga: The Practice of Myth & Sacred Geometry**

With the poetry of a passionate artist - and the perspectives of an intuitive scientist, Oman Ken has written a visionary book. Utilizing his unique system of daily practices, he lays out the vision and pathway for a more peaceful and compassionate world.

--- *Reverend Max Lafser, Unity minister and former chairman of* **The Center For International Dialogue**

I know first-hand the power and beauty of a 365 daily transformation practice. Oman's deep reflection and soul searching has devoutly created this profound and poetic work. Use this book as a daily practice to soar into the heights of your soul. You will forever be transformed.

---*José R. Fuentes, Co-Founder and Facilitator of the Sedona Integral Group*

Oman's book, Journey of *The Great Circle,* is too rich with meaningful poetic and creative thinking not to be experienced. Through his 365 contemplative exercises, he brings a great gift to the human family for our next leap in wholeness. I celebrate this new work, for I know the reader will be assisted in their spiritual unfoldment.

--- *Bruce Kellogg, Unity minister*

Journey of *The Great Circle* is Oman Ken's epic masterpiece to passionately hone and master the best in us. Four seasonal volumes of brilliant creativity weaving consciousness, science, art, history, and evolutionary spirituality. Stunningly written and organized. You will be blessed.

--- *Enocha Ranjita Ryan, Transformational Healing Artist*

As a minister, I would highly recommend Oman's book to inspire other ministers with meaningful themes for Sunday talks. Each of the 365 contemplative narratives is rich with powerful ideas and inspiration. Oman's book is such a meaningful gift for humanity as well as a practical pathway to a better world at this crucial moment in human development.

--- *Marshall Norman, former Unity minister of Madison, Wisconsin*

Journey of
The Great Circle

DAILY CONTEMPLATIONS FOR CULTIVATING INNER FREEDOM
AND LIVING YOUR LIFE AS A MASTER OF FREEDOM

AUTUMN VOLUME

OMAN KEN

BALBOA.PRESS
A DIVISION OF HAY HOUSE

Copyright © 2021 Oman Ken.

All rights reserved. No part of this book may be used or reproduced by any means, graphic, electronic, or mechanical, including photocopying, recording, taping or by any information storage retrieval system without the written permission of the author except in the case of brief quotations embodied in critical articles and reviews.

This book is a work of non-fiction. Unless otherwise noted, the author and the publisher make no explicit guarantees as to the accuracy of the information contained in this book and in some cases, names of people and places have been altered to protect their privacy.

Balboa Press books may be ordered through booksellers or by contacting:

Balboa Press
A Division of Hay House
1663 Liberty Drive
Bloomington, IN 47403
www.balboapress.com
844-682-1282

Because of the dynamic nature of the Internet, any web addresses or links contained in this book may have changed since publication and may no longer be valid. The views expressed in this work are solely those of the author and do not necessarily reflect the views of the publisher, and the publisher hereby disclaims any responsibility for them.

The author of this book does not dispense medical advice or prescribe the use of any technique as a form of treatment for physical, emotional, or medical problems without the advice of a physician, either directly or indirectly. The intent of the author is only to offer information of a general nature to help you in your quest for emotional and spiritual well-being. In the event you use any of the information in this book for yourself, which is your constitutional right, the author and the publisher assume no responsibility for your actions.

Any people depicted in stock imagery provided by Getty Images are models,
and such images are being used for illustrative purposes only.
Certain stock imagery © Getty Images.

Cover art designed by Oman Ken – and created by Mark Gelotte.

Graphic art designed by Oman Ken – and created by Mark Gelotte.

Photography of Oman Ken by Charles Ruscher

ISBN: 978-1-9822-7191-6 (sc)
ISBN: 978-1-9822-7192-3 (e)

Print information available on the last page.

Balboa Press rev. date: 09/14/2021

✳ CONTENTS ✳
Themes and Metaphors of Autumn

✳ DEDICATION ✳

This book is dedicated to the teachers
who serve and educate the children of the world
pointing them to the discovery of their creative potential,

to the spiritual teachers
who help guide others to live a life of inner freedom
and discover who they really are,

and to the teachers of science
who help their students investigate the nature of reality
and "what is true".

It is of great advantage for us to be consciously aware
of our current philosophy of life
so we can continue to sculpt and hone our personal beliefs
into empowering beliefs that express ever-greater freedom
and more actively participate
in benevolently contributing our unique gifts and talents
to the positive progression of the world.

✳ WHAT IS – JOURNEY OF *THE GREAT CIRCLE* ✳

JOURNEY OF *THE GREAT CIRCLE* is a collection of 365 contemplative narratives designed as a daily transformative practice for the purpose of personal transformation. The annual collection of narratives is divided into four volumes, Winter, Spring, Summer, and Autumn each beginning on either the solstice or equinox. Each of the 365 narratives has a specific spiritual theme to help you gain a more expansive understanding of what really matters - and points you to how to live a life with peace of mind and inner freedom.

The various themes of the narratives involve insights from spirituality, quantum physics, the evolutionary perspective, the study of visionary archetypes, healing, and transformative practice. **Journey of *The Great Circle*** can be thought of as "a spiritual map of an awakening life".

A life of inner freedom is when one consciously realizes the perfection that's always unfolding within - and within all of life. Living with this awareness allows the natural states of peace, happiness, joy and harmony to effortlessly arise. It is a life of one who has devotedly learned to love others and all of life unconditionally - and who has gained the joyful awareness of serving the wellbeing of others. In these writings, one who attains this level of mastery is referred to as a **Master of Freedom**.

We are all natural-born storytellers with a mandate from *Life* to generate the most fulfilling and creative story of life we can imagine. Every day is a new opportunity to make our life story a little more glorious, a little more fulfilling, a little more creative. We are the authors of this story in every moment of our lives based on the intentions we choose, either consciously or unconsciously. For most people, in order to have the most glorious, fulfilling, creative, and peaceful life requires some form of spiritual practice necessitating conscious attention each day.

Journey of *The Great Circle* utilizes a transformative system of daily practices that can help you:

1) Experience a life of peace, happiness, joy, harmony, and fulfilling creative expression.

2) Prepare for the day's activities and surprises that await you so you can meet each situation from the "sanctuary" of heart wisdom, gratitude, and centeredness.

3) Connect to the inner guidance of the heart so you may live you life with ease and grace.

4) Learn to love every expression of life unconditionally.

5) Maintain a conscious alignment with *a Greater Power*. *A Greater Power* has been called myriad names, including but not limited to, *the Source of Life, the Infinite Presence of Love, God, the Great Spirit,* and *the Infinite Intelligence of the Universe.*

When **Journey of *The Great Circle*** is used on a daily basis it will help cultivate inner freedom and assist you in fulfilling your sacred destiny of an awakened life as a **Master of Freedom**.

To consciously know
what life is truly about
and what really matters
transforms everything.

✳ PREFACE – THE GENESIS ✳

I WAS STANDING ALONE on a large wooden stage in front of a thousand people performing my original songs with my two dear companions - my acoustic guitar and my lyrical voice. I had also created a photographic slide show to visually animate the poetic images of my songs, which projected on a large screen behind me.

As the strings of my guitar rang out, I was offering the last song of a two-week concert tour where I had traveled through the lush Northwest in late spring. As the musical notes of this final composition came to an end, I felt something was very wrong. I could feel a turbulent energy within my ailing body crashing through every cell. My physical form was in some kind of crisis, and from that moment on, my life would never be the same.

The Story of How This Book Came To Be

Life seems to lead each of us on an adventurous journey in which we must ultimately make important choices based on the many possible roads and different turns that come before us along the way. When we were young, most of us conjured up some sort of future vision about how our life would unfold when we grew older. Yet usually for most of us, there was a plethora of surprises and unpredictable twists along life's journey. This book is the surprising result of one of those twists.

In 2005, after numerous years of steadily declining health, a mysterious illness had become a major challenge, and I became deeply frustrated and depressed. I lost most of my physical energy and was very fatigued and exhausted. A heat sensation would rush up into my head each day accompanied by reddish flushing of my chest, neck, and head. At times I felt an internal shaking in my body that was strange, frightening, and uncomfortable. Because of these curious symptoms, I had to adjust my entire life. My musical career came to a halt, and I had to adapt to a new expression of who I was and what I did. I was no longer able to tour around the country performing concerts and retreats with my music. I lost all motivation and energy to record music in my home studio as I did in previous years. And I was barely able to perform at short local events - such as conferences and weddings in order to pay monthly bills.

Because of these increasing physical challenges, I spent many years and lots of money seeing numerous doctors, naturopaths, nutritionists, chiropractors, hypnotherapists, spiritual counselors, health wizards, and a "host of pretty cosmic characters" to find a resolution to my situation. I did get a little help here and there, but for the most part, nothing seemed to work ongoing. My health kept declining slowly. I got very angry at life. At God. At the *Infinite Intelligence* that was supposed to be good and fair. What was happening to me did not feel fair.

I thought of myself as "a spiritual person" because I did a host of "spiritual things". I meditated every day, read spiritual books, attended self-help workshops, exercised regularly, ate a fantastic array of organic food, projected what I thought was a positive attitude toward life, served people with my uplifting music, donated money to environmental organizations - and therefore in my mind,

I did everything "right". Why would someone like me, who is "spiritual" and is doing everything "right", suffer from a physical condition that felt so "wrong"? Over time, I was getting more and more depressed, even suicidal. After a long period of feeling this way, I got very tired of living a depressed life and decided to take more responsibility for my healing.

When I made this shift in awareness, one of the ways I chose to responsibly deal with my ongoing depression was to re-dedicate my life to my spiritual practice. I did this by spending more time in Nature, so I could deeply contemplate my personal situation. I wanted to find out what, if anything, I was supposed to learn about myself from this challenging opportunity I was dealing with.

At that time I had been living in Sedona, Arizona for eighteen years. I received the inner guidance to spend one day a week out in Nature alongside a beautiful wooded creek called Oak Creek and use this time to explore my inner spiritual quest. Each week at the water's edge I would spend five to seven hours in contemplation and inquiry, and then wrote down any insights or realizations. I wanted to use this time in Nature to gain insights about what I could discover about myself from my increasing health challenges and how they might relate to my life-long quest of spiritual awakening, however I understood it.

Thus this weekly ritual of sitting beside the creek, quieting my mind, and waiting began. And then insights started to come. And they continued to emerge each week with different spiritual themes and different life perspectives for me to consider. The thought came to me that it would be easier to remember these insights at a later time if I could find a simpler form to record them, rather than writing long paragraphs of prose as in a spiritual journal. Previously, I had done a lot of journal writing, but I noticed I had a tendency to not go back and read my journals very often. Therefore, I wanted to devise another way to record my thoughts.

I decided to use the basic circular form of the Native American medicine wheel with its four cardinal points and a center point. I picked four primary concepts of each theme or idea I was exploring during my contemplations and wrote them down in four short phrases or sentences in the location of the four cardinal directions (west, south, east and north).

I named these thematic circles Contemplation Circles. Each Contemplation Circle was focused around a spiritual theme that would help point me to *a Transcendent Reality* and to an expanded vision of living my life with inner freedom. I perceived these circles as spirtual maps of consciousness - or theme targets - or wheels of distinction that empowered and supported my spiritual journey and the restoration of my health. Through these ongoing contemplations, I have received beneficial insights that have served the wellbeing of my body, heart, and mind, and have helped me to expand the way I love and accept myself.

Over many years of working with these Contemplation Circles on a daily basis, I began to see applications for them in various aspects of my spiritual practice. They started to organically have a life of their own. I was inwardly guided regarding how to use them in contemplation practices, affirmative prayer, foundational transformative practices, and to gain ever-larger perspective of my life, including my physical challenges.

In 2007, I experienced a transformational workshop called the Big Mind Process facilitated by Genpo Roshi, a Buddhist teacher and author. I was deeply moved by the ability of this process to bring a person to a direct experience of profound states of transcendence so quickly and effectively. The next morning, I began to create my own Contemplation Circles around my experience of the Big Mind Process. It felt natural to use a set of specific circles in a sequential form in my daily meditations. The result was very powerful. The depth of my meditations took on a new level of sublime communion, and I began to notice a much greater experience of self-love and acceptance of my life.

I used this system of meditation for a year, continuing to receive fulfilling results - and was then guided to put this meditation process into a form that could be shared with others. The first book I wrote is called, **Master of Freedom**. This book was written as a universal creation story that portrays "The Great Story" of the creation of the Universe, the 13.8 billion year process of infinitely intelligent evolution. **Master of Freedom** is the archetypal story of life awakening throughout the Universe - in relation to our current human journey of transformation, the spirituality of humanity. It offers a poetic glimpse of our sacred destiny, which is to live an awakened life of inner freedom - and to learn to love all of life unconditionally.

Then in November of 2008, I was given the inner guidance to take 365 of my 400-plus Contemplation Circles and organize them in such a way as to write a thematic narrative for every day of the year. I started writing these narratives on December 21, 2008, the Winter Solstice. That year, I wrote a 350-word narrative for 365 consecutive days. This daily set of contemplative narratives, accompanied by its adjacent Contemplation Circle, I called **Journey of The Great Circle**.

I do not call myself a spiritual teacher, nor am I some kind of healer, psychological counselor, or expert of esoteric spiritual studies. I am simply a conscious person who is passionate about living life fully and discovering what really matters, but also a person, like many, who has suffered a great deal during my life adventure. Yet by some form of *grace*, I have embraced the conscious awareness to take responsibility for my healing, and through inner transformative work have gained a greater experience of inner freedom.

Initially, I did not begin this time of deep contemplation in Nature with a pre-conceived idea to write a book. The creative process of these contemplations grew over time on its own, and I feel this book was written through me rather than by me. I was benefiting tremendously from these contemplations and insights, living with greater peace, happiness, joy, and harmony, and my guidance informed me to put them into a book for the benefit of others.

The Daily Practice of Being an *Artist of Life*

JOURNEY OF *THE GREAT CIRCLE* is a daily transformative program to assist people interested in developing larger perspectives of what life is truly about in order to cultivate an ongoing experience of inner freedom and an awareness of loving oneself and others unconditionally. It uses *the evolutionary perspective* to help create an understanding of the "Bigger Picture" of our human reality.

This system of contemplative practices focuses on the daily practice of being an *artist of life* in which a person lives in a state of inner freedom, maintains an ongoing alignment with *Life*, and learns to effectively contribute his or her creative gifts and talents in service to others - and to all of life. In this series of narratives, living in inner freedom is described as an awakened individual (referred to as a **Master of Freedom**) who has discovered how to live life masterfully and who has learned to respond to every experience with gratitude, surrender, and complete acceptance of what is.

The insights from **Journey of *The Great Circle*** assist in understanding that this universal awakening is a part of the intrinsic evolution that's taking place everywhere in the Cosmos. Thus it's taking place on our little blue planet - and is also taking place within you and me. Every person has the potential to be a conscious self-reflective human being becoming aware of the natural unfolding of evolutionary principles within the Universe and throughout the Earth. When we become aware of, and deeply study, *the evolutionary perspective* (the unfolding perspective of the Universe that has been naturally evolving for 13.8 billion years) and we perceive how we are all an integral part of this constant and ever-expanding evolution, we then begin to understand that this *journey of spiritual awakening* is one of the most natural processes unfolding within every human being. It is just one step in the never-ending unfolding journey within a vast Universe of Infinite Awakenings.

The Intention for Journey of *The Great Circle*

This book is designed to assist individuals to respond to life's challenges with harmony and grace, as well as to understand the blessing and obligation it is to contribute one's unique gifts and talents to the creation of a more glorious world. In other words, these narratives are designed to inspire people to cultivate inner freedom and to joyously offer their creative gifts to others as an *artist of life*.

My intention in sharing this book
is that it be helpful
in discovering the magnificence
of who you really are.

My hope
is that the contemplative practices in this work
may aid you
to more easily navigate your life
to a place of peace and inner freedom.

❋ INTRODUCTION – POLISHING THE DIAMOND ❋

Bringing Light to *the Art of Life*

IMAGINE WALKING THROUGH AN ART MUSEUM that displays many exquisite masterpieces of paintings and sculpture. Now visualize that it's late at night when all of the lights are turned off - and every room is completely dark. In this moment you would not be able to see anything in the museum. All of the magnificent works of art would be right in front of you, but without any light to illuminate them, you couldn't enjoy them.

Now imagine that you light a match. The sudden light from the match would allow you to get a glimpse of some of the artistic majesty around you. Yet if you turned on a strong flashlight, it would provide even more illumination for you to enjoy a bigger spectrum of the art collection. And, of course, if the main lights in the museum were suddenly turned on, you would be able to appreciate the total experience of beauty and grace from all the masterpieces around you.

Certainly before the overhead lights were turned on, the art and sculpture were right there close to you the entire time, but were veiled and hidden in the dark. But with the aid of the light, you were able to observe what was always present.

Similar to the lit match, the flashlight, or the main lights in the museum, ever-greater spiritual awareness (ever-larger perspectives of what our life is truly about and what really matters) is like a powerful light that comes into "the mansion of our heart and mind" to illuminate the reality we perceive. More expansive perspectives of reality transform "the darkness of our mind", so we can easily see the truth, goodness, and beauty that is always there. What is always present within us, and what *the Essence of Life* yearns for us to fully experience, is the radiant magnificence of who we really are. We are constantly being invited by *Life* to rediscover our ever-present magnificence - by turning on the light of our conscious awareness.

There is a constant stream of *Transcendent Energy*, a *Field of Unlimited Creativity*, which surrounds us and permeates within us in every moment. This *Boundless and Transcendent Creativity* is who we really are. Yet sometimes "the darkness" of our habitual belief in separation, fear, and other loveless thoughts can inhibit us from seeing our own beauty, our own "magnificent work of art". Every one of us is a living masterpiece that is ever-evolving, a creative work in progress. Our life is the outer creative expression of our inner development. We are continually learning to unveil the exquisite beauty and majesty of who we truly are. Each day we fashion the blank canvas of our life to create the next version of our masterpiece. Every day we're embarked on a journey of learning to artfully live our lives in a way that expresses the natural states of peace, happiness, joy, and harmony. These are the natural states of our *True Eternal Nature*.

Greater spiritual awareness is what naturally nurtures the creative artist within us - or what we can call *the artist of life*. There are many time-tested ways to cultivate *the artist* within us - and to turn on "the light of our spiritual awareness", including meditation, self-inquiry, deep contemplation, and devotional prayer - to name a few. Yet another important way is to fully recognize that in the present moment, our life is always unfolding perfectly just as it is - for life simply is the way it is. This sublime recognition is a radical acceptance of our life.

The Daily Practice of *the Art of Life*

Like being helplessly and powerfully drawn toward some mysterious invisible magnet, we seem to be constantly pulled by unseen forces that attempt to compel us to seek for something other than what we already are. Our modern society, as well as the unconscious people around us, sometimes tell us that we are not OK the way we are, that we are somehow flawed and need to be fixed, that something within us is not right, and that what is wrong in us must be changed into what others believe is right.

The unconscious result of our society's dysfunctional conditioning is that it keeps pulling us away from the creative power of the present moment. This kind of social conditioning persists in attempting to catapult us to some future reality where, at some illusory time, our lives will hopefully be fixed, changed, holy, or enlightened. It falsely promises that we will finally be transformed into what we've been taught by others to believe life should actually look like.

If we habitually succumb to "the mysterious pull of this magnet", this collective illusion propagated within our society, then we typically begin our personal quest to be fixed, or to rid ourselves of our flaws, by first trying to eliminate our suffering. And sometimes from a religious point of view, this illusory quest compels us to attempt the pursuit of spiritual enlightenment - or some kind of spiritual transformation, so we may someday be like the elevated saints and gurus we have learned to venerate.

Of course there is nothing wrong with gaining inspiration from the wealth of great spiritual wayshowers that have come before us, especially if they're pointing us to our own innate power and invincible *True Nature*. Yet seeking to be fixed, as if we were broken, can become the kind of illusory spiritual quest in which we join millions of other people across the globe in seeking something to magically transform our lives, but which in actuality, we already have and already are. *We already are, and have always been, the perfect expression of truth, goodness, and beauty that the Infinite Intelligence of the Universe perfectly unfolds within us through a natural process of universal and personal evolution.* We are all living in a boundless *Field of Unlimited Creativity* which is always present to further our inner development and spiritual evolution.

As we intentionally open our heart so we may explore an even deeper and more meaningful spiritual quest, we begin to feel the inner attraction of an authentic "spiritual magnet", our true *journey of awakening.* This *journey of discovery* is primarily about the full realization of who we really are. This "attraction" is the natural tug of *the Transcendent Impulse* within us. It is the natural impulse to learn that, in the present moment, our life is unfolding perfectly just as it is.

Over time we begin to recognize the perfection unfolding within the creative expressions in every form of life. We are part of that perfection which includes each living creature on our planet and every phenomenal structure within the Universe. This awareness allows us to be truly grateful for everything, to humbly surrender our attachments and resistance, to fully accept ourselves just as we are, and to celebrate the essential Oneness of which we are a part.

This is *Life's* universal invitation to love and accept ourselves completely and unconditionally with all of our individual flaws and personality traits. It's a heightened recognition that the challenging parts of our life are not problems, but rather sacred gifts we can use to "polish the diamond" within us. We use these gifts so we may transform into a more radiant expression of our highest self. We attain this awareness - not by being habitually attached to getting rid of our suffering or our challenges - but by embracing each challenge as "a gift in disguise" offered for our personal and collective transformation. These are life's exquisite opportunities to let our pain or suffering point us to what our life is truly about - and what really matters.

As we arrive at this level of spiritual awareness, we become immune to the societal influences and programming of "the magnet of dysfunctional conditioning". We then experience a transformative shift from living under the unconscious urge of constantly seeking for what we do not have - to celebrating the magnificence of who we already are and joyously living *the art of life*.

Being and Becoming

Living our lives in the present moment is where true creativity exists, as well as the genuine experience of unconditional love. Authentically living in present moment awareness, or Presence, allows us to be consciously aware of two fundamental and paradoxical streams of life that are constantly expressing within us: *Being* and *Becoming*.

Being is the absolute reality where everything in our life is unfolding perfectly just as it is. A life that is unfolding perfectly is one that lives in the sacred sanctuary of present moment awareness. With this awareness there's a knowing that because of the perfection in our life, there is nothing to do and nowhere to go, and that nothing needs to be changed, altered or fixed. *Being* is also an awareness of the Oneness within all of life, and in that Perfect Oneness rests the experience of true happiness and peace of mind.

At the same time, living in Presence allows us to experience the paradoxical and complimentary stream of life called *Becoming*. The journey of *Becoming* is the constant natural yearning within us to develop our highest potential, to strive for ever-higher levels of awareness, to expand into new horizons and uncharted territory of unlimited possibilities, and to poetically "reach for the stars". This ongoing personal growth and inner development comes from an intrinsic longing to contribute to the creation of a more glorious world within an awareness of joy and creativity, rather than from an awareness of needing to fix something that is wrong with us - or the unconscious attachment to relieve our suffering.

Cultivating Inner Freedom

There are many beautifully written self-help books, which certainly play an important role in elevating a person's conscious awareness and alleviating suffering. As it has been already stated, **Journey of The Great Circle** is not about helping you change the outer circumstances of your lives, fix your emotional or psychological flaws, or get rid of your problems. These writings aim to inspire you to live a life of devoted practice so as to cultivate inner freedom, self-love, and an unconditional love for all of life. Yet with this wealth of self-cultivation, the areas of one's life are constructively affected. This book is also designed to point you to the conscious awareness of your *True Eternal Nature*, the supreme holiness and magnificence of who you really are.

It's pretty obvious that everyone has their own set of difficult opportunities to deal with, and there doesn't appear to be any way to bypass life's many challenges. Some challenges can be very hard to cope with, yet challenge is one of the most natural parts of evolving life. For without the dynamic challenges, chaos, and turbulence within the Universe there would be no galaxies, nor stars, nor planets. Thus there would be no intelligent life on Earth, and there would be no conscious awakening within you and me.

Therefore, with intention, we can choose to use our challenges as sacred gifts in order to become ever more free. We can make use of these opportunities to consciously develop a more awakened awareness, for true healing is learning to maintain a perfect balance within us that supports the evolution of all of life. No matter how much money we have, how great our health may be, how wonderful our marriage or significant relationship is, or how successful our career may be unfolding, we will always be presented with challenging situations that will invite us to expand our ability to experience true inner freedom.

Inner freedom does not come from changing the external conditions of our lives, but is fostered from how we're able to respond to the events and challenges of our life from inside the chamber of our heart. The heart is the integral part of us we must keep open and aligned with *the Source of Life*, so the sublime energy of *Limitless Love* can continuously flow through us unimpeded.

Embodying Inner Freedom

Inner freedom is the unconditional love and acceptance of ourselves and others in which we fully realize that our life is unfolding perfectly just as it is. Since the nature of life is to move through continuous cycles of order and chaos, balance and imbalance, challenges will always be an intrinsic and important part of our ever-evolving life. A masterful ability to love and accept life just the way it is, simply witnessing these experiences without judgment, allows for inner freedom to be embodied within the everyday unfolding of life's constant stream of challenges and treasures.

Just as turning on the main lights in a darkened museum allows us to see all the artistic masterpieces present, as we illuminate the light of our own awareness to the supreme majesty and magnificence of who we are, we re-establish our ability to live in self-mastery. In these writings, a person who realizes and lives with this elevated awareness is referred to as a **Master of Freedom**.

Transformative Practice

This innate yearning to embody inner freedom and joyously express our unique creativity is enhanced by developing a system of personal practice that helps us consciously live our visionary intentions. Through the use of daily transformative practices, we "polish the diamond of our inner being" and use the personal expressions of our creativity to help manifest a more peaceful and compassionate world. Transformative practice is what establishes new belief systems, new world views, new perspectives of life, and new behavior. Practice is what also slowly eliminates destructive habits and dysfunctional patterns in our life.

As we develop a more expanded awareness, "life becomes practice" and "practice becomes life". And both our life and our practice are informed and guided by consciously living in a state of Presence, a state of present moment awareness. From this state, we practice *the art of life*, like a musician practices his or her instrument, or a painter practices his or her craft, to co-create with life in sculpting a more beautiful world. Whether we practice the piano or tennis, compose a symphony, develop a life-enhancing personality trait, or help to relieve hunger on our planet, transformative practice is all about living in the joy of being an *artist of life*. It's about jumping into the natural stream of evolving life that inwardly directs us towards truth, goodness, and beauty - and towards expressions of unconditional love and service to others.

The essence of this book is intended to inspire and provide the mechanisms for the power of daily practice. Each day presents a unique awareness perspective to contemplate regarding the nature of your life. Each day provides an opportunity to expand your awareness of what your life is truly about - and what really matters. It is of great benefit to bring these contemplations out into the glory of Nature - to sit next to a creek - or lie upon the earth at the top of a hill - or lean against a tall tree. As you exercise the "muscles" of your *body, heart, mind, and Spirit* each day with steady determination and commitment, you are assisting *Life* in creatively sculpting its next expression of awakening within you.

Remember that you already are, and have always been, a supremely gifted *artist of life*. There is no one else who can create the exquisite masterpieces which only you can create. So while you enjoy your daily practice as you read and contemplate each day's theme within this book of narratives, you are practicing *the art of life*. And remember that your daily practice is not only for your personal benefit. We are all intimately connected as one global family as we ascend the infinite ladder of awareness. Our daily practice benefits all the men, women, children, and myriad creatures of the world. Practice well.

You Are A Diamond

You are a perfect diamond
    Longing to become more perfect
        A luminescent jewel
            Shimmering upon the necklace of this ephemeral world
                Forged from the supreme fire
                    Within the heart of the Universe

You are a multifaceted gem of sublime majesty and grace
    Through which *Life* focuses its celestial starlight
        So it may glisten endlessly within you

You are a beloved *artist of life*
    Fashioning unparalleled hues upon the blank canvas of each new day
        To create the next rendering of your magnificent masterpiece

You are an invincible prism of the *Soul*
    Chiseled into form so *the Fullness* of the Cosmos can savor
        More of the luminous spectrum of its sensual wonders and hallowed glories

You are an ascending aeronaut spiraling heavenwards
    Climbing the infinite ladder of possibility
        Navigating tumultuous storms and immaculate skies
            Terrestrial chaos and galactic order
                The sacred gifts you use to share the omniscient nature of your truest self

You are a sovereign sculptor of untethered intentions
    Each one polishing the ever-effulgent diamond of your life
        So you may launch new portals of pristine freedom
            For the invisible lines of destiny to dance through you

Your mission - to dance with the *Light*
    Your purpose - to polish the perfection
        Your meaning of it all - to give for the good of all

It's just what diamonds
    Who spend their life *Being*
        In the course of *Becoming*
            Do

Everything in the vast Universe
is being creatively shaped into form,
now and forever,
by the unfathomable intelligent artistry
of the limitless *Field of Love*.

✳ HOW TO BENEFIT FROM THIS BOOK ✳

The Daily Narratives and Contemplation Circles

JOURNEY OF *THE GREAT CIRCLE* has been designed to provide a set of contemplative narratives of various spiritual themes to be used as a daily transformative practice for cultivating peace of mind and inner freedom. Engaging daily in this form of inner development, especially for an entire year, you will be inwardly pointed to the most natural ways to experience greater peace, happiness, joy, and harmony.

Each of the 365 contemplative themes has a narrative displayed on the left page and a corresponding Contemplation Circle on the right. The Contemplation Circle illustrates a short summary of the daily narrative in four concise statements or words. Each Contemplation Circle can be used to quickly reconnect and summarize the primary ideas that have been described in the narrative.

The Contemplation Circles are typically read in the clockwise direction starting with the north node (top quadrant) yet there are often variations of how the Circles can be read. Many have arrows pointing in a specific direction for further contemplation. Generally, the counter-clockwise direction of the Circles represents the evolution of consciousness, and the clockwise direction represents the evolution of creation.

The Four Seasonal Volumes

The complete set of 365 contemplative narratives has been divided into four seasonal volumes. Each has a specific theme for its series of daily practices. The Winter Volume is oriented toward practices for the **cultivation of spiritual wellbeing**; the Spring Volume for **wellbeing of the mind**; the Summer Volume for **wellbeing of the heart**; and the Autumn Volume for **wellbeing of the body**.

Each of the four volumes contains sixteen primary Contemplation Circles that are repeated in all four volumes. The specific Contemplation Circle is the same within each volume, but the narrative is different, allowing you to explore and gain a deeper understanding of the main theme.

How to Use the First Two Seasonal Narratives – September 22nd and 23rd

The first two narratives of this volume, September 22nd and September 23rd, explore the spiritual meaning and transcendent qualities of the autumn season. Both of these narratives have two dates printed at the top of the page. This is because the autumn equinox, the first day of autumn, will usually occur on one of those two dates depending on the relationship of the Earth's orbit with the Sun for any given year. The title of the first narrative is written as "Gifts of Autumn – September 22 or 23" and the second is written as "Qualities Within the Seasons of Life – September 22 or 23".

When the autumn equinox takes place on September 22nd, read the first two narratives as they are sequentially laid out. When the autumn equinox occurs on September 23rd, read the narrative entitled "Qualities Within the Seasons of Life" first, and then read "Gifts of Autumn" on September 23rd, the actual day of the autumn equinox for that year.

Transformative Practices

A primary intention of this book is to encourage the use of daily transformative practice as a means to discover effective ways to embody and anchor the ideas and concepts into the heart as a direct experience. Consistent self-cultivation is the center of spiritual development. Throughout each of the four volumes there are a series of transformative practices that may be incorporated into one's daily life. The prominent focus is based upon four foundational transformative practices. These are:

1) meditation, 2) contemplation, 3) appreciation, and 4) prayer.

It is suggested for the spiritual development of the reader that some form of each of these four practices be experienced frequently. Change usually happens slowly and incrementally through constant repetition on a daily basis. In order to master a sport, an art, a science, or a business, one must practice ardently. It takes this same effort to develop our spiritual nature.

You may be interested in exploring the suggested meditative practices in the narrative from January 14th called "Meditation Practices" in the Winter Volume or explore various meditation practices that you discover elsewhere. You can also explore a specific form of the practice of contemplation in the narrative from April 5th called "A Contemplation Practice" in the Spring Volume. Daily appreciation is seemingly straightforward, yet you may get additional inspiration from the July 6th narrative called "Spheres of Appreciation" in the Summer Volume. And you may deepen your exploration of the power of prayer in the October 8th narrative called "The Practice of Prayer" in the Autumn Volume.

Daily Affirmation Statements

At the top of each contemplative narrative is a short affirmation printed in italics. This affirmation expresses one of the key themes within the daily narrative. For best results, the affirmation can be repeated at various times throughout the day. In the back of the book, all affirmation statements are printed for each day within a given volume. They are designed to be copied onto a piece of 8.5" x 11" paper. You can cut along the dotted lines and then take the individual affirmation with you as a reminder of the theme you are embracing for that specific day.

Visionary Archetypes as Transformative Practice

A visionary archetype is similar to the image of a distant horizon, for it represents qualities and virtues of ever-higher levels of human consciousness that we can envision on our personal horizon, yet desire to embody right now in our life. It is a poetic image of our greater potential or possibility, which we have yet to realize, until we have bravely traveled past boundaries of our current beliefs about who we think we are.

Visionary archetypes are symbolic templates that point us to higher stages of inner development and to the qualities and realms of creative expression we strive to achieve. They can be thought of as pictorial representations of superior moral qualities which can empower and motivate us to reach for something greater in ourselves, a promise of a more positive future for our life.

We can use these archetypes as a spiritual tool and blueprint of potential to assist us in imagining a more perfect expression of ourselves, and to hold within us an expansive vision of what is possible. It is suggested that each person seek their own inner guidance regarding how to use these visionary archetypes as a means to envision and embody the highest possibilities of who they really are.

Throughout each volume there are four sets of visionary archetypes that can be used as a transformative practice to envision and embody one's creative potential and spiritual sovereignty. The four sets are: 1) The Archetypes of Spiritual Awakening, 2) The Archetypes of Life Mastery, 3) The Archetypes of Higher Knowledge, and 4) The Archetypes of Conscious Contribution.

The Archetypes of Life Mastery, the Archetypes of Higher Knowledge, and the Archetypes of Conscious Contribution are all visionary archetypes. The Archetypes of Spiritual Awakening are four archetypes that represent our *spiritual journey*, or *journey of awakening*. The ultimate culmination of our *journey of awakening* is consciously living a life of inner freedom represented by the archetype of the **Master of Freedom**. All of the other visionary archetypes are facets of our unlimited potential, pointing to our sacred destiny as a **Master of Freedom**.

A Tool of Inner Guidance

There are additional ways to benefit from this book other than consecutively reading the daily narratives. You can also utilize this book to find guidance and inspiration by opening any volume to any place within the seasonal narratives, reading that specific narrative, and discovering how the narrative applies to your life at that moment. In this way, **Journey of The Great Circle** becomes "a tool of inner guidance" and can be used when you need a form of spiritual guidance or when you are seeking a moment of inspiration for your day.

The Great Circle as "a Spiritual Map of an Awakening Life"

The Great Circle is a map of consciousness and creation. It is a way to clearly understand the dynamics at play in our world and in our life. **The Great Circle** illustrates how our <u>inner development</u> determines and gives creative shape to how our <u>external reality</u> is expressed in our life. It portrays the universal dynamics relating to <u>our inward expansion of awareness</u> mirrored as <u>our outward creative expression</u>.

The primary function of **The Great Circle** as a transformative tool is to simply portray a useful collection of thoughts and ideas for the purpose of deeply comprehending the nature of existence. With this awareness we develop a greater understanding of what our life is truly about and thus cultivate an unconditional love for each expression of life.

There are many examples of traditional iconic images that represent **The Great Circle**, such as the Yin Yang symbol, the Star of David, the Medicine Wheel, and the Sacred Cross. In this book, the following symbolic image, *"The Great Circle* Portal - a Window Into *Being* and *Becoming"*, is also used to visually illustrate **The Great Circle** as "A Spiritual Map of an Awakening Life".

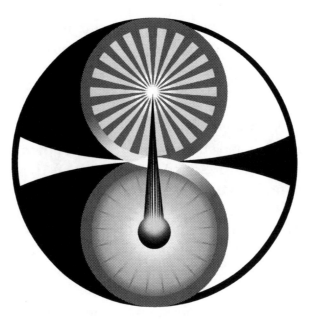

This image has been placed at each chapter of the contemplative practices to subconsciously assist you in deepening your understanding of the universal dynamics that are at play in the world and in your life. It can also be used to cultivate a comprehension of your purpose in life, your life mission, the meaning of life, and an awareness of your *True Nature*. Here is the significance of the Circle:

First, there is both a vertical line and a horizontal line within the larger circle of the image. The vertical line represents *Being* - or *Infinite Intelligence* - or God *(the Divine Transcendent* aspect of life). The horizontal line represents *Becoming,* our *journey of inner development,* our *spiritual journey.*

Over the vertical line within the large circle there is a Vertical Infinity Sign (a figure eight) that perpetually descends to the bottom of the circle and then ascends to the top repeating continuously. This Vertical Infinity Sign represents the constant yearning of our current physical lifetime (bottom circle) to merge with *the Transcendent, the Source of Life* (top circle) and *the Transcendent* (top circle) that constantly yearns to manifest ever-new expressions of creativity in our current physical lifetime (bottom circle). This natural and constant yearning (which is both the longing for spiritual awakening and spiritual embodiment) exists within us and within all forms of life. It is called *the Transcendent Impulse.*

The Vertical Infinity Sign represents *the Transcendent Impulse* as the top circle merging with the bottom circle - Consciousness merging with Creation - God merging with the Universe - *Divinity* merging with humanity - *Spirit* merging with the body - *Infinite Intelligence* merging with the myriad forms of Nature - *The One* merging with the Many.

The top circle within the Vertical Infinity Sign is a cosmic tunnel, like an inter-dimensional portal or quantum vortex, constantly moving towards the center. The center of this circle represents God, *the Source of All That Is, Universal Consciousness.*

The bottom circle has a Black Centerpoint or Singularity which represents material form, the physical body, or a focused point of creative manifestation.

The thick black line from the center of the top circle to the center of the bottom circle represents the perpetual alignment and Oneness of our current physical incarnation with *the Divine Transcendent (God, Infinite Intelligence, the Source of Life).*

Master of Freedom Logo

This image represents our *Fully Awakened Self,* one's *True Eternal Nature* completely experienced and lived within one's physical body. It is the embodied realization of a person who lives a life of inner freedom, loves all of life unconditionally, and serves the good of all with their creative gifts and talents. It is every person's sacred destiny to embody the *Awakened Self* and fully experience life as a **Master of Freedom.**

Infinite Awakenings Logo

This image represents the perpetual evolution - or the constant "awakenings" - that naturally take place in every aspect of Nature symbolized by the diamond, the flower, the bird, and the human being.

At one time, millions of years ago, there was only a plethora of green vegetation on the planet. The beautiful manifestation of flowers had not yet arrived on the evolutionary scene. But over time and with gradual development, evolving life eventually found a way to empower a brand new emergent form to arise; the very first flower.

For the first flower to take shape on Earth, a radical shift in consciousness was required within the plant kingdom. This new expression of vegetative form could poetically be thought of as an "enlightenment" or "awakening" of the plant kingdom. A similar kind of radical shift in consciousness also occurred in the mineral kingdom with the first diamond - and millions of years later, in the animal kingdom with the first flight of a bird.

The same expansive evolutionary impulses in consciousness are happening right now throughout the world as they continuously have from the beginning of the Universe. Each person on the planet is now, consciously or unconsciously, evolving and developing into his or her destiny as an awakened human.

The Story of Awakening Within the First Narratives

In the conceptual design of **Journey of The Great Circle**, there is a poetic interweaving of themes within the first four contemplative narratives of each volume. Together these four narratives reveal "a hidden archetypal story" regarding every person's *spiritual journey of discovery*.

The first four narratives in the Autumn Volume are:
1) Gifts of Autumn
2) Qualities Within the Seasons of Life
3) The Great Story of Awakening
4) *Journey of Awakening*

The daily practice of contemplative narratives can easily be accomplished without the understanding of this conceptual design. Yet for those who are interested, the concept of how these four narratives are woven together is described at the end of the book in the section called "The Story of Awakening Within the First Narratives".

Life as Practice

One of the foundational themes within the contemplative narratives of **Journey of The Great Circle** is to experience the spiritual power of daily transformative practice. In order to embody something that we desire in our life, it usually requires dedicated practice and committed perseverance.

When we intend to align our awareness with *the Source of Life*, it also takes practice to embody this alignment as an ongoing experience in every moment. When we intend to be grateful for all that we're learning from every experience of our life, it takes practice. When we intend to live a life of inner freedom, it takes practice. When we intend to love all of life unconditionally, it takes practice.

If a person is committed to the practice of learning to play the piano, in the beginning it requires a lot of focused attention on every detail of how to move the fingers across the keyboard. Yet over time as one implements daily exercises and perseverance, eventually playing the piano becomes natural and effortless. It is as if some invisible *Field of Energy* is playing through the person - as the piano becomes a natural creative extension of his or her body.

The same thing occurs with spiritual practice. For with the daily dedication of placing our attention on the spiritual desires of our heart, we naturally and effortlessly learn how to respond to life's glories and challenges with ease, grace, and conscious responsibility. This is what these 365 daily contemplative narratives are designed to help you manifest in your life. There comes a sacred moment on our journey of discovery when we deeply recognize the authentic joy of practicing each day to be the best version of ourselves. And in that sublime moment, daily transformative practice becomes one of the most fulfilling and meaningful facets of our life.

Therefore practice with all the vibrant joy in your heart so you may walk through this life, gracefully and naturally, as a **Master of Freedom**.

The young bud of a rose holds the promise
of a beautiful blossom and a delightful fragrance
which lies waiting at the true center of the flower.

The vast creativity and unlimited potential
within the essence of every person
lies waiting at the silent center of one's being.

DAILY CONTEMPLATION PRACTICES FOR AUTUMN

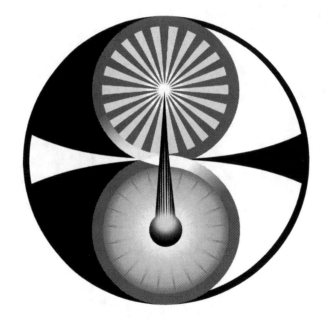

1

THE DANCE
OF THE INFINITE
SEASONS

GIFTS OF AUTUMN

Celebrating the seasonal cycles is a way to gain new insights into the true purpose of my life.

Once again, for those who live in the northern hemisphere of the Earth,
It's the time for the annual terrestrial event called *the autumn equinox*,
The cyclic patterning within Nature when the path of the Sun overhead
(Which travels from east in the morning to west in the evening)
Provides us with a moment of equal daytime and equal night,
In other words - with an equal amount of light and darkness.

This yearly "midpoint of the Sun's path" between the two solstices symbolizes within our lives
A natural quest to establish a balance of both our internal and external worlds,
Our masculine and feminine energies, our expansive and expressive yearnings.

This is the time during the year when the apparent path of the Sun that journeys above us
Returns to the same trajectory across the sky as at the moment of *the spring equinox*
(Which also represents a balance of light and darkness - of activity and rest),
And yet *the equinox of autumn* reveals its own particular qualities.

Autumn symbolizes a time of consciously deepening our commitment to our spiritual work
Arising from "the seeds of intention we've planted in the gardens of our heart during spring"
Which have yielded an abundance of opportunities to learn what really matters,
Develop our awareness, and gain new insights into the true purpose of our life.

It also represents a time to harvest the vision of what we believe is possible,
Something new within us that's now being manifested into outward expression,
As well as a time to reap the bounty of what we've **"planted in the spring of our life"**.

Inherent in this season is "a natural air of appreciation", for autumn stands for
A time in which we cultivate our **gratitude** for all of the blessings around us
And for what we're learning from every experience we encounter.

Today as we gaze into the wonders of Nature,
We can observe the leaves of deciduous trees beginning to change colors,
The fibrous stalks of green vegetation starting to become brittle,
And the luscious flowers of our gardens in the early stage of withering.

Nature reminds us that it's a time to further explore and **develop our unlimited potential**,
That life is in a process of constant change, maturation, and renewal,
And that renewal and maturation are always taking place within us as well.

The occasion of the autumnal harvest traditionally brings together a community of people
Offering ways to celebrate one another and strengthen a reverence for life.

For autumn also points us to a deeper recognition of our interconnectedness with all of life
And **the joy of contributing our gifts to the wellbeing of others - and the world**.

This time of the transformational season of autumn and the annual celebration of the harvest
Is a reminder for us to celebrate our lives every day of the year.

Circle of the Gifts of Autumn
(Transcendent Qualities Within the Seasons of Life)

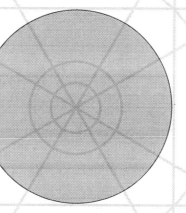

INWARD EXPANSION
A TIME TO REAP THE
BOUNTY - AND HARVEST
THE VISION - OF WHAT
I BELIEVE IS POSSIBLE,
WHICH I'VE "PLANTED IN
THE SPRING OF MY LIFE"

CONTRIBUTION TO THE WORLD
A TIME TO CELEBRATE MY
INTERCONNECTEDNESS
WITH ALL OF LIFE
AND THE JOY OF SERVING
THE WELLBEING OF
OTHERS AND THE WORLD

GRATITUDE
A TIME TO DEEPEN
MY GRATITUDE
FOR THE BLESSINGS
OF MY LIFE
- AND FOR WHAT
I'M LEARNING FROM
ALL OF MY EXPERIENCES

LIMITLESS DEVELOPMENT
A TIME TO FURTHER
DEVELOP MY POTENTIAL
REMEMBERING MY LIFE
IS IN A PROCESS
OF CONSTANT CHANGE
AND RENEWAL

QUALITIES WITHIN THE SEASONS OF LIFE

Life is a mirror reflecting back to me all that longs to be developed, released, and transformed.

Every colorful flower produces its own distinct fragrance,
    Each type of fruit offers its own particular taste,
        Every sliver of a rainbow's spectrum has a completely different hue,
            And as well, each season of the year expresses its own unique qualities.

Each of the four seasons - **winter**, **spring**, **summer**, and **autumn**,
    Represents specific love-centered qualities and visionary characteristics
    Which can help connect us to what really matters
    And point us to insights that support our unfolding wellbeing.

By contemplating and exploring **the qualities of each season**,
    We can gain greater awareness of what our life is truly about
    And learn to cultivate our innate yearning to love more fully.

For example, there's a certain quality of autumn that inwardly points us to dedicating our life
    To developing our potential - and expanding our awareness of what really matters,
        For the essence of this season reminds us to live our life with inner freedom
        Which then points us to the qualities of alignment and renewal in winter.

In spring, there is an intrinsic desire to outwardly express the gifts of our personal creativity,
    While in summer, there's a natural longing to deepen our kindness and to serve others.

Another quality that winter symbolizes is a quiet period of self-reflection and spiritual inquiry,
    And this solace empowers our inborn yearning for self-care, or contribution to oneself,
        Whereas contribution to family is an integral quality which corresponds to spring,
        Contribution to community is central within the season of summer,
        And contribution to the world prevails within autumn.

In spring, there's a seasonal urge to contribute our creative gifts and talents,
    While summer represents a natural drive
        Toward deepening our love and compassion for others.

The annual seasonal wheel turns to autumn again, which points us to our inner development
    And that we're constantly being invited by *Life* to learn to love unconditionally,
        Whereas winter attunes us to being fully present in every moment.

Finally, summer also represents the awakening and transformative quality of surrender,
    Autumn, the quality of gratitude for what we're learning from every experience,
        Winter directs us toward an awareness of our Oneness with all of life,
        And spring is aligned with the quality of acceptance
            In which we embrace that our life is unfolding perfectly just as it is.

Metaphorically, each season seems to have its own distinct fragrance, its own particular taste,
    Its own individual and unparalleled hue - in other words, its own transcendent qualities,
        And we're constantly invited to investigate these qualities ever deeper within us
        So we may discover for ourselves "the seasons of our awakening".

Circle of Qualities Within the Seasons of Life

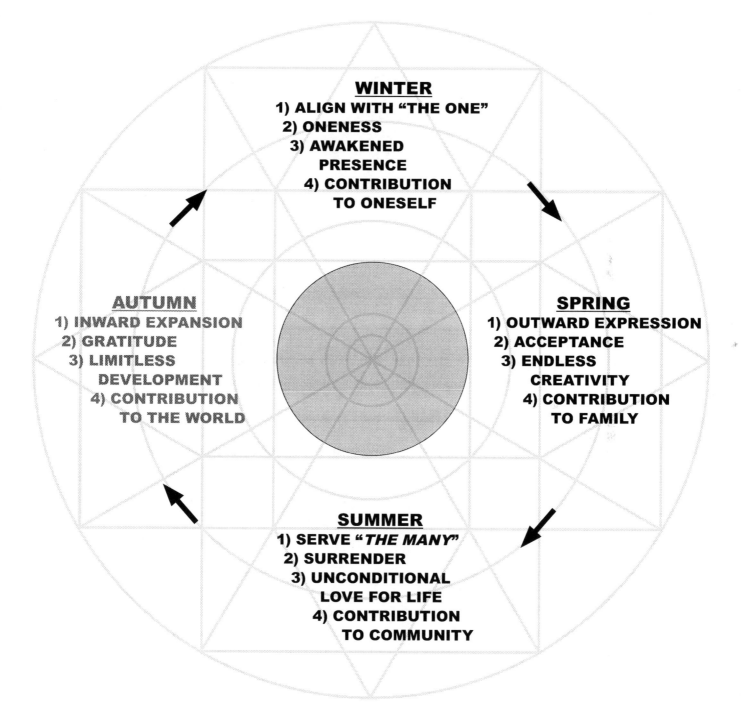

WINTER
1) ALIGN WITH "THE ONE"
2) ONENESS
3) AWAKENED
   PRESENCE
4) CONTRIBUTION
   TO ONESELF

AUTUMN
1) INWARD EXPANSION
2) GRATITUDE
3) LIMITLESS
   DEVELOPMENT
4) CONTRIBUTION
   TO THE WORLD

SPRING
1) OUTWARD EXPRESSION
2) ACCEPTANCE
3) ENDLESS
   CREATIVITY
4) CONTRIBUTION
   TO FAMILY

SUMMER
1) SERVE *"THE MANY"*
2) SURRENDER
3) UNCONDITIONAL
   LOVE FOR LIFE
4) CONTRIBUTION
   TO COMMUNITY

THE GREAT STORY OF AWAKENING

Every morning I align my awareness with the Source of Life - and with what really matters.

The four principal qualities depicted within the season of autumn are each integral components
Contributing to a much larger pattern of an ever-unfolding story of spiritual awakening.

Autumn's qualities of inward expansion, gratitude, development, and contribution to the world,
Are four key components of four different "chapters of life" or "systems of awareness"
Which together form *a journey of transformation - a journey of awakening.*

Most people have heard the saying, "A circle has no beginning and no end"
And yet, paradoxically at the same time, each distinct point along a circle
Can also be thought of as "a beginning point" - or "an ending point".

We begin with the first chapter of our *journey of awakening*, **The Great Circle**, (see Sept. 28th)
Derived from joining the first quality from each of the four seasons on the previous page.

This includes our inward expansion (our learning), our outward expressions (our creativity),
Aligning with "*The One*" (with *the Source of Life)*, and serving "*The Many*" (all beings).

This chapter of our story declares that for every higher stage of development we attain,
New forms of our creative expression, or of "healing", are then manifested in the world.

The four **Pillars of Awakening** are essential qualities for our spiritual growth (see Oct. 12th)
Which, as we embody them, transform us from living our life in fear - to living in *Love,*
And, thus, they form the second chapter of our transformative story.

When we become mired and confused by the challenges of daily living,
Surrender, acceptance, and Oneness may, at times, seem more difficult to access,
Whereas gratitude for what we're learning from every experience of life
Is always a good "beginning point" to help transform any situation.

Next - limitless development, unconditional love, endless creativity, and awakened presence
Are all key facets of the **Master of Freedom**, our Fully Awakened Self, (see Jan. 21st)
The full integration of our Compassionate Heart merged with *Infinite Presence.*

The unfolding story leads us to the last chapter, **the Spheres of Contribution**,
In which contribution to the world is a most natural expression of our *awakening journey*
Rising out of contribution to oneself, family, and community. (see Nov. 13th)

And as our consciousness continues to awaken, we eventually discover
That "the world around us" is essentially and literally the same as "ourselves",
For all creatures of the Earth are our extended family and our global community.

Each of these four "systems of awareness" or "aspects of our life journey"
Is a key chapter in **a Great Story** about the natural unfolding of our spiritual awakening.

For when we refer to *the Infinite and Eternal Source of Life*, there is no beginning or ending -
Yet as far as the awakening of our ever-evolving world, every day is a new beginning.

Circle of The Great Story of Awakening
(My *Spiritual Journey* In Relation to the Infinite Seasons of Life)

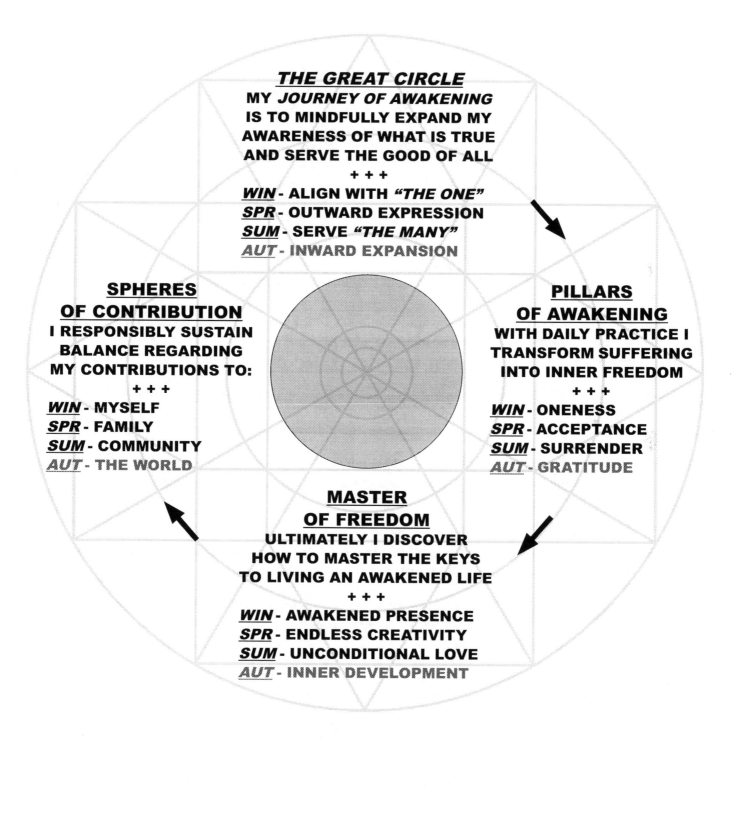

THE GREAT CIRCLE
MY *JOURNEY OF AWAKENING*
IS TO MINDFULLY EXPAND MY
AWARENESS OF WHAT IS TRUE
AND SERVE THE GOOD OF ALL
+ + +
WIN - ALIGN WITH *"THE ONE"*
SPR - OUTWARD EXPRESSION
SUM - SERVE *"THE MANY"*
AUT - INWARD EXPANSION

SPHERES
OF CONTRIBUTION
I RESPONSIBLY SUSTAIN
BALANCE REGARDING
MY CONTRIBUTIONS TO:
+ + +
WIN - MYSELF
SPR - FAMILY
SUM - COMMUNITY
AUT - THE WORLD

PILLARS
OF AWAKENING
WITH DAILY PRACTICE I
TRANSFORM SUFFERING
INTO INNER FREEDOM
+ + +
WIN - ONENESS
SPR - ACCEPTANCE
SUM - SURRENDER
AUT - GRATITUDE

MASTER
OF FREEDOM
ULTIMATELY I DISCOVER
HOW TO MASTER THE KEYS
TO LIVING AN AWAKENED LIFE
+ + +
WIN - AWAKENED PRESENCE
SPR - ENDLESS CREATIVITY
SUM - UNCONDITIONAL LOVE
AUT - INNER DEVELOPMENT

JOURNEY OF AWAKENING

Living my life in service to others is an actual demonstration that I have truly awakened.

Many religious traditions from around the world have their own unique way of declaring
That the life of every person on the planet (whether they consciously know it or not)
Is essentially *a spiritual journey* - **a journey of awakening**.

And for most of these traditions, the first stage of this transformative journey is **development**,
In other words, it's the journey of expanding one's awareness of what life is truly about,
Learning what really matters, and developing one's creative potential.

So as *to awaken* (i.e. *to learn to love all of life unconditionally)* we can expand our awareness
By fostering more inclusive perspectives of life that engender more empathy and care.

There is a natural impulse within us that constantly invites us to develop our unlimited potential
And to learn the key dynamics at play in our lives so we can progress out of ignorance,
Experience authentic inner freedom, and discover who we really are.

Expanding our awareness about what is true then offers us the opportunity
To undertake the next stage of our journey - **to consciously transform ourselves**.

Through self-examination, keeping our heart open, and engaging in transformative practices,
We can change our dysfunctional habits and loveless beliefs
Into more compassionate, caring, and love-centered ways of living in this world.

As we sustain an alignment with *the Source of Life* and follow the guidance available to us,
We can transform old habitual patterns and ways of behavior
Into our next higher expression of a healthy and harmonious person.

Over time, our *spiritual journey* advances us to the third stage referred to as **mastery**,
Which is to embody and integrate this awakened awareness in our daily life
Through our alignment with *the Source of Life* - and our transformative practice.

Throughout the past, various traditional religious groups have taught their followers
That the primary goal of the *journey of awakening* was personal spiritual freedom,
And that a seeker's only true desire was simply "to be one with God".

This personal union with God, or "enlightenment", was said to deliver the spiritual seeker
From *maya (the illusions of the world)* to freeing one from attachment and suffering.

Yet today, many people are understanding that an essential step of this *awakening journey*
(Beyond personal spiritual freedom or "enlightenment") is also **contribution**,
Which is discovering ways and taking action to serve the good of all.

Authentic enlightenment (which is another word for true inner freedom)
Is an emergent leap in consciousness to an even greater participation in the world
By serving the needs of others, which ultimately *is the same* as serving ourselves -
For this fourth stage, **contribution**, is an actual demonstration
That we have truly awakened.

Circle of the *Journey of Awakening*
(Key Stages of the Transformative Quest For Inner Freedom)

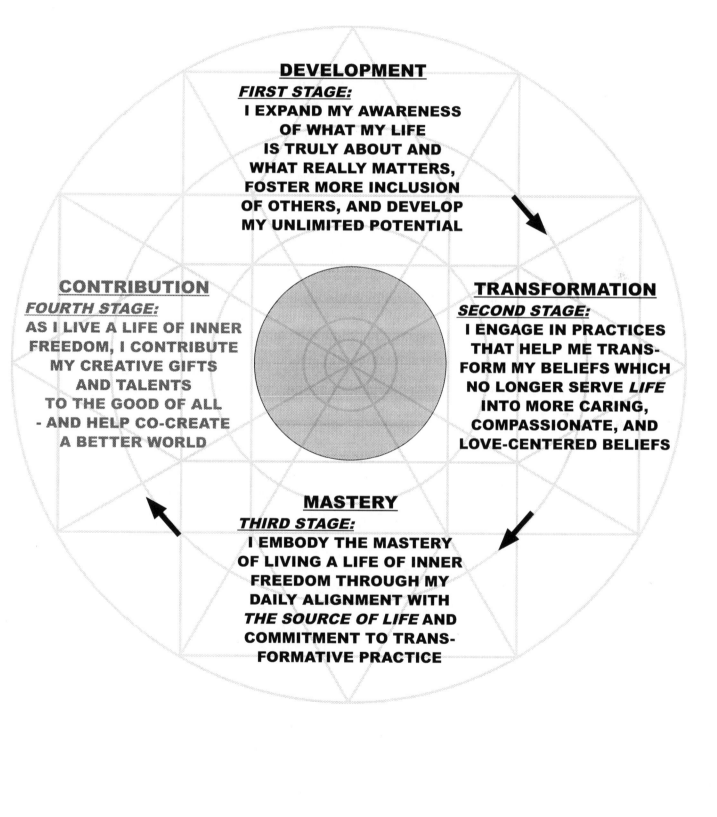

DEVELOPMENT
FIRST STAGE:
I EXPAND MY AWARENESS
OF WHAT MY LIFE
IS TRULY ABOUT AND
WHAT REALLY MATTERS,
FOSTER MORE INCLUSION
OF OTHERS, AND DEVELOP
MY UNLIMITED POTENTIAL

CONTRIBUTION
FOURTH STAGE:
AS I LIVE A LIFE OF INNER
FREEDOM, I CONTRIBUTE
MY CREATIVE GIFTS
AND TALENTS
TO THE GOOD OF ALL
- AND HELP CO-CREATE
A BETTER WORLD

TRANSFORMATION
SECOND STAGE:
I ENGAGE IN PRACTICES
THAT HELP ME TRANS-
FORM MY BELIEFS WHICH
NO LONGER SERVE *LIFE*
INTO MORE CARING,
COMPASSIONATE, AND
LOVE-CENTERED BELIEFS

MASTERY
THIRD STAGE:
I EMBODY THE MASTERY
OF LIVING A LIFE OF INNER
FREEDOM THROUGH MY
DAILY ALIGNMENT WITH
THE SOURCE OF LIFE AND
COMMITMENT TO TRANS-
FORMATIVE PRACTICE

THE QUESTIONS THAT EMERGE FROM AN AWAKENED LIFE

Serving others is actually the same as serving myself - for we are all part of one Eternal Self.

When a light rain gently falls from the sky during the late afternoon
While the Sun is peaking through the low clouds, it's a good time to observe a rainbow
Curving across the sky from one end of the horizon to the other.

Now imagine the epic evolutionary journey of humanity as "a long visual arc of discovery"
In which the beginning of this unfolding arc represents *primitive human awareness*
And the other end of the arc depicts *a fully awakened human.*

We might also imagine that this "arc of humanity's epic unfolding" is like a colorful rainbow
That touches the distant horizon at one starting point along the rainbow,
Ascends high into the sky above, and then returns again to the Earth
At another point much farther along the horizon.

Or another way of imagining this "arc of humanity" is to visualize the top half of a circular clock
Where 9 o'clock signifies *primitive awareness* (or *total concern for the needs of self*)
And 3 o'clock implies *a fully awakened human* (or *the impulse to serve others*),
While 12 o'clock, being the exact midpoint between the two,
Represents that *the thoughts of concern for only the self*
And those of *service to others* are both in one's awareness -
Yet it's the key point where one shifts toward service.

This visualization can help us understand that at the point along the clock starting at 12:01,
People begin to be more caring for <u>others</u> than merely for the personal needs of <u>self</u>.

Each of us, in our own unique way, is a cosmic traveler on this *journey of evolving humanity,*
And every one of us can be placed somewhere on "the long arc of this life clock"
Depending on our current level of inner development and conscious awareness.

With each day, *the Source of Life* invites us to shift our awareness from our petty selfish needs
To an awareness that serving others <u>*is actually the same*</u> as serving ourselves,
For all people are part of one *Eternal Self,* one global family.

We all seem to be participants journeying into new uncharted territory
Where we're transforming our lives from habitually living within the patterns of fear
To a conscious life of inner freedom which serves the wellbeing of others -
In other words, shifting from being "a victim of fear" to "a Servant of Love".

There's no "right or wrong", "good or bad" place we should be on this arc of evolving humanity
For we're all just where we need to be in our current process of learning and developing
Just as children are where they need to be - learning at their current grade level -
And doing the best they can within their current school program.

Yet no matter what point that we're presently at along the path of this unfolding rainbow arc,
There's always a natural yearning deep within inviting us to respond to the questions:
"What can I contribute today?" - "Where can I help today?"
"How much can I give today?" - "Who can I serve today?"

Circle of the Questions That Emerge
From an Awakened Life

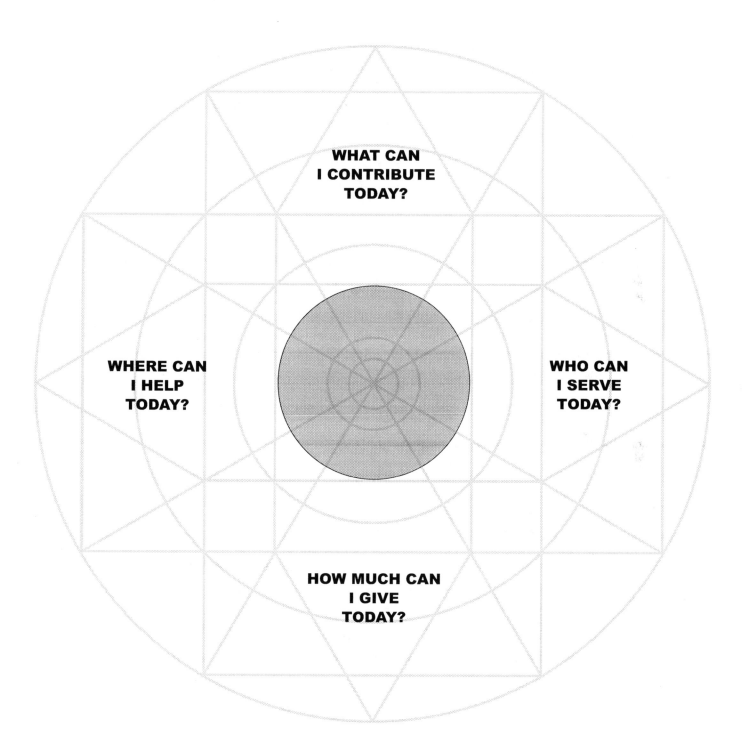

WHAT CAN
I CONTRIBUTE
TODAY?

WHERE CAN
I HELP
TODAY?

WHO CAN
I SERVE
TODAY?

HOW MUCH CAN
I GIVE
TODAY?

THE UNITY OF EXISTENCE

I fully accept that my life is unfolding perfectly - and is an integral part of one Unity.

Every morning when we wake up, we open our eyes to an array of diverse polar opposites,
A world where we may experience <u>warm days</u> - which then morph into <u>cool nights</u>,
A world where we are bathed in the nurturing streams of the dawning <u>light</u> -
Which then transform into evening <u>darkness</u>.

If we visualize ourselves on the surface of the Moon gazing back at the Earth
In order to temporarily gain a much different perspective of our planet,
The above dual polarities would then be seen as two integral parts of a "unity",
A wholeness that can only be viewed from this very distant vantage.

As we return to our familiar vantage back on Earth where these two polarities exist separately,
Each polar opposite has its own distinct identity, its own individual traits,
And from this relativistic viewpoint, both polarities can't exist at the same time.

From the common perspective of living in the world, <u>darkness</u> cannot exist if <u>light</u> is present,
And <u>winter</u> cannot exist when the season of <u>summer</u> is unfolding.

Yet in order to deepen our comprehension of the sublime nature of existence,
We can enter into the sacred place within us that holds the grandest vantage possible,
A vista where **consciousness** and **creation** are two integral parts of a whole,
Where **God** and **the Universe** are two essential aspects of one unity,
An awareness that views reality from an entirely different paradigm
Where both facets of existence must exist at the same time.

The Unity of Existence is the union of an inner non-physical world with an outer physical world,
The bond of internal awareness with external reality, the joining of *Being* with *Becoming*,
The merging of ***Infinite Intelligence*** with **every material form of life**.

So to more fully explore the Unity of Existence, let's inquire into the following two statements:
   1)*There cannot be creation without consciousness,*
     Yet there also cannot be consciousness without creation.

   2)*There cannot be a Universe without God,*
     Yet there also cannot be God without a Universe.

Could it be that both components of a physical dimension and a non-physical dimension
Must intimately dance and intertwine together for *existence to truly be?*

The majestic tapestry of the vast Universe is an unfolding weaving of light and darkness
From the interplay within the Perfect Unity of ***"The One"* merged with *"The Many"***.

The numerous polarities that occur on Earth which arise within the turning of the seasons
All join together to form a universal dance of **the Unity of Existence**
Which is perfectly choreographed as the merging of consciousness and creation,
The sacred union of masculine and feminine, the blending of yang and yin,
"Cosmic dance partners" on our *journey of infinite awakenings.*

Circle of the Unity of Existence

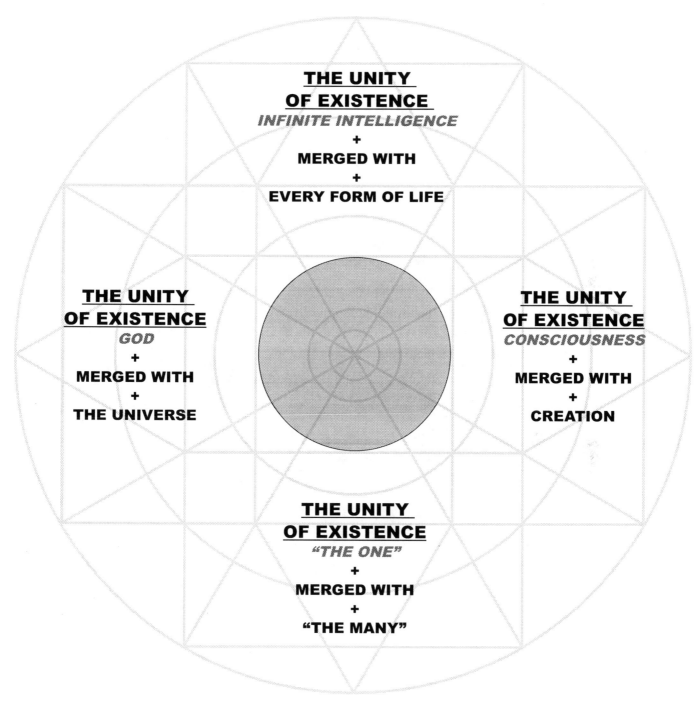

**THE UNITY
OF EXISTENCE**
INFINITE INTELLIGENCE
+
MERGED WITH
+
EVERY FORM OF LIFE

**THE UNITY
OF EXISTENCE**
GOD
+
MERGED WITH
+
THE UNIVERSE

**THE UNITY
OF EXISTENCE**
CONSCIOUSNESS
+
MERGED WITH
+
CREATION

**THE UNITY
OF EXISTENCE**
"THE ONE"
+
MERGED WITH
+
"THE MANY"

II

THE POETRY
OF
THE GREAT CIRCLE

THE GREAT CIRCLE

Life is a journey of self-mastery of my outer transformations mirroring my inner development.

The Great Circle is "a spiritual map of an awakening life"
>Which portrays our transformation and healing directly mirroring our inner development,
>>And this circle helps to illuminate the mystery and paradox
>>>Regarding the relationship of our physical and non-physical dimensions.

In each moment both our physical and non-physical aspects are part of the perfection of **Being**
>And yet, at the same time, we are also here to help the world **Become** more perfect.

The mystery of life may never be completely understood with the faculties of the human mind,
>Yet numerous symbolic images have been used for centuries
>>To help point humanity to the sacred place within
>>>Where one might discover (and personally experience)
>>>>A deeper comprehension of this eternal mystery.

In China, there is a Taoist teaching that helps to illumine
>The existential paradox portrayed within **The Great Circle**,
>>And this teaching states, *"I am in the Universe - the Universe is in me -*
>>*The Universe and I are one"*.

The first phrase of this teaching, ***"I am in the Universe"***,
>Points us to the circle's lower quadrant and to a recognition that in the present moment,
>>We can learn to experience that our life is unfolding perfectly just as it is.

It also directs us to the sublime knowing that each one of us
>Is an exquisite unique strand within the Great Web of Life
>>And, paradoxically at the same time, we are connected and one with everything.

The phrase ***"the Universe is in me"*** refers to both the right and left quadrants of the circle,
>Which points us to the dynamic forces of infinite creativity working within the Universe
>>And that these same forces of <u>development</u> and <u>creativity</u> are also working in us.

The last phrase which states, ***"the Universe and I are one"***
>Points us to the upper quadrant of **The Great Circle**
>>And brings to light that our *True Nature* is eternal and unbounded,
>>>Intimately merged with *"The One"* Source of All That Is,
>>>>And this teaching invites us to awaken to our *Eternal Nature*.

The Great Circle depicts *our evolving creativity* mirroring *our evolving consciousness*,
>The <u>inward</u> expansion of our awareness mirrored as our <u>outward</u> creative expressions,
>>Our <u>inner</u> development out-pictured in our body as our <u>outer</u> transformation.

From one perspective of reality, there appears to be four distinct seasons of the year,
>Yet, simultaneously, they can also be seen as the unity of one revolution of the Sun.

Similarly, there seems to be four different aspects to the constant turning of **The Great Circle**,
>Yet it's also the unity and integration of one continuous unfolding of *the Mystery of Life*.

The Great Circle
(A Spiritual Map of an Awakening Life)

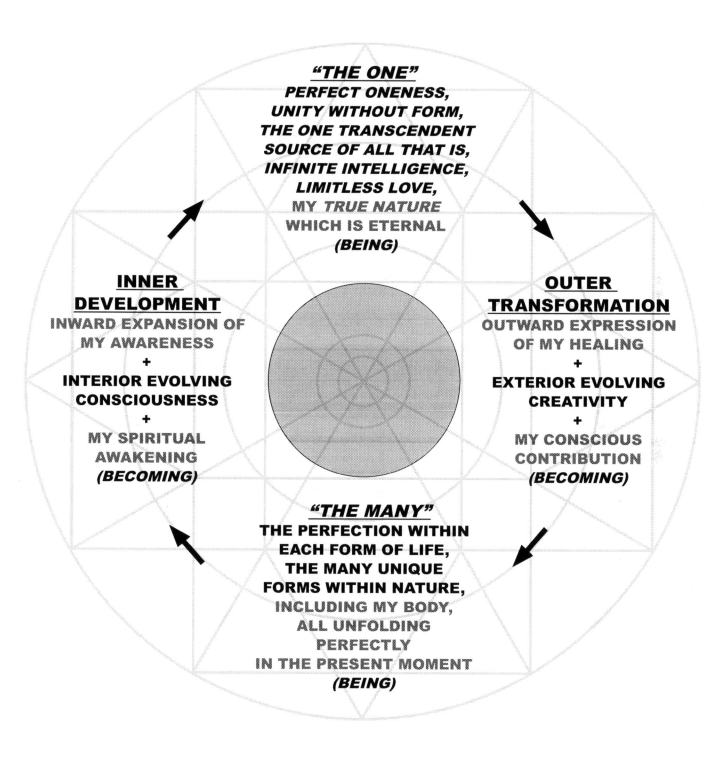

"THE ONE"
PERFECT ONENESS,
UNITY WITHOUT FORM,
THE ONE TRANSCENDENT
SOURCE OF ALL THAT IS,
INFINITE INTELLIGENCE,
LIMITLESS LOVE,
MY *TRUE NATURE*
WHICH IS ETERNAL
(BEING)

**INNER
DEVELOPMENT**
INWARD EXPANSION OF
MY AWARENESS
+
INTERIOR EVOLVING
CONSCIOUSNESS
+
MY SPIRITUAL
AWAKENING
(BECOMING)

**OUTER
TRANSFORMATION**
OUTWARD EXPRESSION
OF MY HEALING
+
EXTERIOR EVOLVING
CREATIVITY
+
MY CONSCIOUS
CONTRIBUTION
(BECOMING)

"THE MANY"
THE PERFECTION WITHIN
EACH FORM OF LIFE,
THE MANY UNIQUE
FORMS WITHIN NATURE,
INCLUDING MY BODY,
ALL UNFOLDING
PERFECTLY
IN THE PRESENT MOMENT
(BEING)

THE GREAT CIRCLE OF GIVING AND RECEIVING

As I give to others I also receive - for giving and receiving are one flow within the Circle of Life.

In the early formative stages of the evolving Universe,
  The first stars could not have been created from massive clouds of hydrogen atoms
    Without the interplay of both attractive and repulsive forces of atomic particles.

Billions of years later, new elements couldn't have formed from a supernova explosion of a star
  Without the interplay of both molecular breakdown and its resultant chemical bonding.

Today on Earth, flowers cannot propagate without the interplay of both a pistil and a stamen,
  And, of course, a human baby inside a mother's womb cannot be conceived
    Without the interplay of both a woman and a man.

Similarly from "a Big Picture vantage", the very nature of existence is also a dynamic balance,
  An intertwined union of opposite, yet complimentary, principles or impulses.

These polar impulses of existence can be said to continually "dance back and forth"
  Between an invisible non-physical dimension - and a visible physical dimension,
    Between an inward expansive realm - and an outward expressive realm,
      In other words, between the interplay of consciousness and creation.

Existence is the perpetual unfolding of an invisible interior realm of ever-evolving development
  That is mirrored into the physical world by *the Infinite Intelligence* of the Universe
    As the visible exterior realm (material form) of every creative manifestation.

From this cosmic perspective, the compassionate experiences of our giving and our receiving
  Are interwoven as one natural flow - for both are integral facets of the one Circle of Life.

Our **giving** to others, from this viewpoint, can be understood as an inward expansive impulse,
  For it is the natural yearning within us to awaken our next possible horizon of kindness,
    To **cultivate a greater awareness of generosity**,
      To go beyond previous boundaries of who and what we believe we are,
        And by doing this, reach higher levels of compassionate sharing.

Furthermore, our **receiving** can be understood as an outward expressive impulse,
  For it's our ability to **embrace the "gift" (the giving)** as a new avenue for our creativity
    Which (if we are receptive to it) can be expressed outwardly in our life
      By using the gifts we receive from others to help co-create a more peaceful world.

The Great Circle illustrates that as we give, we also naturally receive,
  For giving and receiving are part of one wholeness - knowing that as we give to another
    We are giving to every part of life, and therefore to ourselves as well.

This continuous cycle that connects **giving** and **receiving**,
  That links the development of a greater awareness of generosity
    With embracing gifts from others as new avenues of our creativity in the world,
      That joins "two cosmic dancers" in a dynamic universal balance,
        Constantly pulsates in us to help co-create a more glorious world.

The Great Circle of Giving and Receiving
(In Relation to the Expansive and Expressive Impulses of Life)

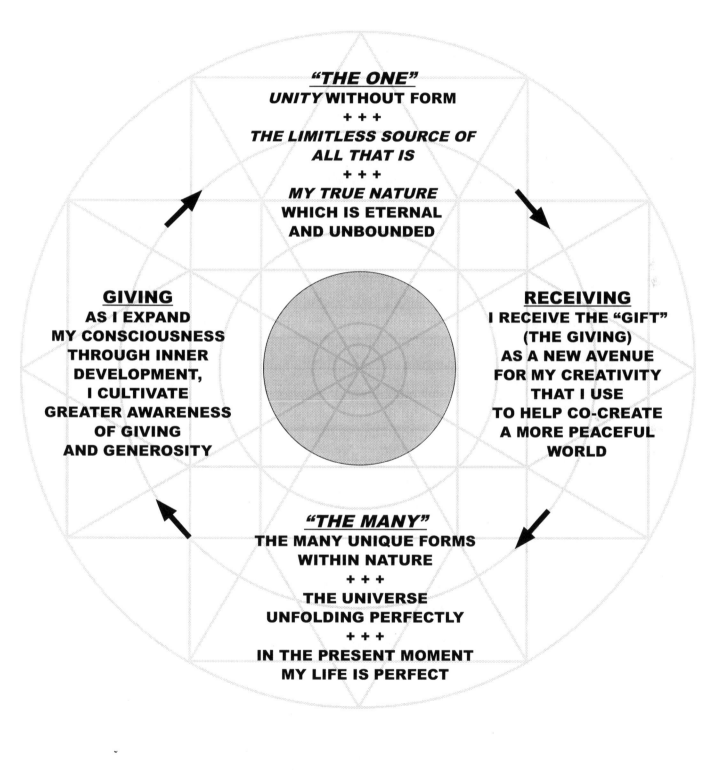

"THE ONE"
UNITY WITHOUT FORM
+ + +
THE LIMITLESS SOURCE OF
ALL THAT IS
+ + +
MY TRUE NATURE
WHICH IS ETERNAL
AND UNBOUNDED

GIVING
AS I EXPAND
MY CONSCIOUSNESS
THROUGH INNER
DEVELOPMENT,
I CULTIVATE
GREATER AWARENESS
OF GIVING
AND GENEROSITY

RECEIVING
I RECEIVE THE "GIFT"
(THE GIVING)
AS A NEW AVENUE
FOR MY CREATIVITY
THAT I USE
TO HELP CO-CREATE
A MORE PEACEFUL
WORLD

"THE MANY"
THE MANY UNIQUE FORMS
WITHIN NATURE
+ + +
THE UNIVERSE
UNFOLDING PERFECTLY
+ + +
IN THE PRESENT MOMENT
MY LIFE IS PERFECT

THE GREAT CIRCLE OF THE SACRED CROSS

Expanding my awareness of what is true is mirrored within the many expressions of my creativity.

For thousands of years of recorded human history, there have been numerous sages,
　　As well as mystics, shamans, and masters who were intuitively aware
　　　　Of a higher knowledge regarding the fundamental dynamics of existence
　　　　　　And illustrated this awareness in various versions of **The Great Circle**.

These spiritual intuitives found many creative ways to symbolically represent this knowledge
　　By producing a variety of emblematic icons which visually expressed their awareness,
　　　　Such as the Taoist circle of Yin and Yang, the Jewish figure of the Star of David,
　　　　　　The Native American medicine wheel, and the Christian cross.

The cross is a prime religious image that has been used extensively throughout the world,
　　For example, it was displayed by the Druids in Britain as the Celtic cross,
　　　　Within the ancient Egyptian culture in the form of the hieroglyph the ankh,
　　　　　　And, of course, throughout Christianity as the cross of the Christ,
　　　　　　　　To name just a few.

These iconic religious symbols carried several layers of meaning for different groups of people,
　　From the most literal, to the metaphorical, and also to the hidden esoteric meaning
　　　　In which the latter held "the higher teachings" regarding the nature of existence.

From an esoteric or mystical perspective, **the vertical line of the sacred cross**
　　Represents the inherent impulse and natural yearning within all people
　　　　To expand their awareness of what is true, to develop their unlimited potential,
　　　　　　And ultimately to learn to love all of life unconditionally.

This inward expansive impulse is *the evolution of consciousness* striving to reach new heights
　　And represents the innate longing within each of us
　　　　To awaken our consciousness to the realization of who we really are.

The horizontal line symbolizes the process of outwardly manifesting our growing awareness
　　As it's mirrored and expressed in our life as our creativity, transformation, and healing.

The point at the top of the vertical line
　　Represents *"The One" (the Limitless Source of All That Is, Infinite Intelligence)*
　　　　Which mirrors our spiritual awakening into the world as our creative contributions.

The point at the bottom of the vertical line
　　Represents *"The Many"* forms and structures unfolding perfectly within the Universe,
　　　　As well as, in the present moment, the perfect unfolding within our own life.

The cross illustrates the universal dynamics of *the evolution of consciousness and creativity*,
　　And for you and I, the way our inner development manifests as our outer transformation.

When we look at the iconic illustration of **the cross** from this "Big Picture perspective",
　　We can see within its symbolic image both the Universe unfolding perfectly before us
　　　　As well as the perpetual blossoming of our own *journey of awakening*.

The Great Circle of the Sacred Cross

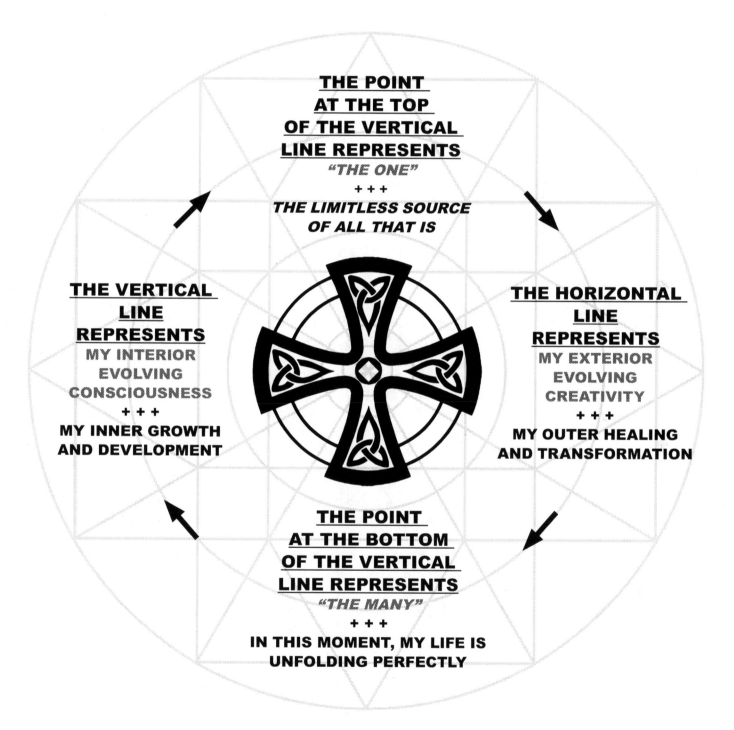

**THE POINT
AT THE TOP
OF THE VERTICAL
LINE REPRESENTS**
"THE ONE"
+ + +
*THE LIMITLESS SOURCE
OF ALL THAT IS*

**THE VERTICAL
LINE
REPRESENTS**
MY INTERIOR
EVOLVING
CONSCIOUSNESS
+ + +
MY INNER GROWTH
AND DEVELOPMENT

**THE HORIZONTAL
LINE
REPRESENTS**
MY EXTERIOR
EVOLVING
CREATIVITY
+ + +
MY OUTER HEALING
AND TRANSFORMATION

**THE POINT
AT THE BOTTOM
OF THE VERTICAL
LINE REPRESENTS**
"THE MANY"
+ + +
IN THIS MOMENT, MY LIFE IS
UNFOLDING PERFECTLY

MANY SPIRITUAL PATHS ON *THE JOURNEY OF AWAKENING*

Every genuine spiritual path leads me to the same awakened realization of my Eternal Nature.

"The magnetic pull of spiritual awakening" (the invitation from *Life* that's tugging on all hearts)
Is one of the most natural impulses within the perfect unfolding of the Universe,
And it's an inner drive constantly inviting us to develop and expand our beliefs
No matter what religion or philosophical system of which we may be a part.

The unique culture and environment of the people within a particular region of the world
Is what predominantly shapes the form of religious belief that a group embraces
And usually is practiced as one of two primary impulses of the evolutionary drive.

One impulse, that of *vertical evolution (the evolution to higher stages of consciousness),*
Is the **Yang** impulse expressed in China by a spiritual sect known as the Taoists,
And is an intrinsic longing to be one with *the flow of Life*, referred to as *The Tao.*

In India, some Hindu sects refer to this <u>vertical expansive impulse</u> as **Transcendence**,
A spiritual impulse to merge with *Brahman (Universal Consciousness, God).*

In Tibet, this yearning was expressed by Buddhists as **Heart Wisdom**,
The inward impulse to reach a sublime spiritual awakening known as *enlightenment,*
And within parts of the western world, Christian mystics referred to it as **Eros**,
The yearning to be one with *the Father, the transcendent Mind of God.*

<u>The expressive impulse of *horizontal evolution* (development of a current level of awareness)</u>
Was depicted within these four religious cultures, respectively,
As **Yin**, a fervent longing to contribute to the good of others and to all of life,
As **Moral Integrity**, a natural yearning to be a virtuous person,
As **Compassion**, a selfless desire to be in service to others,
And as **Agape**, the drive to live with a kind and loving heart.

As an awakened Taoist on this quest, one finally realizes the mystical truth, **"I am the Tao"**,
As an awakened Hindu on *the spiritual journey*, one understands, **"I am Brahman"**,
As an awakened Buddhist, one recognizes **"I am Bodhisattva"**,
And as an awakened Christian, **"I am the Way, the Truth, and the Life"**.

The religious phrase, **"The Way"**, is another name for our *journey of awakening*
Leading us to the perfect union of our Compassionate Heart (the Servant of Love),
Which is merged and integrated with *Infinite Presence (Limitless Source of Life).*

The spiritual traditions listed above are just four examples of the numerous names or paths
For the various religious expressions of our natural human yearning
To awaken our consciousness to the realization of our *Eternal Nature.*

For all of these spiritual paths described above - and for every other path one might take,
"The magnetic pull of *the journey of awakening*" is the same,
But the outward form can take many different shapes,
Wear many diverse colorful garments,
And sing many unique devotional songs.

Circle of Many Spiritual Paths on
the Journey of Awakening
(Four Examples from the Diverse World Religions)

**THE WAY OF
THE TAO**
(AWAKENED TAOIST)
YANG – A LONGING
TO BE ONE WITH
THE FLOW OF LIFE
+ INTEGRATED WITH +
YIN – A LONGING
TO CONTRIBUTE TO
THE GOOD OF OTHERS

**THE WAY, THE TRUTH
AND THE LIFE**
(AWAKENED CHRISTIAN)
EROS – THE IMPULSE TO
MERGE WITH *THE TRAN-
SCENDENT MIND OF GOD*
+ INTEGRATED WITH +
AGAPE – THE IMPULSE TO
LIVE WITH A KIND AND
COMPASSIONATE HEART

**THE WAY OF
BRAHMAN**
(AWAKENED HINDU)
TRANSCENDENCE –
THE IMPULSE TO BE
ONE WITH *BRAHMAN*
+ INTEGRATED WITH +
MORAL INTEGRITY –
THE IMPULSE TO BE
A VIRTUOUS PERSON

**THE WAY OF
THE BODHISATTVA**
(AWAKENED BUDDHIST)
HEART WISDOM –
A YEARNING TOWARD
SUBLIME AWAKENING
+ INTEGRATED WITH +
COMPASSION –
A SELFLESS DESIRE
TO SERVE OTHERS

VERTICAL EVOLUTION

Life is constantly inviting me to awaken to, and embody, higher stages of consciousness.

From countless analytical observations of the wonders of Nature and the Cosmos
    (Using an objective, deductive, and evidence-based investigation),
        Science has established that everything in the Universe is constantly evolving.

All of the myriad expressions of life are intertwined in a perpetual transmutative journey
    Of evolving from one creative form to another.

If you were to take an imaginary magnifying glass and gaze deep into "the heart of evolution",
    You could observe there are two primary, but complimentary, components of evolution.

One of these primary components can be called **vertical evolution**,
    In other words, <u>the evolution of progressing to higher stages of consciousness</u>,
        And the second component is **horizontal evolution**,
            I.e. <u>the evolution or development within a current stage of consciousness</u>.

The symbolic image of *the cross*, with both its vertical and horizontal lines,
    Is a visual representation of these intertwined evolutionary components
        Which are individually expressed as two different universal processes.

Regarding our human evolutionary journey, *vertical evolution* is like "a ladder of awareness"
    That *Life* is constantly inviting each person on the planet to climb
        In which "every rung of the ladder" is **a specific level of human development**.

Every level that a person attains on this journey of life is more expanded than the one before
    And, therefore, each new level requires more conscious awareness to sustain it.

The intrinsic human drive within us to reach for an awareness of who we really are
    Is the spiritual foundation of our *vertical evolution*.

Vertical evolution can also be likened to the wide spectrum of a colorful rainbow
    In which some of the rainbow's basic colors are at the bottom of the spectrum
        And its more radiant expansive colors are displayed toward the top.

It's natural for every person who travels *an awakening journey* (a *journey of discovery*)
    To first explore and experience the, so-called, "lower vibratory colors",
        And then with the expansion of one's awareness and opening of one's heart,
            Begin to progress upward through "the ascending color spectrum"
                So as to experience **higher waves** of life's many vibratory stages.

Each **consecutive stage** of human consciousness must first be fully embraced
    In order to learn and embody the life lessons of that specific stage,
        And then in time, move on, or transcend, to the next higher stage of awareness.

These sequential upward-spiraling steps of **The Great Chain of Being**
    Are like a cosmic dance we perpetually dance, an endless journey we are embarked on,
        Taking small but persistent steps to our destiny of loving all of life unconditionally.

Circle of Vertical Evolution
(Evolution of Progressing to Higher Stages of Consciousness)

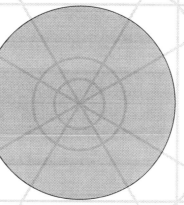

LEVELS
VERTICAL EVOLUTION –
THE ASCENDING LEVELS
OF HUMAN
DEVELOPMENT, LIKE "A
LADDER OF AWARENESS"
THAT EACH PERSON
IS CONSTANTLY BEING
INVITED TO CLIMB

WAVES
VERTICAL EVOLUTION –
THE SPECTRUM
OF HUMAN AWARENESS,
FROM LOWER TO HIGHER
WAVES OF CONSCIOUS-
NESS, THAT ALL PEOPLE
ARE DESTINED
TO MOVE THROUGH

STAGES
VERTICAL EVOLUTION –
THE CONSECUTIVE
STAGES OF HUMAN
CONSCIOUSNESS THAT
ARE TO BE EMBRACED
AND TRANSCENDED SO
ONE MAY ATTAIN HIGHER
STAGES OF AWARENESS

**THE GREAT CHAIN
OF BEING**
VERTICAL EVOLUTION –
THE SEQUENTIAL
UPWARD STEPS OF "THE
GREAT CHAIN OF BEING"
THAT EVERYONE,
IN TIME, EVENTUALLY
ASCENDS

HORIZONTAL EVOLUTION

Today I consciously deepen my relationships and connections with the people in my life.

Horizontal evolution (i.e. the evolution or development of our current stage of consciousness)
Is defined by a different and distinct quality than its counterpart - *vertical evolution*
(I.e. the evolution of our progressing to higher stages of consciousness).

Vertical evolution is the natural longing within each of us to expand our awareness,
To rise to a higher level of consciousness, to reach for something greater.

Whereas *horizontal evolution* is the natural impulse within us
That yearns to cultivate and increase our current talents, skills, or states of awareness
At our present level or stage of personal development.

Horizontal evolution can also be thought of as that part of us
Which focuses on **how to be in relationship and in communion** with other people
And with the other countless creatures and ecosystems of the natural world.

Within Nature, *horizontal evolution* is what manifests the interrelatedness of bees and flowers,
The organic creativity of trees to produce an oxygen rich atmosphere,
The various interdependent functions of numerous bacteria with animals,
And is the intimate emotional bonding that grows between two people.

We can use the visual image of a typical tall office building with its many consecutive floors
To help us understand the difference between *vertical and horizontal evolution*.

Vertical evolution is like the movement of a person who is on one floor of the structure
Attempting to ascend upward to the next higher floor (a higher stage of awareness)
Within "our imaginary office building".

Horizontal evolution is like remaining on the floor of the building where you are
(Your current <u>stage</u> of awareness) and then remodeling all the rooms on that floor
To make them more beautiful or more functional **(<u>states</u> of awareness)**.

All of the various rooms on one particular floor
Are like the numerous **types of human development**
That we each consciously desire to investigate and cultivate
At one specific stage of life - or stage of awareness.

There are many areas, or what's been defined as **lines of individual human development**,
Which we are all in a process of learning to cultivate and **integrate in our lives**,
And **a few examples of these developmental lines are:**
Morality, cognition, emotional maturity, creativity, and spirituality.

Each of us is not only continuously climbing our vertical evolutionary "ladder of awareness",
But we're also constantly being invited by *Life* to compassionately serve one another
And contribute our unique creative gifts and talents to the world
By consciously redesigning and refining
The sacred place within our hearts in which we currently abide.

Circle of Horizontal Evolution
(Development of My Current Stage of Consciousness)

COMMUNION
THE EVOLUTION
OF DEEPENING
MY RELATIONSHIPS
AND COMMUNION
WITH OTHER PEOPLE
- AND WITH ALL ASPECTS
OF THE NATURAL WORLD

STATES
THE EVOLUTION
AND CULTIVATION OF
MY CURRENT TALENTS,
SKILLS, OR STATES
OF AWARENESS WITHIN
MY PRESENT STAGE
OF DEVELOPMENT

INTEGRATION
THE EVOLUTION
OF HOW I INTEGRATE
THE 1) PERSONAL,
2) CULTURAL,
3) SOCIAL, AND
4) NATURAL WORLD
FACETS OF MYSELF

LINES AND TYPES
THE EVOLUTION OF ALL
MY INDIVIDUAL AREAS
OF SELF-DEVELOPMENT
THAT GROW INTO HIGHER
FORMS OF EXPRESSION
WITHIN MY CURRENT
STAGE OF AWARENESS

THE EVOLUTIONARY IMPULSE

The Natural Intelligence that animates the Universe is the same Intelligence that animates me.

Since the dawn of humanity the world has been full of mysterious and unexplainable events,
　　And there have always been people who have tried to figure out how they happen.

Many, so-called, "miraculous occurrences" have been de-mystified by science over time
　　Through the acquisition of greater scientific knowledge.

For example, the properties of a specific kind of stone referred to as lodestone,
　　Once held a bizarre-like quality in which the stones magically attracted pieces of iron
　　　　Until scientists explained this attraction as an invisible force called magnetism.

Another invisible energy that we all know from basic physics is when an apple falls from a tree,
　　There is an unseen force of gravity pulling the apple towards the ground.

And furthermore, when a Geiger counter is placed near a piece of radioactive material,
　　We can physically observe the result of the hidden force of radioactivity
　　　　Imperceptibly impacting the sensors of the Geiger counter.

In a similar manner to the three natural and invisible forces listed above,
　　There is also a ubiquitous unseen impulse acting within the entire Universe
　　　　Which animates, shapes, and directs the Cosmos as it constantly evolves.

For fourteen billion years, this invisible and infinitely intelligent impulse of evolution
　　Has been infusing all of known reality
　　　　So as to fashion its unique and profoundly diverse patterns of creativity.

The Evolutionary Impulse can be described as life's *Natural Intelligence*
　　That animates every material form along a path of perpetual creative unfoldment.

It can be thought of as ***the Infinite Creativity* within all of existence**
　　That intelligently shapes and organizes higher expressions of manifested form,
　　　　Such as galaxies, stars, oceans, myriad life forms, and every human being.

The Evolutionary Impulse is (from a religious perspective) **the Universal Force of God**
　　That guides development and manifestation within all forms of the natural world.

It is the *Force* that "attracts together" sub-atomic particles, the planets in their solar orbits,
　　All interdependent ecosystems, as well as two lovers who experience romantic passion.

The Evolutionary Impulse can also be described metaphysically as **the Field of Love**
　　That intentionally shapes *Universal Light* into the many forms of creation *(Power)*
　　　　Producing atoms, molecules, weather patterns, and complex organisms, etc.

You and I are like grains of sand resting upon "the tightly stretched fabric of the Cosmos"
　　And listening to the hallowed frequencies of the Universe's celestial music
　　　　As this *intelligent impulse of life* vibrates through us
　　　　　　And invisibly sculpts us into our next novel pattern of creative expression.

Circle of *the Evolutionary Impulse*

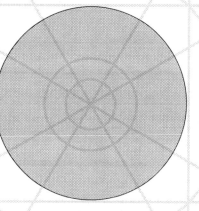

LIFE'S NATURAL
INTELLIGENCE
THE EVOLUTIONARY
IMPULSE – THE NATURAL
INTELLIGENCE
THAT ANIMATES EVERY
MATERIAL FORM ALONG
A PATH OF PERPETUAL
CREATIVE UNFOLDMENT

THE UNIVERSAL
FORCE OF GOD
THE EVOLUTIONARY
IMPULSE –
THE GOD FORCE THAT
GUIDES DEVELOPMENT
AND MANIFESTATION
WITHIN ALL FORMS OF
THE NATURAL WORLD

INFINITE
CREATIVITY
THE EVOLUTIONARY
IMPULSE – THE INFINITE
CREATIVITY THAT
INTELLIGENTLY SHAPES
AND ORGANIZES EVER
HIGHER EXPRESSIONS
OF MANIFESTED FORM

THE FIELD
OF LOVE
THE EVOLUTIONARY
IMPULSE –
THE FIELD OF LOVE THAT
INTENTIONALLY SHAPES
UNIVERSAL *LIGHT*
INTO THE MANY FORMS
OF CREATION (*POWER*)

GOD AS "THE TRANSCENDENT"

In the silence of my heart, I am aware of my Oneness with the Limitless Consciousness of Life.

The mystery of God is an elusive enigma that cannot be fully understood by the rational mind,
Yet for thousands of years poets and philosophers have tried to find words and phrases
Which help point us to this transcendent conundrum.

In recent times, contemporary philosophers have postulated that God has three distinct facets,
Or "three faces of God" - in other words, three individual aspects of the same mystery.

As a metaphor to help us understand this mystery, "the three faces of God" are analogous
To the three separate characteristics of water at diverse temperatures,
For ice, liquid, and water vapor are all expressions of the same element of water
But, due to varying temperatures, are each experienced in distinct forms.

Similarly, God as "The Creation", God as "The Beloved", and God as "The Transcendent"
Are also three simultaneous expressions of one *Absolute Power within the Universe*
Yet experienced by different people in distinctive ways at various times,
And expanding our understanding of each "face of the divine"
Can help us more effectively navigate our *journey of awakening*.

Many Native American tribes, the Celtic religions, and a multitude of shamanic traditions
Know God as a divine expression of **"The Creation"**, *Spirit* grounded within the Earth,
And for these groups, God is experienced within every part of Nature.

The fundamental Christian and Islamic religions (among various other sects around the world)
Know God as an expression of **"The Beloved"**, the Sacred Thou, the Holy Other,
And for them, God is experienced directly through a personal loving relationship
With a divine *Supreme Being, Father-Mother God, the Beloved One.*

The great mystics, the Hindu Advaitists, and many Eastern and esoteric spiritual traditions
Know God as an expression of **"The Transcendent"** *(Oneness, Being, Perfection)*
For God is primarily experienced by them as *Limitless Consciousness*.

This distinct "face of the divine" that has been referred to as God "The Transcendent"
Can be described as *the one Source of All That Is*, which is eternal and formless,
Yet from which every form of physical expression emerges into the world.

The various names of **God as "The Transcendent"** can be conveyed in many ways,
Such as *the Absolute, Pure Awareness, Perfect Wholeness,* or *Infinite Presence.*

"The Transcendent" (which is the first person perspective of the divine) is the facet of God
That has also been poetically expressed as *the Unbounded Ocean of Being.*

Every river of manifestation and every stream of creation comes from it - and is pulled to it
By *an Exalted Power*, and ultimately merges into this boundless *Ocean of the Divine.*

There is no place within the expanse of the Universe, or within a single heart of humanity,
Where this *Ocean* is not.

Circle of God as "The Transcendent"
(First Person Perspective of the Divine)

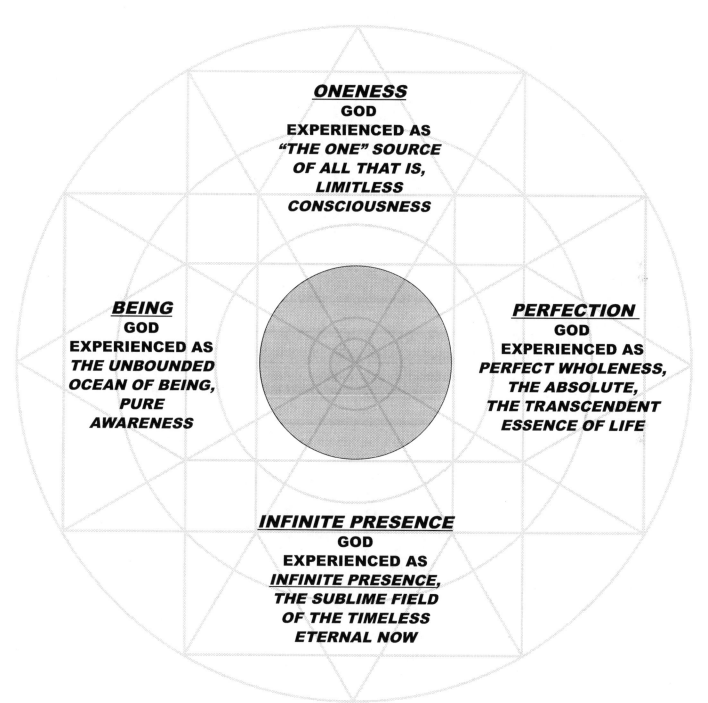

ONENESS
GOD
EXPERIENCED AS
"THE ONE" SOURCE
OF ALL THAT IS,
LIMITLESS
CONSCIOUSNESS

BEING
GOD
EXPERIENCED AS
THE UNBOUNDED
OCEAN OF BEING,
PURE
AWARENESS

PERFECTION
GOD
EXPERIENCED AS
PERFECT WHOLENESS,
THE ABSOLUTE,
THE TRANSCENDENT
ESSENCE OF LIFE

INFINITE PRESENCE
GOD
EXPERIENCED AS
INFINITE PRESENCE,
THE SUBLIME FIELD
OF THE TIMELESS
ETERNAL NOW

CHI

I align with the Source of Limitless Power so that Life Force energy easily flows through me.

When a building contractor erects a new modern home
    Its construction includes a vast network of electrical wires
        Which are laid within the interior framework of the walls
           So as to create a system of available wire
               Designed to allow electric power to flow throughout the building.

The individual electric wires have no intrinsic power of their own
    Since they are simply "the hollow conduits" intended to channel streams of energy
        But, obviously, must be directly connected to a power source
           In order for "the magic of electricity" to pass through them.

When a contractor decides it's time for the system to be connected to the source of power,
    Then the free flow of electricity can circulate everywhere throughout the home
        And electric power can be available via its intricate labyrinth of wires.

Our physical human form has come into being based on millions of years of evolution
    Directed by *the Infinite Intelligence* of the Universe
        And, over time, has developed intricate energy circuits, or meridian channels,
           Which allow **Life Force energy** to circulate throughout our body
              In a similar manner that electricity
                 Moves through the individual wires of a house.

This *Life Force energy* can be thought of as **the natural *Vital Force* within the Universe**
    That circulates throughout every unique form of life.

All living creatures on Earth experience this *Vital Force* of rejuvenation, healing, and renewal,
    And for thousands of years, the Chinese have referred to this force by **the word "Chi",**
        Which also means *Living Spirit* - or *Universal Energy*.

The entire Cosmos is filled and animated by the force of **Chi**
    That perpetually moves through all phenomena and every expression of life.

Like the unseen power of an electric current which circulates through the wires of a home,
    ***Chi* is the invisible *Living Spirit* that permeates within all beings**
        And within all of creation.

Animals and plants appear to circulate this energy naturally and effortlessly,
    But only we humans seem to have the ability to unnaturally impede its flow
        With our habitual mental constrictions of fear and loveless thinking.

Therefore, it's up to each of us to maintain a flow of *Chi* throughout our body
    By staying consciously aligned to *the Source of Limitless Power.*

Chi is like the invisible breath *(Life Force)* offered by a Master Musician *(one's Eternal Self)*,
    Which circulates through the hollow chamber of a flute (one's physical body)
        Giving vitality to the instrument and empowering the music for "the dance of life".

Circle of *Chi*

LIFE FORCE ENERGY
CHI –
THE *LIFE FORCE* ENERGY
THAT ANIMATES, GIVES
VITALITY TO, AND FLOWS
THROUGH EVERY LIVING
CREATURE

UNIVERSAL ENERGY
CHI –
THE UNIVERSAL ENERGY
THAT RENEWS EVERY
EXPRESSION OF LIFE
AND MOVES THROUGH
ALL PHENOMENA

VITAL FORCE
CHI –
THE NATURAL
VITAL FORCE
WITHIN THE UNIVERSE
THAT CIRCULATES
THROUGHOUT EVERY
UNIQUE FORM OF LIFE

LIVING SPIRIT
CHI –
THE INVISIBLE
LIVING SPIRIT
THAT PERMEATES
WITHIN ALL BEINGS
AND WITHIN
ALL OF CREATION

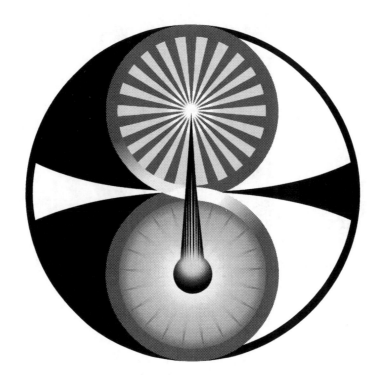

III

BODY AWARENESS PRACTICES

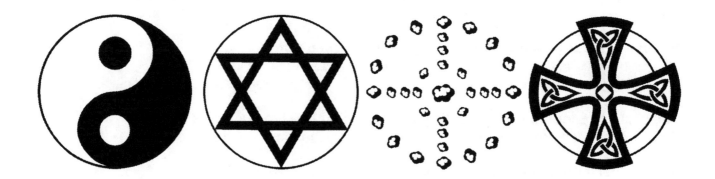

FOUNDATIONAL TRANSFORMATIVE PRACTICES
My daily transformative practices help me cultivate a life of peace and inner freedom.

If certain individuals in today's world want to be competitive in professional sports,
  They must be dedicated to a host of routine practices that constantly improve their skills.

For example, professional golfers will work with a coach to help enhance their *power swing*
  So they can continually refine their accuracy and focused concentration.

Today's pro golfers will also spend time developing their *inner game of mental training*
  By cultivating the power of imagination to help them attain their goals,
    As well as engaging in physical exercises which tone the muscles of their bodies.

Similarly, in the realm of the theatrical arts which includes professional acting,
  Seasoned actors will constantly devote time to work on fundamental exercises
    That form the foundation for them to improve their creative talents.

Some of these exercises involve working with the sound or articulation of their voice,
  Developing a deeper and more creative access to their emotional expression,
    Keeping the body fit and able to move freely and expressively,
      And using their imagination to support their mental training.

So if we are truly determined regarding our desire to continually develop "the art of living",
  Then we can also do what the professionals do to consciously develop themselves
    Which is to engage in a lifestyle of effective transformative practices
      That help us cultivate inner freedom.

If our intention is to express more kindness and compassion in our daily life,
  Be more able to hear and respond to the inner guidance available to us,
    Consciously access higher creativity to solve challenges and inspire others,
      Or develop ways to contribute our unique gifts and talents to the world,
        Then there are specific beneficial practices that are foundational.

The first foundational transformative practice is meditation,
  The practice of experiencing inner silence so as to still our mind,
    Align our awareness with *the Source of Life,* and awaken to our *Eternal Nature.*

Another is **contemplation**, the practice of reflecting on "the Big Questions" of life
  In order to consciously expand our awareness of what our life is truly about.

There are numerous other transformative practices that can be helpful,
  Such as **appreciation** and **prayer** which are basic to our spiritual development.

There are many progressive thinkers and contemporary philosophers who have speculated
  That the development from these kinds of transformative practices may be essential
    To help our species evolve to the next new emergent form of human life.

Whether or not this evolutionary step happens anytime soon, most caring people can sense
  That the world will be a much better place as we learn to truly share our authentic love.

Circle of Foundational Transformative Practices
(Primary Ways to Cultivate and Maintain Inner Freedom)

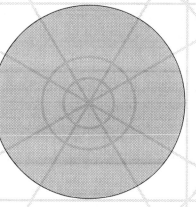

MEDITATION
**THE PRACTICE
OF EXPERIENCING INNER
SILENCE SO AS TO STILL
MY MIND, ALIGN MY AWARE-
NESS WITH *THE SOURCE
OF LIFE*, AND AWAKEN
TO MY ETERNAL NATURE**

PRAYER
**THE PRACTICE
OF ASKING *LIFE*
HOW I AM TO SERVE,
AND CONTRIBUTE TO,
THE WELLBEING OF
OTHERS - AND ACTING
ON WHAT I RECEIVE**

CONTEMPLATION
**THE PRACTICE OF
CONSCIOUSLY EXPAND-
ING MY AWARENESS
BY REFLECTING ON
"THE BIG QUESTIONS"
REGARDING WHAT MY
LIFE IS TRULY ABOUT**

APPRECIATION
**THE PRACTICE OF BEING
THANKFUL FOR THE GIFTS
I RECEIVE EACH DAY,
BEING GRATEFUL MY LIFE
IS UNFOLDING PERFECTLY,
AND FULLY APPRECIATING
MYSELF FOR WHO I AM**

THE PRACTICE OF PRAYER

I pray for the wellbeing of others through consciously co-creating with the Source of Life.

Some anthropologists postulate that humans have been experimenting
    With the notion of "praying to the gods" for over fifty thousand years.

Prayer can be a compassionate act of consciously sending benevolent energy to others
    With the hope of restoring order, harmony, or wellbeing in their lives.

It can be a creative act of aligning our awareness with *a Greater Power (God, Source, Life),*
    In order to intentionally help others - or to better ourselves in some way.

In the last few thousand years, most religions from around the world
    Have developed formal rituals and structures for how prayers are to be performed.

During this same period, there have also been many secular institutions and individuals
    Who doubted, and questioned, the true power of prayer
        Believing it to be religious fantasy.

In recent times, modern science has tried to resolve this dilemma
    By conducting many controlled studies on the efficacy of prayer as a spiritual practice
        To determine if it has the ability "to bring good to the lives of others".

Numerous studies have concluded that both individual prayer and prayer performed in groups
    Have positive influences on others through the focused power of our creative thought.

Each one of us can discover this for ourselves by choosing to become "a spiritual scientist"
    To determine (within our own life) if there's a positive influence from focused prayer.

The practice of prayer can be thought of as our conscious co-creation with *a Greater Power*
    And consists of four distinct steps that are displayed in the circle on the following page.

First we **align our awareness with *the Source of Life*** (the *Infinite Presence of Love, God,*
    Or whatever we personally call *the Intelligent and Transcendent Power of Life)*
        And ask to be "inwardly given" an intention for the situation we are praying for.

Then, based on the inner guidance we receive regarding our prayer,
    We **use our creative imagination to bring focused clarity to our intention,**
        Which in science terms means we draw from *the quantum field of all possibilities.*

Next we **activate the heart energy of our intention**
    By empowering it with an elevated emotion, such as joy - or love for life.

The last step is to **hold our intention in our mind with grateful certainty**
    While knowing and acting as if our prayer has already manifested.

As "a spiritual scientist" we can engage life as an ongoing living experiment
    So as to constantly discover greater awareness of the true nature of our life -
        Or in this case, to discover the true power of prayer.

Circle of the Practice of Prayer
(A Transformative Practice of Conscious Co-Creation)

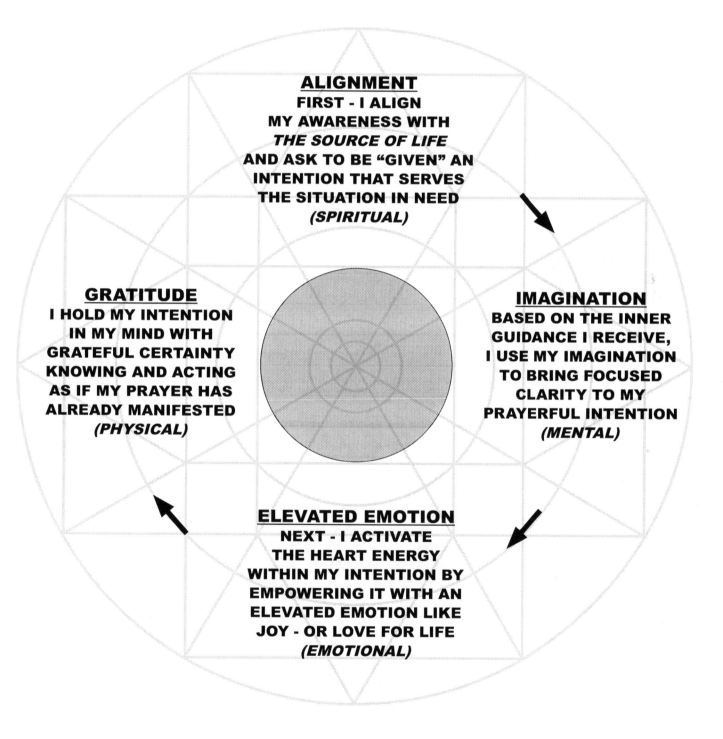

ALIGNMENT
FIRST - I ALIGN
MY AWARENESS WITH
THE SOURCE OF LIFE
AND ASK TO BE "GIVEN" AN
INTENTION THAT SERVES
THE SITUATION IN NEED
(SPIRITUAL)

GRATITUDE
I HOLD MY INTENTION
IN MY MIND WITH
GRATEFUL CERTAINTY
KNOWING AND ACTING
AS IF MY PRAYER HAS
ALREADY MANIFESTED
(PHYSICAL)

IMAGINATION
BASED ON THE INNER
GUIDANCE I RECEIVE,
I USE MY IMAGINATION
TO BRING FOCUSED
CLARITY TO MY
PRAYERFUL INTENTION
(MENTAL)

ELEVATED EMOTION
NEXT - I ACTIVATE
THE HEART ENERGY
WITHIN MY INTENTION BY
EMPOWERING IT WITH AN
ELEVATED EMOTION LIKE
JOY - OR LOVE FOR LIFE
(EMOTIONAL)

VARIOUS DIMENSIONAL FORMS OF EXERCISE

I maintain health and vitality so I may more effectively contribute my creative gifts and talents.

A rainbow in the sky is a phenomenal manifestation of ordinary rays of sunlight
    That are projected through falling rain, which acts as a large prism
        And divides the sunbeams into its many distinctive colors.

Each of the individual colors we perceive within a rainbow's spectrum
    Are, of course, all part of one unified ray of light.

In grade school, we learned there are three primary colors within light: blue, yellow, and red -
    And then later we discovered that each of these three colors
        Vibrates at different specific frequencies.

The color blue has the higher vibrational frequency,
    Whereas yellow is within the middle frequency range, and red has the lowest frequency.

Metaphorically, the radiant energy of a human being can be likened to "a single ray of light"
    That, when projected through "the prism of existence",
        Is then divided into three distinct bodily and dimensional expressions:
            The physical body, the vibrational body, and the quantum body.

Our *quantum body* is organized and formed by our higher frequencies, similar to the color blue,
    And contains our most fundamental intentions and our causal primary impulses.

Our *quantum body* gives rise to our *vibrational body*, which is made up of many vibratory fields
    That pulse within us as subtle energy and the flow of *Universal Life Force*,
        And, in the above model, is represented by the middle range color of yellow.

From these two higher frequency expressions (that is, *the quantum and vibrational bodies)*,
    The physical body then comes into manifestation as the most dense and solid form
        Symbolized by the color red - the lowest frequency of the primary colors.

As we gain more knowledge of, and a direct experience with, the different bodily expressions,
    We become aware that if we consciously intend to maintain radiant health and vitality
        For all three unique expressions of our body,
            We must provide appropriate forms of exercise for each of them.

To keep our **physical body** healthy, there are many types of exercise that stretch and tone
    Our muscles and internal organs, such as **yoga**, **weight training**, and **aerobics**.

There are also specific forms of exercise for our **vibrational body** that maintain
    The circulation of *Life Force* or *Chi* - like **Tai Chi**, **Qigong**, and **Moving Meditation**.

And our **quantum body** can be harmonized and balanced with certain awareness exercises,
    Such as **sound healing**, **sacred geometry**, and **imagination meditations**.

By frequently using these exercises, the rainbow spectrum of our magnificently evolved body
    Can continue to sustain its natural radiance.

Circle of Various Dimensional Forms of Exercise
(Transformative Practices)

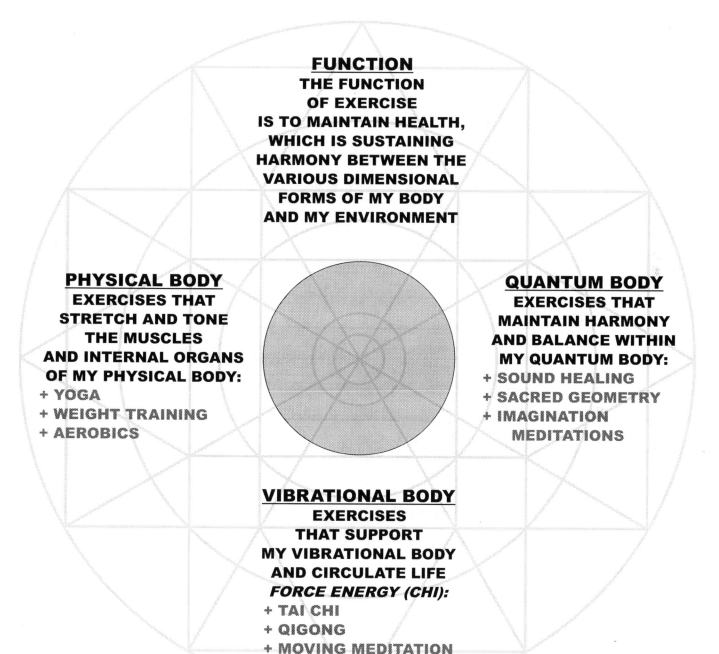

FUNCTION
THE FUNCTION
OF EXERCISE
IS TO MAINTAIN HEALTH,
WHICH IS SUSTAINING
HARMONY BETWEEN THE
VARIOUS DIMENSIONAL
FORMS OF MY BODY
AND MY ENVIRONMENT

PHYSICAL BODY
EXERCISES THAT
STRETCH AND TONE
THE MUSCLES
AND INTERNAL ORGANS
OF MY PHYSICAL BODY:
+ YOGA
+ WEIGHT TRAINING
+ AEROBICS

QUANTUM BODY
EXERCISES THAT
MAINTAIN HARMONY
AND BALANCE WITHIN
MY QUANTUM BODY:
+ SOUND HEALING
+ SACRED GEOMETRY
+ IMAGINATION
  MEDITATIONS

VIBRATIONAL BODY
EXERCISES
THAT SUPPORT
MY VIBRATIONAL BODY
AND CIRCULATE LIFE
FORCE ENERGY (CHI):
+ TAI CHI
+ QIGONG
+ MOVING MEDITATION

IV

THE SONG
OF EMBODIED
LOVE

THE NATURAL STATES THAT EMERGE FROM BEING

As I align my awareness with the Source of Life I attune myself to the natural state of peace.

When the first radios appeared, if one wanted to align the internal tuner to a specific frequency
So the radio could receive a clear broadcast channel,
One had to finely adjust a tuning knob located on the front.

Similarly, there is an aspect of our life that's also like tuning ourselves to a radio channel
As we finely attune our mind and heart to a vast field of *Natural Intelligence*
So as to receive a clear transmission from the limitless essence of who we really are.

As we align our awareness daily with *the Source of Life (God, Infinite Intelligence),*
We gain access to greater experiences of **peace**, **happiness**, **joy**, and **harmony**,
Or what has been referred to as **the natural states that emerge from *Being*.**

The more we discover effective ways of maintaining this alignment,
For example, through moments of deep stillness, by choosing elevated thoughts,
By being well rested and relaxed, by cultivating health and wellbeing,
And by doing what we can to fully feel our emotions,
The more effortlessly we experience these natural states.

On the other hand, when we encounter excessive stress, imbalance, or confusion,
Or when we're overly concerned with the many problems that arise in our life,
It can become difficult to experience these states.

How often one experiences peace and harmony, joy and happiness,
Usually depends on one's level of inner development and conscious awareness.

If, because of ignorance, we experience our life only at a basic level of mere survival needs,
Then the considerable fears and struggles of our everyday reality
Can greatly inhibit our ability to perceive these natural states of *Embodied Love.*

When our inner development is still immature and untrained,
We can, sometimes, be overwhelmed by the power and control of our egoic proclivities
And, thereby, only attain short periods of experiencing these higher states.

Yet as we expand our awareness of *Absolute Perfection* - and of *Oneness with All That Is,*
Our embodied experience of these natural states becomes more developed
And we start to encounter them as a more enduring part of our life.

Eventually, through the conscious development that comes from our various life experiences,
Through personal inner growth, through presence, and through our alignment with *Life,*
We can reach a more expansive and compassionate level of awareness
Where we learn to embody these states as our everyday way of being.

We are all on a *journey of awakening* in which we're constantly learning to stay attuned to *Life*
In order to receive clear guidance of how to realize true inner freedom
(I.e. - to experience the natural states of peace, harmony, joy, and happiness)
As an ongoing celebration of living this exquisite life.

Circle of the Natural States That Emerge From *Being*

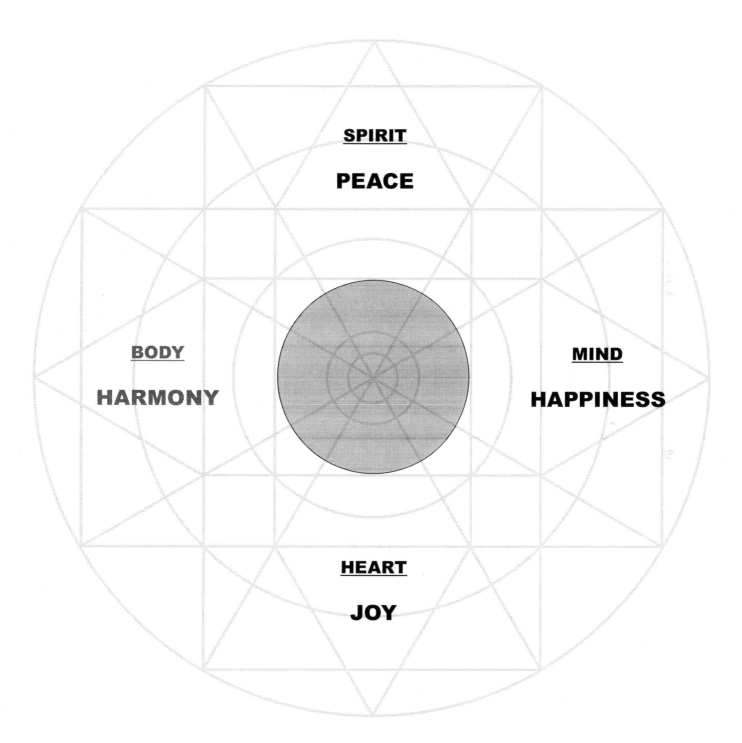

SPIRIT

PEACE

BODY

HARMONY

MIND

HAPPINESS

HEART

JOY

THE NATURAL STATE OF HARMONY

Today I feel in harmony with Life as I respond to the natural yearning within me to serve others.

If a metal pendulum within a clock is in motion swinging back and forth
    While the clock is hanging on a wall made out of wood,
        And you take a second pendulum clock
           Which you hang on the same wall close to the first clock
              While its pendulum is swinging as well,
                Then eventually, over time, the two moving pendulums
              Will begin to swing together in harmony.

The pendulum of the second clock will respond to the frequencies from the first clock
    As it attempts to harmonize with the pulsing vibrations it feels through the wooden wall.

In time, the second pendulum will slowly synchronize its rhythms with the other clock
    Because of a phenomenon that science calls *resonance*.

In science *harmony* is the concordance, or agreement, of two individual frequencies
    That, when combined, create a new resonant frequency.

As a metaphor, we can think of the first clock as analogous to *the Infinite Intelligence of Life*,
    And when we (symbolized by the second clock) take time to be silent and listen within
        In order to consciously attune our awareness to this *Natural Intelligence*,
           Then through the harmony created by a universal resonance,
              We experience an alignment with *the Source of Life*.

Our alignment with *Life* connects our awareness with the innate yearning in our heart
    To cultivate a compassionate life - and respond to a natural impulse to serve others.

Furthermore, **harmony can also be thought of in terms of *transcendence***
    Which can be known as a direct experience of transcendent Unity (Oneness with *Life*)
        Resonating within our heart and physical body.

True harmony comes from understanding - and living from the following universal perspective:
    "For the *whole* to be healthy and in balance,
        Each *part (each individual)* must support the *whole (the collective)*".

For example, we must be responsible to maintain our own health and wellbeing
    So we may effectively serve the health and wellbeing of others.

As we sustain our own wellbeing and align with *the Source of Life*, we more easily awaken to
    The knowing that serving another person *is essentially the same* as serving ourselves,
        Because we're all intimately connected as one human family.

The natural state of harmony that's always resonating within our physical body
    Can be experienced in the present moment as a perpetual transcendent Unity.

And thus, over time, we learn to recognize that **to truly be in harmony with *Life***
    Is to be one with, and attuned with, the natural yearning to serve others.

Circle of the Natural State of Harmony

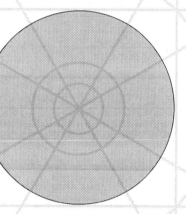

ALIGNMENT
HARMONY –
WHEN I AM ALIGNED
WITH LIFE, I CONNECT
MY AWARENESS WITH
THE NATURAL IMPULSE,
OR YEARNING, TO BE
IN SERVICE TO OTHERS

CONCORDANCE
HARMONY –
(IN SCIENTIFIC TERMS)
THE CONCORDANCE
OF TWO FREQUENCIES
THAT, WHEN COMBINED,
CREATE A NEW
RESONANT FREQUENCY

TRANSCENDENCE
HARMONY –
A DIRECT EXPERIENCE
OF TRANSCENDENT
UNITY (ONENESS WITH
LIFE) RESONATING
WITHIN MY HEART
AND PHYSICAL BODY

AGREEMENT
HARMONY –
THE SUPPORT
AND AGREEMENT OF ALL
PARTS (INDIVIDUALS)
THAT ARE IN A HEALTHY
ACCORD WITH
THE *WHOLE (COLLECTIVE)*

PILLARS OF AWAKENING

I am grateful for what I'm learning from every experience of my life.

The journey of awakening is a simple concise phrase
    Which represents the inward development that occurs for each person
        Who consciously cultivates a life of inner freedom (the mastery of *Being*).

Life is constantly inviting each of us to awaken to our next higher stage of awareness
    Along this ever-unfolding journey of personal growth and development.

There are two foundational components required to progress along our *journey of awakening:*
    1) To expand our awareness of what our life is truly about and what really matters,
        And 2) to awaken our consciousness to who we really are - our *Eternal Nature*.

The first component, gaining greater awareness of what our life is truly about
    Is like finding the special "keys" that unlock more possibilities of what life can become.

Four "keys" or "attributes" that are essential for us to embody on our *awakening journey*
    Are **gratitude**, **surrender**, **acceptance**, and awareness of our **Oneness** with all of life.

Imagine for a moment that this *journey of awakening*
    Is like walking through a series of locked rooms in a large stately house,
        Which ultimately leads to the Great Hall at the center of "the mansion of your life".

Now imagine that you have always possessed all of the keys to unlock and enter each room
    But they have been *hidden* deep within your inner being - and must be rediscovered.

As you approach the locked door to the first room, you realize within you the key of **gratitude**,
    Revealing the gift of being grateful for what you're learning from every life experience,
        Which allows you to enter the initial room - only to find the next door locked.

From a moment of insight, you recover another vital key, the key of **surrender**,
    As you let go of the attachments to your desires,
        And surrender to *a Greater Power, the Limitless Source of Life*,
            Which then enables you to gain entrance to the second room.

Acceptance that your life is unfolding perfectly just as it is
    (Fully embracing what life has given you without judgment or resistance)
        Is the next key you retrieve within you that opens the third door.

In the fullness of time, you find the last key - your awareness of your **Oneness** with all of life,
    Which admits you to the Great Hall (a symbol of embodying your *Fully Awakened Self*).

Each of the four seasons of the annual cycle - winter, spring, summer, and autumn,
    Symbolically points us to one of these "keys", or **Pillars of Awakening**.

The season of autumn, which represents the ongoing development of our unlimited potential
    And a time to be thankful for the richness and blessings from all of our life experiences,
        Has a way of pointing our hearts to the transformative quality of *gratitude*.

Circle of the Pillars of Awakening
(Attributes For Cultivating Inner Freedom and a Life of Mastery)

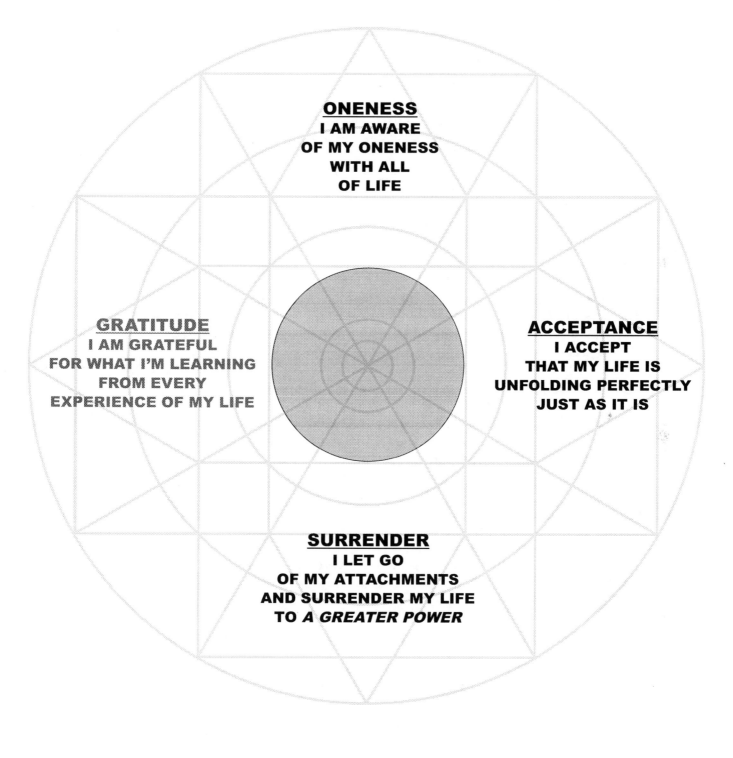

ONENESS
I AM AWARE
OF MY ONENESS
WITH ALL
OF LIFE

GRATITUDE
I AM GRATEFUL
FOR WHAT I'M LEARNING
FROM EVERY
EXPERIENCE OF MY LIFE

ACCEPTANCE
I ACCEPT
THAT MY LIFE IS
UNFOLDING PERFECTLY
JUST AS IT IS

SURRENDER
I LET GO
OF MY ATTACHMENTS
AND SURRENDER MY LIFE
TO _A GREATER POWER_

GRATITUDE

I feel grateful for the sublime gift of simply being alive.

When we take time to sit alone on the banks of a mighty river
    And pensively watch the river's current continually passing in front of us,
        We can easily sense the force of its rushing waters
            And feel its inherent power.

And possibly, we can tune into *the constant force of an unseen energy*
    That's invisibly directing the water downstream
        With a dynamic intent of purpose and directionality,
            Guiding the river as it ultimately joins some distant ocean.

If you were to throw a single leaf from a tree into the coursing water,
    The leaf will appear to merge with the current and essentially become part of the river
        As it glides effortlessly in the direction of the river's natural flow.

The leaf will, in a manner of speaking, "surrender itself" to this great surge of power
    And harmonize with the moving water.

The awakening attribute of **gratitude** can be likened to a leaf floating down a river,
    For one aspect of **gratitude is feeling blessed to be in sacred <u>harmony </u>with *Life***
        When we're consciously aligned with *"the River of Limitless Love"*
        And we accept our life is unfolding perfectly in each moment.

Gratitude can be thought of as **the radiant experience of opening our heart**
    And feeling the natural flow of authentic <u>joy</u> that courses through us.

There is an ongoing stream of *Life Force energy* that always wants to surge through our body
    And when we attune ourselves with its *Source*,
        We naturally allow this energy to flow through us unimpeded.

Gratitude is also our experience of feeling blessed with true <u>happiness</u>
    That emerges from the gift of simply being alive.

Of course, *"The River"* symbolically represents *the Source of Life*
    (In other words - *the Infinite Intelligence of the Universe, God, Ultimate Reality).*

Thus **gratitude is our experience of feeling richly blessed with a sublime <u>peace</u>**
    That arises as we align our awareness with *the Source of Life*.

As we genuinely become appreciative of the diverse gifts we encounter each day,
    We discover so many things to be grateful for, but the grandest gift of all is life itself.

It may be helpful to think of ourselves as analogous to a leaf that rides upon *"the Mighty River"*,
    And yet this same *"River of Life"* is perpetually flowing within us.

Therefore simultaneously, in some mysterious and unfathomable way,
    We <u>are</u> both *"the River"* and *"that which consciously journeys upon the River"*.

Circle of Gratitude
(In Relation to the Natural States of *Being*)

PEACE
GRATITUDE –
THE EXPERIENCE
OF FEELING RICHLY
BLESSED WITH A SUBLIME
PEACE THAT ARISES
AS I ALIGN MY AWARENESS
WITH *THE SOURCE OF LIFE*

HARMONY
GRATITUDE –
THE EXPERIENCE
OF FEELING BLESSED
TO BE IN HARMONY
WITH *LIMITLESS LOVE* AS
I ACCEPT THAT MY LIFE IS
UNFOLDING PERFECTLY

HAPPINESS
GRATITUDE –
THE EXPERIENCE
OF FEELING BLESSED
WITH TRUE HAPPINESS
THAT EMERGES
FROM THE GIFT
OF SIMPLY BEING ALIVE

JOY
GRATITUDE –
THE EXPERIENCE
OF FEELING BLESSED
TO BE IN THE NATURAL
FLOW OF AUTHENTIC JOY
AS I MAINTAIN AN OPEN
AND LOVING HEART

THE CYCLE OF ABUNDANCE

I embrace the natural "cycle of abundance and need" as an essential part of the Circle of Life.

It seems normal that we humans naturally long for, and attempt to continually reach towards,
An ongoing experience of abundance as part of how we want our lives to unfold.

For, of course, why wouldn't we prefer to have sustained abundance, unceasing fulfillment,
And want to be at the top of our game at all times?

At one level this idea seems desirable, yet by trying to hold onto an endless state of *increase*
Many people might actually be living their lives in a way that is illusory, or unnatural,
And they may be unaware, or in denial, of the natural and cyclic processes of life.

We all live in a physical world of numerous dual polarities, a reality of frequent changes
In which Nature, and all of its creatures, go through cycles of <u>increase</u> and <u>decrease</u>,
The perpetual shifting from <u>expansion</u> to <u>contraction</u>, and then back again.

The Earth annually revolves around the Sun, creating seasonal cycles of <u>growth</u> and <u>decay</u>,
In which during spring, a time of increase, flowers grow toward their fulfillment
And then blossom into the wondrous expressions of summer,
Only to decay in autumn or winter as a natural part of the Circle of Life.

Most seasonal weather patterns generate periods of moderate weather conditions
Which allow for many years of predictable abundant harvests,
But eventually include times of harsh extreme temperatures and circumstances
Which tend to limit the size of the harvest for those years.

Economies also go through natural periods of booming <u>ascent</u>, or seemingly endless growth,
Yet somewhere along the cycle they, sooner or later, turn the corner toward a <u>decline</u>.

And every species upon the Earth must experience the natural cycle
Of its family members or "loved ones" who, for a while, live lives of expansive growth,
Then mature and die, which seems to be a crucial part of the Circle of Life
Giving way for the next generation to carry on the work of its ancestors.

As we embrace this larger perspective of these natural cycles of **increase** and **decrease**,
This vantage can help us learn to be grateful for each experience taking place in our life.

With conscious awareness of the cyclic changes that naturally shift from **need** to **abundance**,
It becomes easier to flow with each situation - and learn to embrace our life just as it is.

This perspective also helps us feel greater empathy for the challenging experiences of others
Who are encountering these constant rhythms of change.

Our life is like a mountain climber ascending the north face and finally arriving at the peak,
But then recognizing we cannot stay at the summit forever.

And so we descend down the mountain slope to once again return to the valley floor
Always eager for the appropriate moment to passionately climb to the top another day.

Circle of the Cycle of Abundance
(The Natural Rhythms of Life)

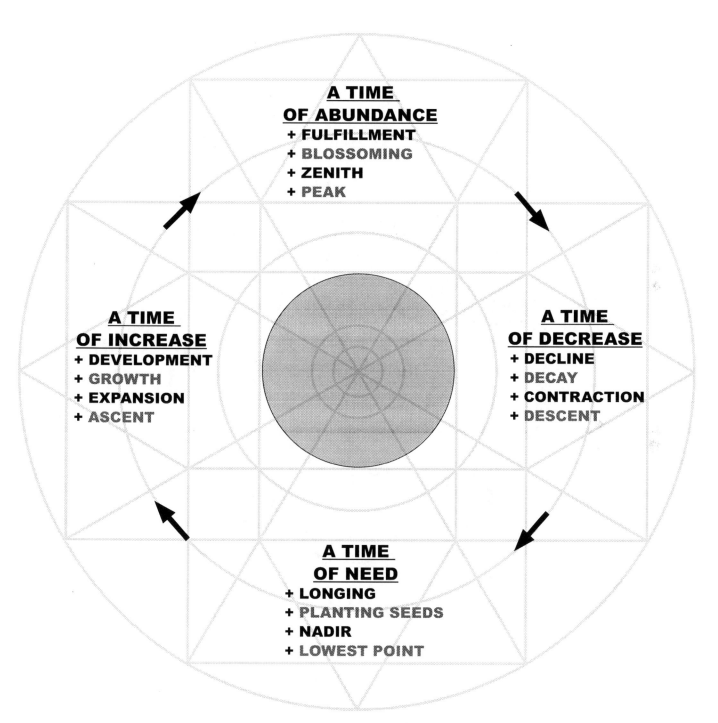

**A TIME
OF ABUNDANCE**
+ FULFILLMENT
+ BLOSSOMING
+ ZENITH
+ PEAK

**A TIME
OF INCREASE**
+ DEVELOPMENT
+ GROWTH
+ EXPANSION
+ ASCENT

**A TIME
OF DECREASE**
+ DECLINE
+ DECAY
+ CONTRACTION
+ DESCENT

**A TIME
OF NEED**
+ LONGING
+ PLANTING SEEDS
+ NADIR
+ LOWEST POINT

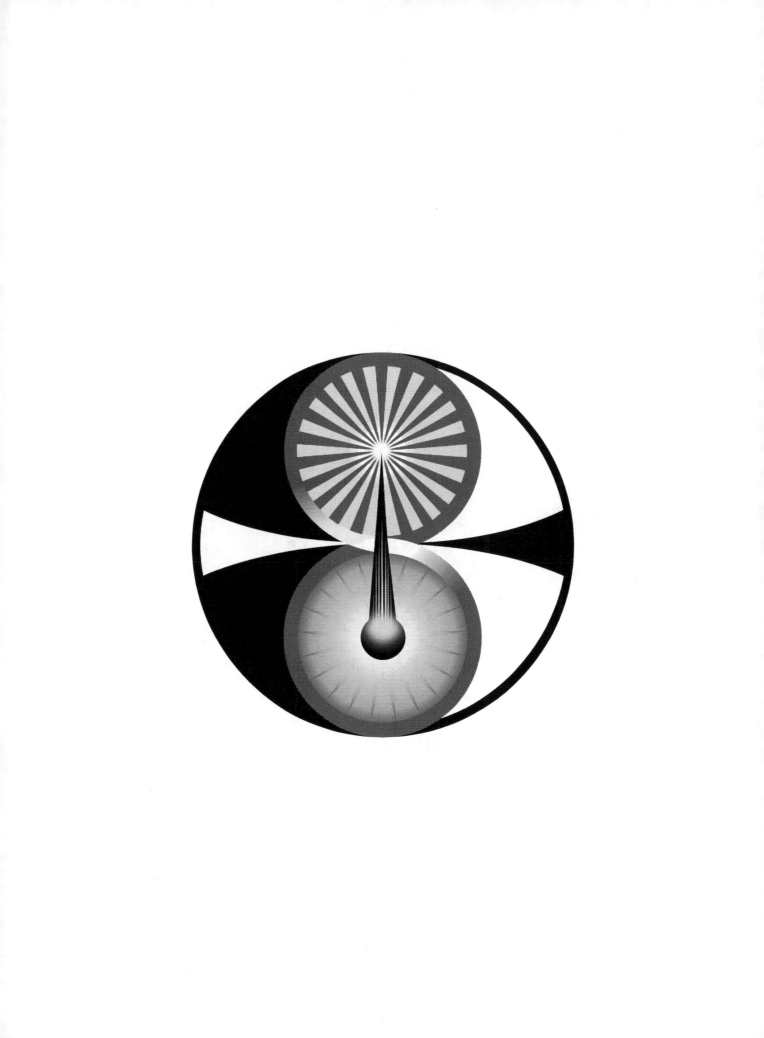

V

BODY
AWARENESS
PRACTICES

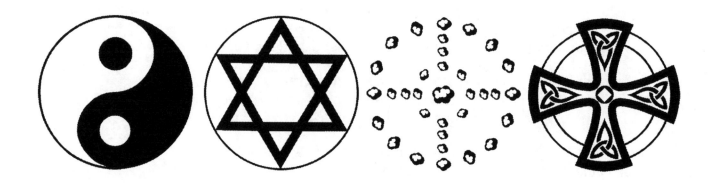

WELLBEING OF THE BODY

I consciously keep my body in a state of health and balance using daily self-care practices.

Every competent factory foreman that works in a manufacturing plant
    Knows if he or she is to keep their production machines well-oiled and in good order,
        A disciplined regimen of constant maintenance must be followed.

Of course, our physical bodies are so much more than mere machines,
    Yet it will certainly benefit us to employ various regimens of self-care
        If we desire to keep our bodies in a state of health and balance.

Every night we go to sleep so our body can regenerate itself,
    Which is like plugging our internal batteries into *the universal battery charger*
        In order to continually recharge our body for our next day's energy requirements.

Behavioral scientists have demonstrated that when we humans do not sleep
    For a period of more than three or four days, we begin to experience a type of insanity.

Thus, it's necessary to receive **adequate rest** every night so our body can be restored,
    And so we're able to respond sanely to our personal world and its daily challenges.

The idea of maintaining **proper nutrition and hydration** for the body may seem obvious,
    Yet for some people, food is merely a vehicle to acquire sensual culinary pleasures
        Or is used as a momentary escape from one's emotional burdens.

We must always remember that the primary function of our food
    Is to provide the nutrition required to fuel our bodies and give us the energy we need.

All organisms from every part of our planet require motion to live
    And in order to maintain wellbeing, they must experience sufficient movement.

When we stop moving our bodies due to stationary lifestyles or a lack of **physical exercise**,
    The internal organs and systems of our bodies cannot function at their optimum levels,
        And thus, if we want to live vibrantly, we must experience adequate movement.

The contemporary notion of **living simply in harmony with Nature**
    May bring up idyllic images of residing in a rustic log cabin surrounded by lush woods
        In some utopian pastoral or mountain setting.

Yet when we're consciously aligned with *the Source of Life*
    Which is the *True Essence* and very core of our being,
        We can learn to live in the busiest metropolis on Earth, or in any environment,
            And still discover the harmony our heart yearns for.

Living in harmony has to do with our ability to effectively simplify our daily activities enough
    So we're able to hear the *inner guidance* that's always directing us each day.

Physical wellbeing requires that we pursue a wise regimen of constant maintenance and care
    So our body is kept "well oiled" - and is at all times ready and able "to follow our heart".

Circle of Wellbeing of the Body
(Transformative Practices)

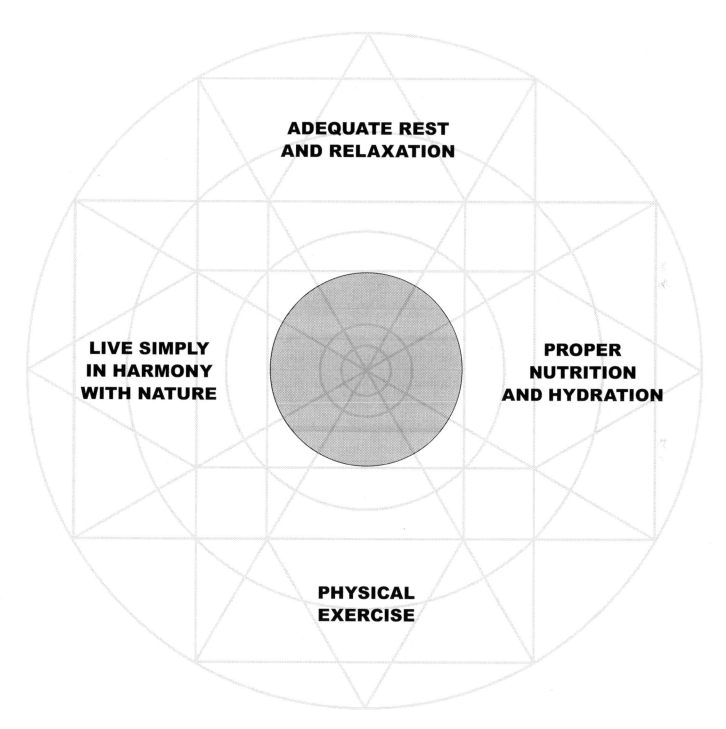

ADEQUATE REST
AND RELAXATION

LIVE SIMPLY
IN HARMONY
WITH NATURE

PROPER
NUTRITION
AND HYDRATION

PHYSICAL
EXERCISE

NUTRITION

I nourish my body with energy from the Sun that has been transformed into vital nutrients.

When a person is standing under a brightly lit streetlight at night,
    You can easily perceive both the person who is actually standing under the light
        And also their shadow, which is projected onto the ground by the streetlight.

Of course in this scenario, the actual living person is seen as "the solid reality"
    And their "shadow" is a dark area generated by "the real person" in the path of the light.

In our contemporary culture which has produced fast-paced living and dysfunctional lifestyles,
    Much of *modern food* has lots of "shadow facets" that some people are addicted to,
        And regarding nutrition, many forget to place their attention on what is "real".

Thousands of years ago, when primitive humans were first emerging on the African plains,
    The instinctual purpose of food was to ingest plants and animals
        In order to obtain the necessary fuel
            That would sustain the "real" energy needs of the physical body.

Instinctively, we all sense proper nutrition comes from the kind of food we consume
    Which adequately replenishes the required nutrients to the cells of our bodies.

Over time as various cultures developed, the taste of food and how it was visually presented
    Would, sometimes, gain more attention than the basic instincts of nutrition,
        And the focus of the food's nutrient value became less and less important.

Recently during our modern era, there has been a pursuit for brand new forms of food
    To be made quickly, economically, and flavorful without much concern for its nutrition.

Furthermore, in order to make the growing of food more efficient and economically profitable,
    Factory farms began to grow vegetables with the aid of pesticides and toxic fertilizers,
        Which eventually created depleted soils deteriorating the food's overall quality.

Using the above visual image of a person standing under a streetlight at night,
    We can see that *nutrition* is analogous to "the actual person who is the solid reality",
        And processed foods, fast food outlets, convenience, greedy profitability,
            And a lack of regard for its quality are similar to "the person's shadow".

But it's extremely detrimental to the health of our body, and the overall health of our nations,
    If all we do is focus on "the shadow aspects of our food"
        Since **nutrition comes from the natural vitamins, minerals, and enzymes**
            Which supply the "real" building blocks for a healthy body.

Of course, meals should taste good, and by using organic natural foods and common sense,
    They can certainly be both nutritious and full of scrumptious delightful flavors.

When we remember that Nature's **nutrition actually originates from sunlight**
    That has been transformed into vital nutrients providing our body with energy,
        Then we can more easily shift our focus from "the shadow" to "the radiant light".

Circle of Nutrition
(A Transformative Practice)

ENERGY
NUTRITION COMES
FROM THE PLANTS
AND ANIMALS I EAT,
WHICH ARE THEN
CONVERTED INTO
THE FUEL AND ENERGY
THAT SUPPORT MY BODY

NUTRIENTS
NUTRITION COMES
FROM THE KIND
OF FOOD I CONSUME,
WHICH REPLENISHES
THE REQUIRED
NUTRIENTS
TO ALL OF MY CELLS

BUILDING BLOCKS
NUTRITION COMES
FROM THE NATURAL
VITAMINS, MINERALS,
AND ENZYMES
WHICH SUPPLY
THE BUILDING BLOCKS
FOR A HEALTHY BODY

SUNLIGHT
NUTRITION COMES
FROM THE LIGHT
OF THE SUN WHICH HAS
BEEN TRANSFORMED
INTO VITAL NUTRIENTS
THAT PROVIDE
MY BODY WITH ENERGY

MOVING MEDITATION

I keep the channels within my body open so the Energy of Life may naturally flow through me.

Universal Life Force (Chi) is intrinsically flowing through every one of Nature's creatures
Including all microbes, trees, flowers, animals, and, of course, every human being.

The constant and natural flow of this *Vital Energy* of the Cosmos
Is one of the most fundamental dynamics within the Universe.

After eons of evolutionary development, early humans acquired
The kind of expansive mind and sensitive heart
Which have allowed the human species to become the only creatures on Earth
That are consciously self-reflective.

Yet self-reflective capacities (as do all expanded abilities) can also bring about a downside,
In other words - a potential pathology that may be experienced in one's heart or mind.

Due to a lack of awareness, our mind can make choices that may generate self-inflicted stress
And our heart can hold onto difficult emotions which may stifle and constrict our body.

Mental stress or emotional constriction that's unconsciously produced within us
Blocks the natural flow of *Chi*, or *Life Force*, which wants to flow through us unimpeded.

If this occurs in our life, we can sometimes take action to eliminate the source of the problem
As well as remove these blockages by practicing specific transformative exercises
That support the circulation of *Chi* to course through our vibrational body,
Such as Tai Chi, Qigong, or Moving Meditation.

Moving Meditation is a simple movement awareness exercise that anyone can easily learn
To help support the flow of *Chi* throughout the subtle fields of the vibrational body.

To do this exercise - find a quiet place, stand erect with your spine straight, feet a little apart,
Knees slightly bent, and place both hands, palms facing each other but not touching,
In front of your navel with your eyes closed.

Begin moving your hands slowly from the navel area outward to each side, and back again,
Repeating these slow, soft repetitive movements for two to twenty minutes
While you visualize *Chi* effortlessly flowing into every cell of your body
And as you imagine any negativity or imbalance flowing out.

Feel energy increasing as you move your hands apart - and a pressure as they come together,
While your mind is focused on an intention of healing - or of vibrant health and vitality.

And, finally, be aware of the cycle of your breath that's directly linked with the *Chi* energy
Moving up the back of your spine and then down the front of your body.

Life is movement - movement is an essential part of life
And we can use **movement**, **intention**, and **breath** to maintain the circulation of ***Chi***
So, each day, *the Vital Energy* of the Universe may naturally flow through us.

Circle of Moving Meditation
(A Transformative Practice)

BREATH
BE AWARE OF YOUR
BREATH THAT IS DIRECTLY
LINKED WITH THE *CHI
ENERGY* AS IT MOVES UP
THE BACK OF YOUR SPINE
- AND DOWN THE FRONT
OF YOUR BODY

SLOW MOVEMENTS
+ STAND ERECT
+ STRAIGHTEN SPINE
+ MOVE HANDS SLOWLY
FROM YOUR NAVEL
OUT TO EACH SIDE,
AND BACK AGAIN
+ REPEAT 2 - 20 MINUTES

INTENTION
WHILE MOVING
YOUR HANDS, FOCUS
YOUR ATTENTION ON
A SPECIFIC INTENTION
OF HEALING, OR
A VISION OF VIBRANT
HEALTH AND VITALTY

VITAL LIFE FORCE
VISUALIZE *CHI,*
OR *LIFE FORCE ENERGY,*
FLOWING INTO EVERY CELL
OF YOUR BODY
WHILE YOU IMAGINE
ANY NEGATIVITY OR
IMBALANCE FLOWING OUT

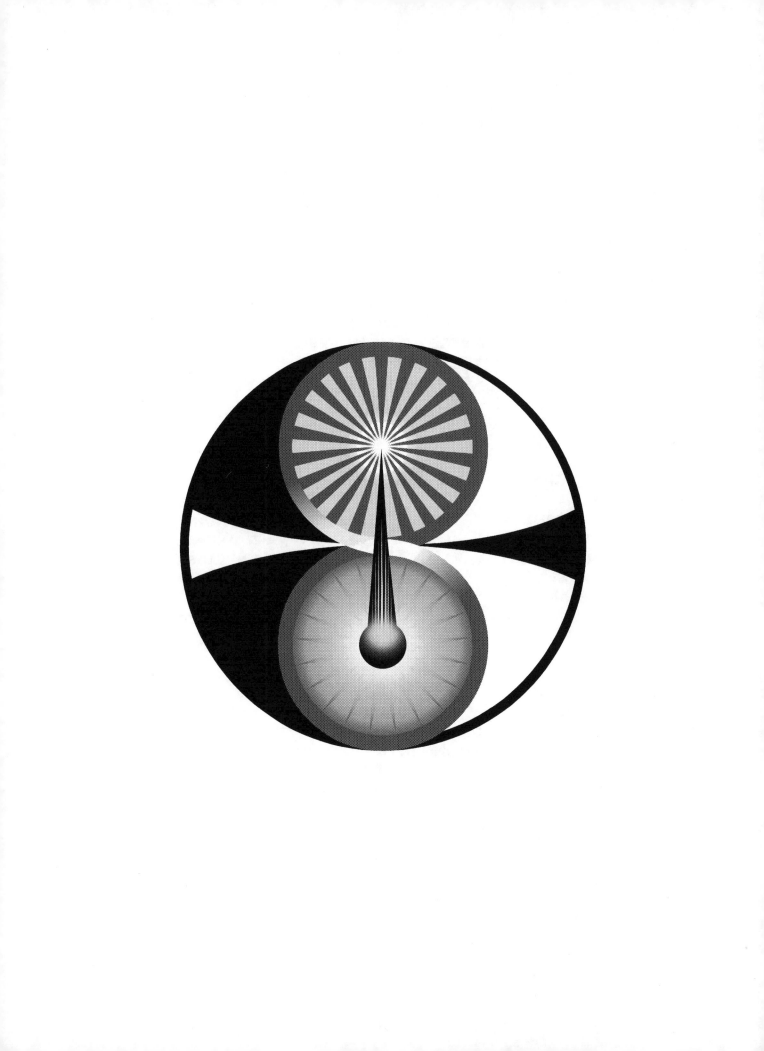

VI

ARCHETYPES
OF HIGHER
KNOWLEDGE

UNIVERSAL ARCHETYPES

Today I use my creative imagination to envision the best, most joyful future I can conceive.

Universal archetypes are visionary images that symbolically represent our <u>future</u> potential
And using these images in an awareness practice to focus our creative imagination
Can help us embody more of our vast potential in our <u>present</u> life experience.

The famous Swiss psychiatrist, Carl Jung, developed in his work the concept of an archetype
And recognized it could be used in various ways in relation to the human psyche,
Such as an image to access heightened possibilities of who we can become
Which are held and exist in, what he called, *the collective unconscious.*

He believed every person has the natural ability to tap into *the collective unconscious*
And, thus, *the energy fields of archetypes* so as to access these dormant possibilities
And use them to constructively transform one's life in benevolent ways.

Humanity's earliest archetypes appeared as certain **primary forms** (Sun, Moon, and stars),
First used by ancient humans as divine embodiments of their newly discovered gods.

Over time, many different archetypes began to emerge as fundamental **forms of Nature**,
Such as special mountains or active volcanoes which symbolized strength and power,
Majestic old trees representing wisdom and understanding,
Or ornate flowers, crystals, and gems expressing beauty and grace.

Other images came from the numerous **animal forms** that were given spiritual attributes,
Such as the bear, wolf, elephant, and lion - to name a few,
Or the many representations of flying birds symbolizing freedom and perspective,
And even various mythological creatures like the Unicorn and Pegasus.

Today, there's also various archetypal **human forms** that have been given mystical power,
Such as *family archetypes* like father patriarch, mother matriarch, and newborn child,
Religious archetypes such as avatars, angels, saints, masters, and sages,
And a multitude of *visionary and hero archetypes.*

Each of these symbolic images listed above can be thought of as a **universal archetype**
Which (if we use them in a representational manner within a transformative practice
As a means to embody in our life a higher vision of what is possible)
Is capable of pointing us to a richer imagination of who we can become.

In the film industry, some movie producers have brought to the screen certain *hero archetypes*
Which can help point us to a greater awareness of our potential,
Such as in the images of Luke Skywalker and Yoda from the movie, "Star Wars",
And in the characters of Frodo and Gandalf
From the classic Tolkien trilogy, "Lord of the Rings".

If we are open to their challenge, all four of these contemporary archetypes are inviting us
To embrace a grander vision of the potential that is latent within us,
An innate call "to soar with our higher angels"
So we can more easily awaken to our infinite possibilities.

Circle of Universal Archetypes
(Symbolic Images that Point to My Greater Potential)

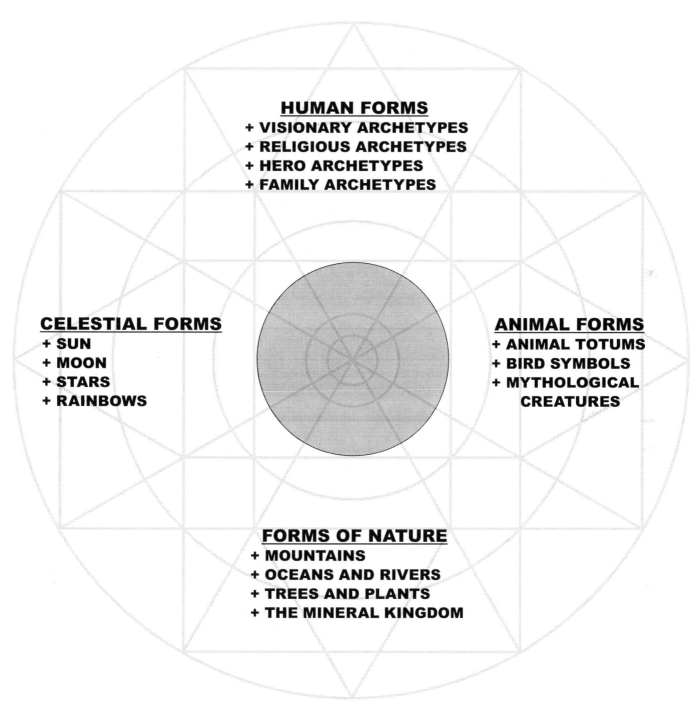

HUMAN FORMS
+ VISIONARY ARCHETYPES
+ RELIGIOUS ARCHETYPES
+ HERO ARCHETYPES
+ FAMILY ARCHETYPES

CELESTIAL FORMS
+ SUN
+ MOON
+ STARS
+ RAINBOWS

ANIMAL FORMS
+ ANIMAL TOTUMS
+ BIRD SYMBOLS
+ MYTHOLOGICAL
   CREATURES

FORMS OF NATURE
+ MOUNTAINS
+ OCEANS AND RIVERS
+ TREES AND PLANTS
+ THE MINERAL KINGDOM

THE GREAT CIRCLE OF THE ARCHETYPES

My creative imagination is a powerful vehicle to help me manifest my unlimited potential.

Every twenty-eight days the Moon performs its "cyclic dance"
    As it journeys along its high orbit and circumnavigates the Earth.

Of course, if you are outdoors during the late evening hours and look up at the night sky,
    You may be able to observe the particular phase the Moon is currently in.

During a full moon (if you are sensitive to it) you might feel a heightened level of energy
    That seems to circulate throughout your body.

At the phase of a new moon, you may sense a period of restful awareness,
    A time of new beginning - or a time of renewal.

The two half moons also have their own inward impulses that can be felt and experienced,
    Which represent the cultivation of inner balance - and our integration with all of life.

In a similar way, we can associate the natural impulses of the seasonal cycles of the Earth
    With four distinct sets of archetypal images because, like the four phases of the Moon,
        Each of the seasons expresses its own relationship to our *spiritual journey.*

The full moon can be matched to the season of summer
    With all of its radiant energy of growth and blossoming,
        While the new moon correlates to winter - a time of rest and rejuvenation.

Each of the four archetypal systems on the following page expresses specific human yearnings
    That correspond to the primary *qualities of the seasons.*

Winter can be connected with **the Archetypes of Spiritual Awakening**,
    A series of four archetypes that, joined together, represents our *journey of awakening*
        Which, over time, leads us to our destiny as a Master of Freedom -
            One who lives a life of inner freedom and service to others guided by *Love.*

The Archetypes of Conscious Contribution can be related to **spring**,
    Where each of the four archetypes represents a natural longing to contribute
        By offering our unique gifts and talents to co-creating a better world.

Summer can be aligned with **the Archetypes of Life Mastery**,
    In which the archetypes symbolize the key virtues, values, and qualities
        That help cultivate inner freedom and embody our destiny of an awakened life.

And finally, **the Archetypes of Higher Knowledge** can be linked to **autumn**,
    Where each archetype points us to a natural longing to develop our unlimited potential,
        Transcend our current level of awareness, learn what our life is truly about,
            And expand our consciousness of who we really are.

Every day, we have a new opportunity to consciously participate in this "cyclic dance",
    The journey of our "ascending orbit of awakening" along the never-ending spiral of life.

The Great Circle of the Archetypes

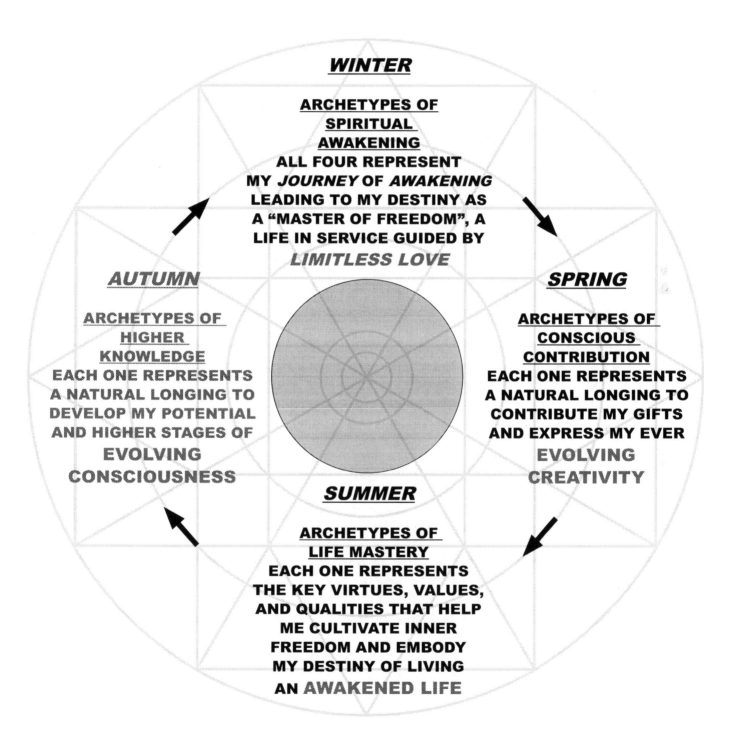

WINTER

ARCHETYPES OF
SPIRITUAL
AWAKENING
ALL FOUR REPRESENT
MY *JOURNEY* OF *AWAKENING*
LEADING TO MY DESTINY AS
A "MASTER OF FREEDOM", A
LIFE IN SERVICE GUIDED BY
LIMITLESS LOVE

AUTUMN

ARCHETYPES OF
HIGHER
KNOWLEDGE
EACH ONE REPRESENTS
A NATURAL LONGING TO
DEVELOP MY POTENTIAL
AND HIGHER STAGES OF
EVOLVING
CONSCIOUSNESS

SPRING

ARCHETYPES OF
CONSCIOUS
CONTRIBUTION
EACH ONE REPRESENTS
A NATURAL LONGING TO
CONTRIBUTE MY GIFTS
AND EXPRESS MY EVER
EVOLVING
CREATIVITY

SUMMER

ARCHETYPES OF
LIFE MASTERY
EACH ONE REPRESENTS
THE KEY VIRTUES, VALUES,
AND QUALITIES THAT HELP
ME CULTIVATE INNER
FREEDOM AND EMBODY
MY DESTINY OF LIVING
AN **AWAKENED LIFE**

ARCHETYPES OF HIGHER KNOWLEDGE

I feel a natural yearning in me to seek the true, the good, and the beautiful within all of life.

Many thousands of years ago as our human ancestors were progressing
    Through their early stages of evolution,
        Some highly developed individuals acquired the mental awareness
           To gaze up into the evening star-strung sky
             And began to contemplate the meaning of life.

Over eons of time, these contemplations led to the emergence of four areas of knowledge
    Which aided our ancestors in expanding their initial sense of life's meaning.

In relation to *the absolute realm of life* (in other words - the transcendent perspective),
    There emerged in them an inherent directive to commune with *a Greater Power*,
        An Exalted Intelligence within all of life that was greater than themselves,
           A Transcendent Presence they believed was the source of everything,
             And a need to fulfill a primal urge to be in harmony with this *Power.*

Then in regards to *the relative realm of life* (in other words - the material-plane perspective),
    There emerged a deep inner yearning to search for, and express,
        Three unique aspects of their inner awareness: <u>truth</u>, <u>goodness</u>, and <u>beauty</u>.

Over time, the search for *truth* (what one believes to be undeniably true)
    Eventually took form and came to be known as the many fields of science,
        The inner striving to discover and develop greater awareness
           Of how the natural world worked, and to apply this knowledge of science
             So life could become easier and more comfortable.

The search for the *good* in life became a philosophical quest
    Of learning how to harmoniously live with one another,
        To co-exist together in cooperation and peace,
           And to formulate a practical system of laws and governance
             That best served the collective needs of the people.

The search for *beauty* (what feels pleasing to one's heart)
    Became a longing to envision and cultivate various forms of artistic expression,
        To explore the infinite possibilities of our human imagination,
           And to experience life as a creative expression of *beauty.*

At this current moment in time as humanity continues to evolve in consciousness,
    Many people are now personally undergoing an emergent process of *awakening*
        As they experience higher and more expansive levels of conscious awareness.

The natural human impulse to seek *the true, the good,* and *the beautiful*
    Is constantly inviting all of us to also seek a more expansive meaning for our life.

This human impulse, symbolically and archetypically, is taking form in every one of us
    As **the Awakened Mystic, the Awakened Philosopher, the Awakened Artist,**
        And **the Awakened Scientist**.

Circle of the Archetypes of Higher Knowledge

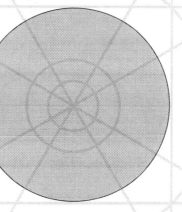

AWAKENED MYSTIC

IT IS THE PART OF ME THAT USES EFFECTIVE WAYS TO MAINTAIN AN **ALIGNMENT** WITH *THE SOURCE OF LIFE* SO I CAN TRULY BE OF SERVICE TO OTHERS

AWAKENED SCIENTIST

IT IS THE PART OF ME THAT DEDICATES MY LIFE AS A LIVING EXPERIMENT SO I MAY GAIN GREATER AWARENESS OF THE *TRUTH* (WHAT IS BELIEVED TO BE UNDENIABLY TRUE)

AWAKENED PHILOSOPHER

IT IS THE PART OF ME THAT FOSTERS HEART WISDOM SO I MAY ESTABLISH THE MOST HARMONIOUS, *GOOD*, AND MEANINGFUL WAYS TO LIVE WITH OTHERS

AWAKENED ARTIST

IT IS THE PART OF ME THAT CULTIVATES ABUNDANT WAYS TO ENJOY AND EXPERIENCE "LIFE AS AN ART - AND AS A CREATIVE EXPRESSION OF *BEAUTY*"

AWAKENED SCIENTIST

I live my life as an ongoing living experiment so I may cultivate greater awareness of what is true.

Prior to the emergence of early humans some primitive hominids, in order to better survive,
Would experiment with their food choices by eating different types of plants
Intuitively hunting for the nutrients and fuel that would give them added strength
And a greater advantage over other species.

Certain hominids were vegetarians and only ate foods such as fruits, leaves, nuts, and roots,
Yet also experimented with strange exotic plants that, occasionally, would kill them.

Other types of hominids evolved to become carnivores,
While still others ate a combination of both vegetation and meat.

Evolutionary science tells us only one of these hominid groups successfully survived
To eventually become our human species we now call Homo sapiens.

Primitive humans would also experiment with the appropriate size of their migratory clans
Trying to determine the proper balance between the ease of feeding a small group
And maintaining enough members for a strong defense against other clans.

Over time, they began to experiment with planting seeds to secure sustainable food supplies,
Initiating the modern reign of agriculture - and creating the means to form large cities.

This was a long unfolding journey, which we can now refer to as an <u>Evolutionary Revolution</u>
That occurred during a period of gradual human exploration and incremental discovery.

This exploration by our ancestors continued for many thousands of years
Until there was a great innovation of knowledge due to an explosion of experimentation
That took place in the sixteenth century commonly called the <u>Scientific Revolution</u>
(Which was an attempt to expand an understanding of the laws of Nature).

This new wealth of knowledge and understanding of how Nature worked
Led to many practical inventions in the <u>Industrial Revolution</u> during the 1700 and 1800's.

Today, we are at an important turning point in our ongoing evolution of human experimentation
In which we're currently experiencing a <u>Spiritual Revolution</u>, an <u>Awakening Revolution</u>,
And now our "human experiment" is to discover a deeper meaning for our lives.

This expansion of meaning is shifting many people into the time of **the Awakened Scientist**,
One who searches for higher knowledge by dedicating their life as a living experiment
So as to cultivate **greater awareness of what is true**.

It is **one who lives a compassionate life**, continually develops **the wisdom of the heart**,
And embraces more inclusive perspectives of reality based on **what life is truly about**.

The image of **the Awakened Scientist** activates our inner longing to be a spiritual explorer,
Travel to the next turn in the perpetual journey, gain greater awareness of the truth,
And investigate the unknown, so all that we do know can be used to serve others.

Circle of the Awakened Scientist
(An Archetype of Higher Knowledge)

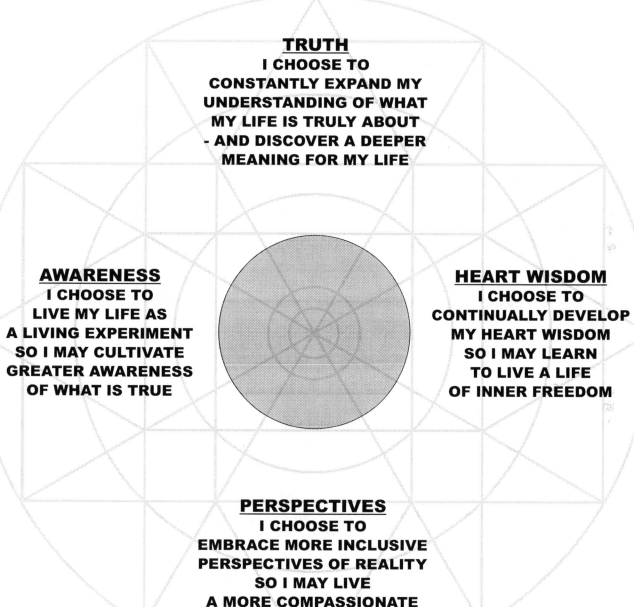

TRUTH
I CHOOSE TO
CONSTANTLY EXPAND MY
UNDERSTANDING OF WHAT
MY LIFE IS TRULY ABOUT
- AND DISCOVER A DEEPER
MEANING FOR MY LIFE

AWARENESS
I CHOOSE TO
LIVE MY LIFE AS
A LIVING EXPERIMENT
SO I MAY CULTIVATE
GREATER AWARENESS
OF WHAT IS TRUE

HEART WISDOM
I CHOOSE TO
CONTINUALLY DEVELOP
MY HEART WISDOM
SO I MAY LEARN
TO LIVE A LIFE
OF INNER FREEDOM

PERSPECTIVES
I CHOOSE TO
EMBRACE MORE INCLUSIVE
PERSPECTIVES OF REALITY
SO I MAY LIVE
A MORE COMPASSIONATE
AND CARING LIFE

FUNDAMENTAL UNIVERSAL PERSPECTIVES

As I expand my perspectives of what my life is truly about it helps me live a more meaningful life.

There's an old and now famous Asian parable about four blind men
Who each encounter an elephant for the first time - yet in their own distinct way.

The first blind man approaches the elephant from behind, holds the elephant's tail
And declares, *"An elephant must be like a rope".*

The second blind man moves toward the large creature, puts his arms around a leg
And proclaims, *"An elephant is like a pillar",*
While the next blind man places his hand on the flat side of its huge belly
And states, *"An elephant must certainly be like a wall".*

The last blind man comes to the front of the mammal, grabs the elephant's trunk
And announces, *"An elephant is like a fire hose".*

All of these blind men are absolutely right from their personal assessment of the animal,
Yet we can also observe that each man has only a partial truth of what an elephant is
Based on their individual point of view - or their unique perspective.

Many people are becoming aware that we live in a multi-perspectival world which requires us
To view all we perceive from multiple perspectives, in order to more fully comprehend it.

If we want to clearly grasp the challenges and opportunities within the great diversity of life,
Including Nature, the institutions of our societies, other people, and our personal life,
We must attempt to include, and to understand, as many possible perspectives
So we may gain a more complete and integrated picture of the whole.

There are four **fundamental universal perspectives** that are inherent in all structures:
1) An interior perspective, 2) an exterior perspective,
3) An individual perspective, and 4) a collective perspective.

The interior perspective defines *an inward expansive impulse* of evolving consciousness
That yearns to expand one's awareness of what is true, develop one's potential,
And describes a person's internal world - which includes the mind and heart.

The exterior perspective defines *an outward expressive impulse* of ever-evolving creativity
That yearns to be creative, express greater diversity, contribute unique gifts and talents,
And relates to a person's body, external environment, Nature, or the Universe.

The individual perspective defines a singular expression of a species of life,
A single category of physical structures, or a distinct animal or person - like you or me.

Finally, there's **a collective perspective** within all things defined as having a relationship with,
And being an integral part of, a larger group such as a family, community, or nation.

Could it be that bringing each of these unique perspectives together into one integrated picture
Can help us all live a more meaningful life by fully comprehending *"the entire elephant"*?

Circle of Fundamental Universal Perspectives
(Four Vantages of Every Life Form, Challenge, or Opportunity)

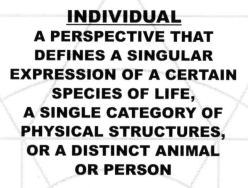

INDIVIDUAL
A PERSPECTIVE THAT
DEFINES A SINGULAR
EXPRESSION OF A CERTAIN
SPECIES OF LIFE,
A SINGLE CATEGORY OF
PHYSICAL STRUCTURES,
OR A DISTINCT ANIMAL
OR PERSON

INTERIOR
A PERSPECTIVE THAT
DEFINES A YEARNING
TO EXPAND AWARENESS,
LEARN WHAT IS TRUE,
AND DEVELOP POTENTIAL
- AND DESCRIBES
THE INTERNAL WORLD
OF MIND AND HEART

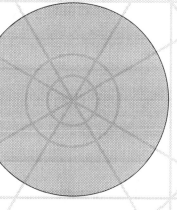

EXTERIOR
A PERSPECTIVE THAT
DEFINES A YEARNING
TO CREATE, EXPRESS
GREATER DIVERSITY, AND
CONTRIBUTE ONE'S GIFTS
- AND RELATES TO ONE'S
BODY, ENVIRONMENT,
NATURE, THE UNIVERSE

COLLECTIVE
A PERSPECTIVE THAT
DEFINES HAVING
A RELATIONSHIP WITH,
AND BEING
AN INTEGRAL PART OF,
A LARGER GROUP OF
LIFE - SUCH AS A FAMILY,
GROUP OR NATION

DIMENSIONS OF EVOLUTION

As I embrace a more inclusive perspective of life, compassion for others blossoms within me.

If you are given a rectangular wooden box
    And are asked to describe its physical measurements to another person,
        You will want to communicate its spatial relationships
            By using a standard measurement system of three dimensions.

In order to describe the three defining outer measurements of the box,
    You will need, of course, to employ the dimensions of length, height, and width.

When we attempt to describe life with its distinctive dimensions - many are now understanding
    That there are also numerous facets, or dimensions, to our evolutionary development.

In order to be effective in developing ourselves - and contributing our creative gifts to the world
    Utilizing the most constructive and expansive manner we possibly can,
        It's beneficial and important to take into account
            All the various dimensions that exist in our life within any given situation.

There are **four fundamental dimensions of evolution**, or distinct developmental influences,
    To be aware of, and to include, if we desire to understand a fuller picture of our life.

There is **psychological evolution** (referred to as an <u>interior-individual dimension</u> of evolution)
    Which is the evolution of the various ascending stages of personal human development,
        Such as the inward expansion of our minds so as to cultivate higher knowledge,
            The opening of our hearts to a greater awareness of love and compassion,
                And the continuous awakening of our spiritual centers.

Relational evolution (the <u>interior-collective aspect</u>) represents an *internal-group impulse*,
    Which points us to the development of our cultural and communal relationships
        As well as our intimate relationships that serve us in learning to love more fully.

Societal evolution (an <u>exterior-collective dimension</u>) is an *external-group impulse*
    Depicting how we organize and structure our communities, institutions, and societies.

And finally, **cosmological evolution** of the physical world (the <u>exterior-individual dimension</u>)
    Is portraying the dynamic unfolding of galaxies, stars, planets, the wonders of Nature,
        And all individual organisms, including humans, from an external perspective.

If we don't look at all the dimensions of evolution when trying to understand how life develops
    (In other words - if we don't include all of the different influential factors
        That are important to understanding our lives, culture, society, and the Cosmos)
            Then we may only perceive a partial picture, only a smaller fragment
                Of whatever aspect of reality we are striving to comprehend.

As we continue to grow in awareness and discover the many advantages
    Of looking at all the diverse dimensions of ourselves, our world, and the Universe,
        We are more able to see "the Big Picture of *Life*", the inclusive nature of reality,
            And from this, learn how to be ever more compassionate with one another.

Circle of the Dimensions of Evolution
(Four Distinct Developmental Influences of My Life)

PSYCHOLOGICAL EVOLUTION
(INTERIOR - INDIVIDUAL)
THE EVOLUTION OF THE VARIOUS ASCENDING STAGES OF MY PERSONAL INNER DEVELOPMENT

RELATIONAL EVOLUTION
(INTERIOR - COLLECTIVE)
THE EVOLUTION OF MY PERSONAL RELATION-SHIPS, AND CULTURAL AND COMMUNAL RELATIONSHIPS

COSMOLOGICAL EVOLUTION
(EXTERIOR - INDIVIDUAL)
THE EVOLUTION OF THE PHYSICAL UNIVERSE AS IT CREATES GALAXIES, STARS, PLANETS, AND LIVING ORGANISMS

SOCIETAL EVOLUTION
(EXTERIOR - COLLECTIVE)
THE EVOLUTION OF HOW SOCIETY ORGANIZES AND STRUCTURES ITS COMMUNITIES AND SOCIAL INSTITUTIONS

LIVING IN A STATE OF CONSCIOUS RELAXATION

Today I fully accept my life just as it is and, thus, I live in a state of conscious relaxation.

When a colorful maple leaf gently falls from a tree in autumn and lands in a flowing stream
The leaf seems to, metaphorically, "surrender to the current"
And finds itself effortlessly traveling downstream with the moving water.

In the above visual image, there's nothing to keep the maple leaf stuck in any one place
Because the leaf has "fully let go" into the current of the stream.

Similarly, if we desire to **live in a state of conscious relaxation**
(Which can also be thought of as - *a peaceful state of present moment awareness),*
We must be like the maple leaf and courageously let go into *the River of Life*
By **surrendering our attachments** of how we want our life to be
And, instead, flow with our life as it is.

Using the practice of daily mindfulness, we can learn to be *the experiencer (the witness)*
Of all the day-to-day experiences of our passing thoughts, emotions, and sensations
And simply observe them as if they're passing clouds within a clear blue sky.

Without any attachment to these momentary phenomena flowing in the perpetual *River of Life,*
We can learn to experience a natural relaxation of our life just the way it is
Rather than clinging to an expectation.

Living in conscious relaxation is **recognizing that our life is unfolding perfectly**
And letting go of our attachments of how we want our life to be - while accepting what is.

For when we **learn to love and accept ourselves unconditionally**
And unconditionally love and accept every aspect of life,
We allow the natural flow of *Life Force energy to move* through us unimpeded.

Could it be that we are here on Earth experiencing life in these bodies
So our *Eternal Self* can realize the ever-expanding lessons of unconditional love?

A big step toward the personal goal of offering our unconditional love to all of life
Is learning to fully love and accept ourselves.

Thus in order to truly surrender our attachments, be grateful our lives are unfolding perfectly,
And love and accept ourselves unconditionally,
We must discover how to **sustain an alignment with *the Source of Life*.**

As we authentically feel this attunement, we're more able to experience a trust in *Life*
That allows us to feel safe and relaxed in every situation.

At this present time, our contemporary culture doesn't provide much training
For us to learn to live in conscious relaxation (to feel safe and loved no matter what).

Yet there's always a constant invitation from *the Natural Intelligence* within us
That yearns to direct us each day down *the River of Life* if we're willing to listen.

Circle of Living In a State of Conscious Relaxation
(Transformative Practices)

ALIGNMENT
AS I LIVE IN A STATE OF
CONSCIOUS RELAXATION,
I SUSTAIN
AN ALIGNMENT WITH
THE SOURCE OF LIFE
SO I MAY MORE EASILY
FEEL TRUST AND SAFETY
IN EVERY SITUATION

PERFECTION
AS I LIVE IN A STATE OF
CONSCIOUS RELAXATION,
I RECOGNIZE THAT
MY LIFE IS UNFOLDING
PERFECTLY - AND I LET GO
OF MY ATTACHMENTS OF
HOW I WANT MY LIFE TO
BE - AS I ACCEPT WHAT IS

SELF-LOVE
AS I LIVE IN A STATE OF
CONSCIOUS RELAXATION,
I LOVE AND ACCEPT
MYSELF JUST AS I AM
WHICH ALLOWS
THE NATURAL FLOW
OF *LIFE FORCE* ENERGY
TO MOVE THROUGH ME

SURRENDER
AS I LIVE IN A STATE OF
CONSCIOUS RELAXATION,
I LET GO
OF ANY ATTACHMENTS
TO MY THOUGHTS,
EMOTIONS,
OR SENSATIONS
AS THEY ARISE EACH DAY

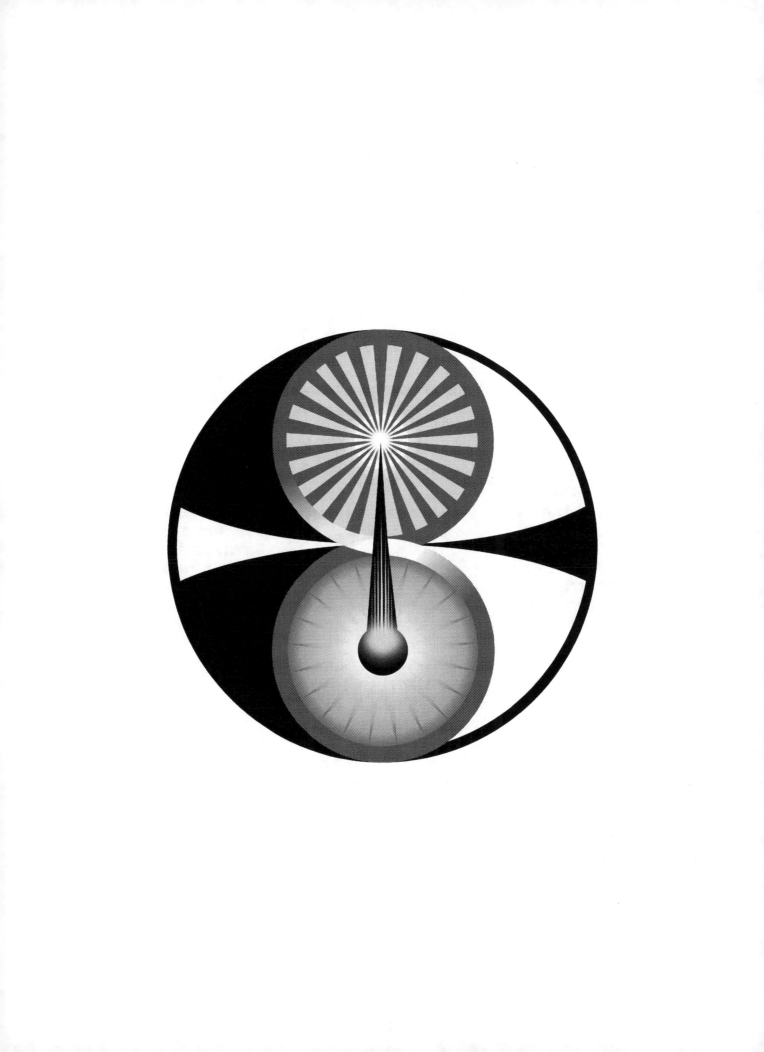

VII

BODY
AWARENESS
PRACTICES

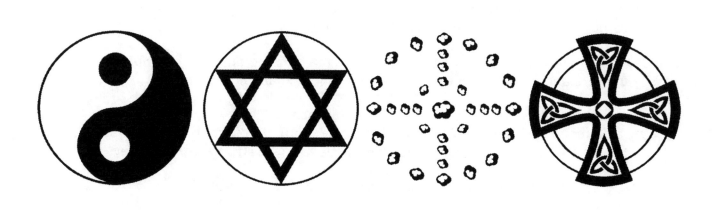

REST

Today I spend time in the sanctuary of silence so I may rest in the rejuvenative "Arms of Life".

At this time of year in many regions of the northern hemisphere,
    We can begin to feel an outer change as the autumn air starts to get crisp and cold.

During this season, the leaves of deciduous trees are "painted with myriad colors",
    Which eventually are released and fall from their branches.

And even a few of the high mountain countrysides
    Have already received their first blanket of snow.

The noticeable change in the air also heralds "a knowing" that winter will be coming
    And numerous creatures of the natural world are responding to their instincts
        To find a place of inactivity and stillness
        Where they can enter into an extended state of **rest**.

For example, bats hibernate every year in dark caverns,
    Reptiles instinctively burrow themselves into the frigid ground,
        Bears regenerate in quiet caves during their annual respite,
            The seeds of most plants lie in patient cessation,
                And much of Nature simply waits for a future time to take action.

Of course for us humans, rest comes from our daily periods of sleep or paused activity
    Which **rejuvenates and re-energizes our bodies, hearts, and minds**.

Without proper rest each day, our <u>body</u> cannot physically maintain radiant vitality
    Which limits our ability to keep our <u>heart</u> open - and nurture our <u>mind</u>.

Rest also comes from the direct experience of transcending our mind
    Through **moments of profound silence, such as during the practice of meditation**
        As we align our awareness with *the Source of Life*.

Each day "an inner call sounds", inviting us to access the portal to our *Eternal Nature,*
    The transcendent place within where we can truly rest in absolute stillness.

Some people may approach moments of meditative silence
    Only as a means to **align themselves with God** as part of a "formal" spiritual practice,
        Yet it's also one of the most natural ways to deeply rest and restore everyday.

And rest can come from **the renewal of our spirit that is brought about**
    As we take time to expand our awareness of what really matters in our life,
        Which then fosters greater heart wisdom and authentic compassion.

Like bats and reptiles that rhythmically hibernate with the seasonal cycles,
    There is, as well, a natural cycle amidst the moments of each day
        When we can rest in the *"Arms of Life"*,
            An inward place we can constantly go to renew ourselves
                And from which we *awaken* to offer our creative gifts to the world.

Circle of Rest
(Transformative Practices)

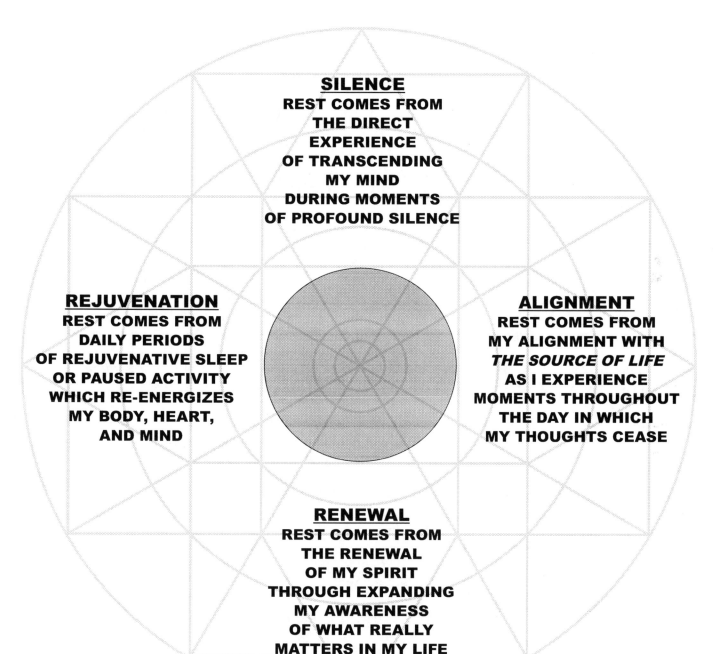

SILENCE
REST COMES FROM
THE DIRECT
EXPERIENCE
OF TRANSCENDING
MY MIND
DURING MOMENTS
OF PROFOUND SILENCE

REJUVENATION
REST COMES FROM
DAILY PERIODS
OF REJUVENATIVE SLEEP
OR PAUSED ACTIVITY
WHICH RE-ENERGIZES
MY BODY, HEART,
AND MIND

ALIGNMENT
REST COMES FROM
MY ALIGNMENT WITH
THE SOURCE OF LIFE
AS I EXPERIENCE
MOMENTS THROUGHOUT
THE DAY IN WHICH
MY THOUGHTS CEASE

RENEWAL
REST COMES FROM
THE RENEWAL
OF MY SPIRIT
THROUGH EXPANDING
MY AWARENESS
OF WHAT REALLY
MATTERS IN MY LIFE

MAINTAINING AN AWARENESS OF WHOLENESS

Everywhere I look in the world around me I perceive Life's Perfect Wholeness.

Fortunately for us humans, we have been blessed to inhabit an oxygen-rich planet
That provides the perfect atmosphere and supply of air for us to live and flourish.

Since air constantly circulates around us, we are always connected to this oxygen-rich air
And yet, most of the time, we're not consciously aware we are breathing it
Because our mind is focused on other thoughts.

Similarly, given that *the Infinite Presence of Love* is present everywhere within the Universe
And there is no place where *Love* is not,
We are inherently always connected to this unbounded *Ultimate Reality*,
But we may not be consciously aware of it
When our mind has placed its attention on a host of other things.

For centuries, "God" has been described using numerous phrases by many religious traditions,
Such as God is *the Creator*, God is *Limitless Love*, God is *Universal Consciousness*,
God is *Pure Awareness*, and God is *the Source of All That Is*, to name just a few.

The various religions of the world have boldly declared there is great benefit
To maintain an alignment with God (or what we can also call *Perfect Wholeness*)
And these traditions have developed a number of spiritual practices to attain this.

One simple practice is to consciously cultivate an ongoing alignment with *the Source of Life*
So we may **be mindful of the *Wholeness* and perfection within everything**.

The development of a greater awareness of *Wholeness* through the practice of meditation
Can help us embody an experience that we are truly one with every expression of life
And attune us to the guidance that's always available for our everyday choices.

Another transformative exercise is to **practice perceiving all manifestations of life**
That are right in front of us (trees, people, cities, mountains, the sky, etc.)
As an integral part of *Perfect Wholeness*.

Perfect Wholeness (the Infinite Presence of Love) is everywhere,
And so as we gaze at our world, can we accept that there's no place where *Love* is not?

We can also **listen to "the music of *Wholeness*"** by hearing all the diverse sounds around us
Like the wind, birds, people, traffic, airplanes, dogs barking, etc.
And practice experiencing them as part of *the symphony of the Divine*.

And as we naturally take in a breath of fresh air,
We can feel we are breathing in *Wholeness* as the animating *Force of Life*
Which different world cultures have called *Chi*, *Prana*, or *Life Force energy*.

Just like the nourishing air that's all around us, we're constantly breathing in *the Energy of Life*,
And we can more easily experience the peace and joy that's always available to us
When we're consciously aware of the *Perfect Wholeness* within all of life.

Circle of Maintaining an Awareness of *Wholeness*
(Transformative Practices)

**BE MINDFUL
OF *WHOLENESS***
I CULTIVATE
AN ALIGNMENT WITH *THE
SOURCE OF LIFE* WHICH
HELPS ME BE MINDFUL
OF THE *WHOLENESS*
AND PERFECTION
WITHIN EVERYTHING

**PERCEIVE
WHOLENESS
EVERYWHERE**
I PERCEIVE ALL
MANIFESTATIONS OF LIFE
(TREES, PEOPLE, CITIES,
MOUNTAINS, THE SKY)
AS AN INTEGRAL PART
OF *PERFECT WHOLENESS*

**LISTEN TO
THE MUSIC
OF *WHOLENESS***
I LISTEN TO ALL OF THE
SOUNDS AROUND ME
(BIRDS, PEOPLE, PLANES,
DOGS) AND EXPERIENCE
THEM AS *THE SYMPHONY
OF THE DIVINE*

**BREATHE
IN WHOLENESS**
I TAKE IN A BREATH
OF AIR AND FEEL
I AM BREATHING IN
WHOLENESS AS
THE ANIMATING *FORCE
OF LIFE (CHI, PRANA,
LIFE FORCE ENERGY)*

PHYSICAL BODY EXERCISES

I maintain a healthy body - and thus, I'm able to share more of my creative gifts and talents.

When a cold mountain stream is freely rushing over rocks and boulders,
    Its active waters are naturally rich with vital life-enhancing energy.

But when the once-moving water is trapped inside a small pool that can't circulate,
    It will begin to turn rank and stagnant.

From the tiniest sub-atomic particles and charged electrons
    To the grandest galaxies, stars, and planets in the Cosmos,
        Every phenomenal expression of form is in ceaseless motion.

Rays of light, weather patterns, the flow of ocean currents, the smallest microbes,
    Even the Earth itself, are all perpetually moving in "a dynamic eternal dance".

Life is intrinsically linked with movement, for everything is in constant motion at an atomic level,
    And in order to develop in a healthy manner, all forms of life require activity.

Our physical bodies require movement to keep our muscles, bones, and organs healthy,
    And to assist our blood and lymph fluids to flow naturally.

"Use it or lose it" is a well-known contemporary phrase
    That's sometimes stated to motivate people to exercise their bodies.

There are four primary systems of **physical body exercise**
    We can utilize to keep the various components of our bodies healthy
        And to foster an overall state of vibrant wellness.

Stretching exercises can keep our muscles and ligaments elastic and flexible
    Of which yoga and free dance are especially suited,
        And even only five to ten minutes a day can be beneficial.

Strengthening exercises, such as weight training, resistance training, and isometrics,
    Strengthen our organs and muscles, while building and maintaining muscle mass.

Running, walking, swimming, and cardio classes
    Are **aerobic exercises** that circulate the flow of nutrients and also cleanse our bodies.

And **toning exercises**, such as East Indian Ayurvedic self-massage
    Or the Chinese system of Do-In, can help us maintain healthy muscle tone
        And can be done daily or periodically throughout the week.

It would be optimal for our bodies if, each week, we could practice a program of exercise
    That included all four of these primary systems.

When we develop a lifestyle in which we maintain a balance of life-enhancing movements,
    Our body, because it has plenty of healthy motion, cannot become stagnant
        And becomes like a flowing stream of vital radiant energy.

Circle of Physical Body Exercises
(Transformative Practices)

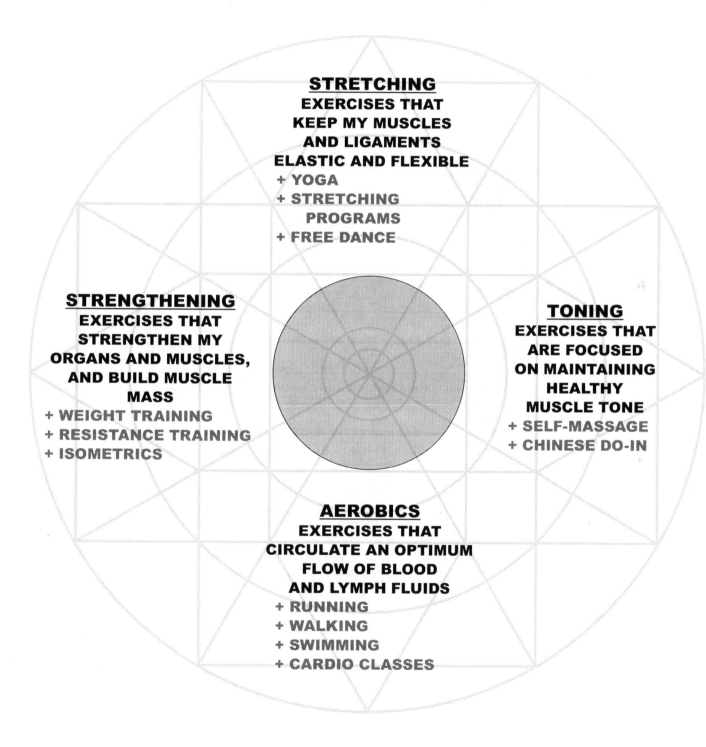

STRETCHING
EXERCISES THAT
KEEP MY MUSCLES
AND LIGAMENTS
ELASTIC AND FLEXIBLE
+ YOGA
+ STRETCHING
   PROGRAMS
+ FREE DANCE

STRENGTHENING
EXERCISES THAT
STRENGTHEN MY
ORGANS AND MUSCLES,
AND BUILD MUSCLE
MASS
+ WEIGHT TRAINING
+ RESISTANCE TRAINING
+ ISOMETRICS

TONING
EXERCISES THAT
ARE FOCUSED
ON MAINTAINING
HEALTHY
MUSCLE TONE
+ SELF-MASSAGE
+ CHINESE DO-IN

AEROBICS
EXERCISES THAT
CIRCULATE AN OPTIMUM
FLOW OF BLOOD
AND LYMPH FLUIDS
+ RUNNING
+ WALKING
+ SWIMMING
+ CARDIO CLASSES

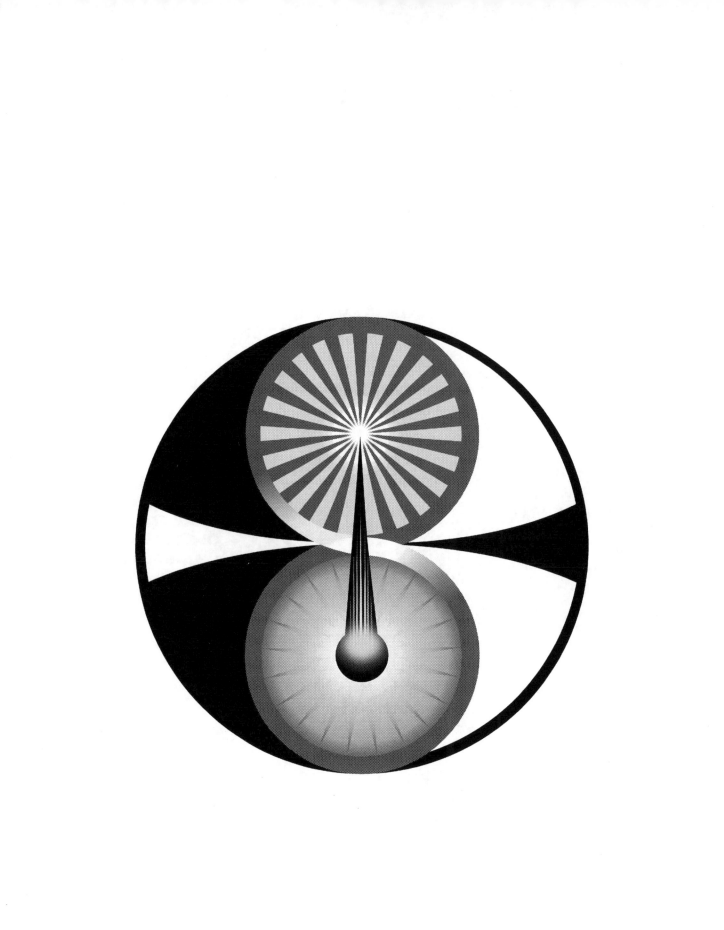

VIII

ARCHETYPES OF SPIRITUAL AWAKENING

ARCHETYPES OF SPIRITUAL AWAKENING

I feel the limitless power of spiritual transformation that is constantly awakening in me.

Many children enjoy spending playtime in the nearby forests
    Collecting colorful bugs, fuzzy caterpillars, and interesting looking creatures,
        Totally mesmerized by the intriguing manifestations of Nature's wonders.

Some kids like to extract tadpole specimens from shallow ponds
    Placing their prizes in glass jars so they can take them home - and watch them grow.

As children observe their tadpoles (which look like tiny fish), they gradually form little rear legs,
    Then front legs, and as they develop, their "tails" begin to disappear.

Nature has created a mysterious transformative process
    In which these miniature fish-looking creatures called tadpoles slowly change into frogs.

Young tadpoles spend the early stages of their lives
    Swimming in the limited underwater world of small ponds,
        Not knowing, one day, they will transform into a completely different form of life
        And develop legs so they can explore the surface of the world as a frog.

Similarly, many people do not know (because they have not discovered or been taught)
    That they are personally going through a powerful and natural transformative process,
        Transforming from a self-centered person into a world-centered person,
        In other words - from a person unconsciously living in fear and limitation
        Into one who lives a life of inner freedom and service to others.

All of us are constantly being invited by a natural evolutionary tug, an inner spiritual yearning,
    To transform ourselves from what we can poetically call **the Young Awakening Self**
        (One who is focused of self-power, control, approval from others, or fear),
        To gradually, with dedication, developing into **the Compassionate Heart**
        (One who lives a life of compassion, care, gratitude, and service).

Within the stories of some old fairy tales, there is a frog that's "awakened" by a kiss
    And is, thereby, magically transformed into a handsome prince or beautiful princess.

When a caring and compassionate person is, so to speak, "kissed by *the Transcendent*",
    In other words - is fully merged and integrated with ***the Infinite Presence of Love***,
        He or she is said to *spiritually transform* into a **Master of Freedom**.

A **Master of Freedom** is one who, in the fullness of time, learns to live a life of inner freedom,
    Who is in service to the wellbeing of others, and who loves all of life unconditionally.

It's a specific stage of spiritual consciousness that's defined as a *Fully Awakened Self*
    In which a person absolutely knows the holy magnificence of who they really are.

Just like our own human journey of life, the earth-bound caterpillar is simply being a caterpillar
    Until an instinctual and miraculous process of *transformative awakening*
        Invites the caterpillar to transform into a graceful butterfly - so it can take flight.

Circle of Archetypes of Spiritual Awakening
(My Spiritual Journey of Personal Transformation)

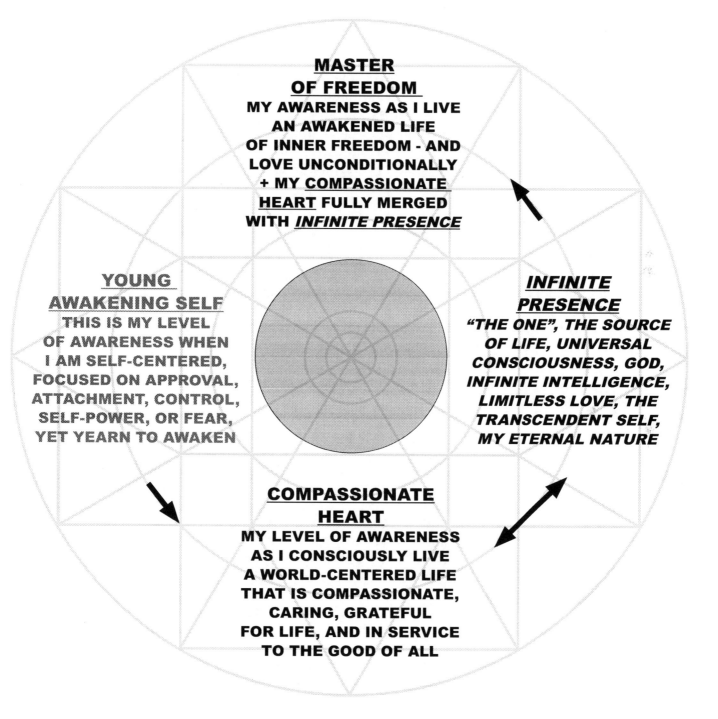

MASTER OF FREEDOM
MY AWARENESS AS I LIVE AN AWAKENED LIFE OF INNER FREEDOM - AND LOVE UNCONDITIONALLY + MY COMPASSIONATE HEART FULLY MERGED WITH *INFINITE PRESENCE*

YOUNG AWAKENING SELF
THIS IS MY LEVEL OF AWARENESS WHEN I AM SELF-CENTERED, FOCUSED ON APPROVAL, ATTACHMENT, CONTROL, SELF-POWER, OR FEAR, YET YEARN TO AWAKEN

INFINITE PRESENCE
"THE ONE", THE SOURCE OF LIFE, UNIVERSAL CONSCIOUSNESS, GOD, INFINITE INTELLIGENCE, LIMITLESS LOVE, THE TRANSCENDENT SELF, MY ETERNAL NATURE

COMPASSIONATE HEART
MY LEVEL OF AWARENESS AS I CONSCIOUSLY LIVE A WORLD-CENTERED LIFE THAT IS COMPASSIONATE, CARING, GRATEFUL FOR LIFE, AND IN SERVICE TO THE GOOD OF ALL

YOUNG AWAKENING SELF

I cultivate a conscious awareness of what is true so I may learn to live a life of inner freedom.

There are many diverse creatures within the natural world
    That have developed novel systems of protection or innovative shielding mechanisms
        So they can defend themselves from the lurking dangers in their environment.

For example - during millions of years of evolution
    Crabs have fashioned a shield of thick exoskeleton over their bodies,
        Armadillos have developed a suit of armored skin,
            Porcupines surround themselves with sharp defensive quills,
                Skunks spray their attackers with irritating toxins,
                    And turtles have formed hard protective shells on their backs
                      Which they retreat into when predators are near.

It's very natural for every form of life to instinctually pursue creative strategies to survive
    And, thereby, to manifest effective means to protect itself from life's menacing perils.

We humans have also produced our own unique ways of protecting ourselves
    From the emotional and psychological dangers of our contemporary world
        By forming a mental structure within our inner being known as *the egoic self*.

In early humans, *the egoic self* was first developed as a means to further personal survival
    In the midst of ever-new psychological challenges that emerged within tribal living.

In our modern world, *the egoic self* has become "the dysfunctional mental armor" within us
    That has contrived the idea "we must emotionally protect ourselves from others"
        And "who we are is our body, our feelings, our thoughts, our self-invented stories"
        Which has formed a protective self-image **we believe we must defend**.

Like a turtle that carries heavy protection on its back, we may routinely hide behind our "shells"
    As a way to temporarily survive the many psychological dangers within our daily lives.

We may also strive to **protect our self-image** from the attacks and opinions of other people
    As well as from our own self-centered illusions we have falsely conceived
        By building various types of walls of separation between ourselves and others
        In order to survive in, what we believe is, an emotionally hostile world.

One way we seek to ensure the continuity of our self-image is decide we **must be in control**
    And try to gain the approval of others, which can, at times, give us "an illusion of safety".

Our life is in a perpetual flow of change - and if we haven't yet developed "a trust in life",
    Then we may live in constant **fear of the unknown** - as well as anxiety of death.

As an evolving species we humans are still quite young as we continue to learn and develop,
    Yet we're discovering that in order to *awaken* to our next stage of spiritual awareness
        We must transform our *self-centered egoic nature*, **the Young Awakening Self**,
        That has helped us survive past perils, but is now no longer required,
        And make space for the emergence of *the Fully Awakened Self*.

Circle of the Young Awakening Self
(Fear-based and Self-centered Strategies to Survive Emotionally)

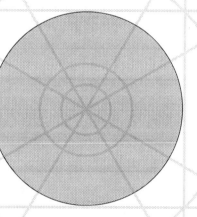

THE FEARFUL MIND
WHEN I'M NOT ALIGNED,
I LIVE IN CONSTANT FEAR
OF THE UNKNOWN, OF
RELIVING THE PAST, OF
CONCERNS ABOUT THE
FUTURE - AND ATTEMPT
TO COVER UP
MY ANXIETY OF DEATH

THE DEFENDER
WHEN I'M NOT ALIGNED,
I IDENTIFY WHO I AM AS
SEPARATE FROM OTHERS
THINKING I AM MY BODY,
FEELINGS, THOUGHTS,
"MY STORIES", CREATING
A FALSE SELF-IMAGE
I BELIEVE I MUST DEFEND

THE CONTROLLER
WHEN I'M NOT ALIGNED,
I THINK I NEED TO BE
IN CONTROL AND GAIN
THE APPROVAL
OF OTHERS
IN ORDER TO ENSURE
THE CONTINUITY
OF MY SELF-IMAGE

THE PROTECTER
WHEN I'M NOT ALIGNED,
I NEED TO PROTECT MY
SELF-IMAGE FROM THE
ATTACKS AND OPINIONS
OF OTHERS BY BUILDING
WALLS OF SEPARATION
SO I CAN SURVIVE
EMOTIONALLY

EVOLUTION OF THE IDENTIFICATION OF SELF

My True Nature is eternal, unbounded, limitless, and one with the Source of Life.

Today's vast knowledge of evolution, derived from over 170 years of scientific research
And from the latest discoveries of DNA studies and gene mapping,
Has shown that every human being is interconnected with every other human.

These findings, along with the myriad discoveries of astronomy, have proved that all humans
Are also biologically interconnected to every other form of life on Earth,
That our planet Earth is a dynamic and evolving part of our Solar System,
That our Solar System is an integral part of the Milky Way Galaxy,
And that this massive galaxy we live in is one of billions of galaxies
Which makes up the known Universe.

By systematically observing and analyzing (to the best of current scientific abilities)
The exterior workings and unfolding of the Cosmos, we can quantitatively accept
That we humans are a small yet exquisite part of an immense evolving Universe.

As well as being an integral part of life's <u>exterior</u> evolution,
There is also an <u>interior</u> dimension of life that is evolving at the same time.

One primary component of our interior dimension is how we look at ourselves psychologically,
In other words - how we identify who and what we believe we are.

Long after the first humans emerged on the evolutionary scene as a new species
Having, at that point in time, only a primitive level of awareness,
Humans began to think of themselves (i.e. basically identified themselves)
As **an individual and isolated physical body**
That they perceived was separate from everything around them.

Over time, early humans developed **a separate ego personality** as a survival mechanism
In which they identified themselves as their thoughts, emotions, and body sensations,
As well as their fear-based pathologies which, generally, became habitual.

Currently within humanity (in which there are many diverse levels of cultural development)
Most people still identify themselves as separate and isolated entities.

Yet countless people from around the world are now *awakening* to an expanded awareness,
Awakening to a greater understanding and embodied experience of who they really are.

These dedicated individuals are realizing their true identity as an ***Eternal and Limitless Self***
That's consciously aligned with *the Universal Self (the Source of All That is)*.

Maybe one day when we have *awakened*, we will finally let go of all identification with anything,
For ultimately it's our destiny to realize that **we are one with *the Source of Life*.**

The evolutionary perspective provides us with a well-defined view of "the Big Picture of reality"
And with an understanding we are all in a natural process of ever-unfolding *awakening*,
A process that's taking us to our next exalted horizon on the eternal Circle of Life.

Circle of the Evolution of the Identification of Self

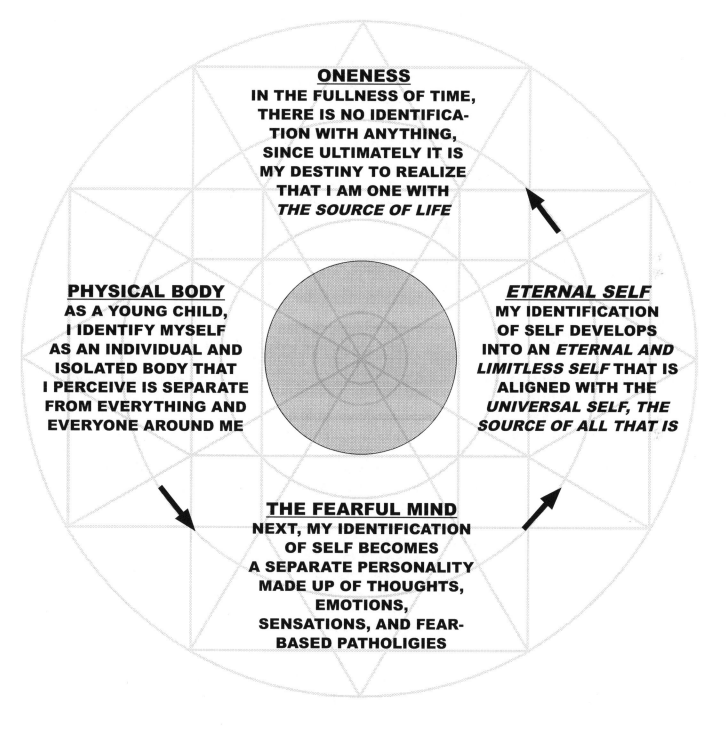

ONENESS
IN THE FULLNESS OF TIME, THERE IS NO IDENTIFICATION WITH ANYTHING, SINCE ULTIMATELY IT IS MY DESTINY TO REALIZE THAT I AM ONE WITH *THE SOURCE OF LIFE*

PHYSICAL BODY
AS A YOUNG CHILD, I IDENTIFY MYSELF AS AN INDIVIDUAL AND ISOLATED BODY THAT I PERCEIVE IS SEPARATE FROM EVERYTHING AND EVERYONE AROUND ME

ETERNAL SELF
MY IDENTIFICATION OF SELF DEVELOPS INTO AN *ETERNAL AND LIMITLESS SELF* THAT IS ALIGNED WITH THE *UNIVERSAL SELF, THE SOURCE OF ALL THAT IS*

THE FEARFUL MIND
NEXT, MY IDENTIFICATION OF SELF BECOMES A SEPARATE PERSONALITY MADE UP OF THOUGHTS, EMOTIONS, SENSATIONS, AND FEAR-BASED PATHOLIGIES

THE FEARFUL MIND

I am constantly guided each day to live my life within the awakened field of absolute safety.

Within Nature's myriad life forms there is an inborn trait science calls *instinct*
 Which is an innate survival impulse that guides creatures through their labyrinth of life.

The reality of life is full of constant challenges, surprises, and adjustments,
 And it is this inward force of instinctual knowing
  Which helps direct living organisms through their daily maze of change.

Without their natural instincts to guide them,
 Caterpillars might "fear" entering their dark cocoons
  "Terrified" their lives may be coming to an end.

Without this inner direction from *the Intelligence of Life*,
 Cicadas might "fear" burrowing into the earth for their long periods of hibernation
  "Afraid" they may be building their own tombs.

Without the instinctual knowing of the natural world,
 Colorful maple trees might "fear" dropping their autumn leaves
  "Frightened" that their leaves may never return again.

We humans also have an instinctual impulse that's constantly communicating with us,
 Yet there is a unique difference between us and the instincts of the rest of Nature.

Humans have both a primal form of instinct - and an evolved form that's called *inner guidance*,
 And in order to be consciously connected to the guidance within us
  We must journey beyond the incessant chatter of our mind
   By becoming quiet - and aligning our awareness with *the Source of Life*.

Inner guidance leads us to greater awareness of what is true - and what really matters,
 For without clarity of what our life is truly about, there is a natural **fear of change**.

Without an authentic feeling of trusting in *Life*,
 There is a natural **fear of the unknown**.

Without the exalted perspectives of higher awareness, there is a natural **resistance**
 To accepting our experiences of life just as they are.

And without a direct experience of our eternal and unchanging nature *(our True Nature)*,
 There is a natural **fear of death**.

For without the inner guidance that comes to us within a "Big Picture perspective" of reality,
 Fear naturally arises in us "to protect us", so to speak, "from the perils of the world".

Our instincts are constantly directing us to evolve beyond our dysfunctional habits
 And always inviting us to reach for the next horizon of expanded possibility for our life
  In order to embrace these higher perspectives and, eventually, to let go of fear
   So we may truly live our life within *the awakened field of absolute safety*.

Circle of the Fearful Mind

FEAR OF DEATH
WITHOUT
A DIRECT EXPERIENCE
OF MY ETERNAL
AND UNCHANGING
NATURE,
THERE IS A NATURAL
FEAR OF DEATH

FEAR OF CHANGE
WITHOUT A CLEAR
UNDERSTANDING
OF WHAT MY LIFE
IS TRULY ABOUT,
THERE IS
A NATURAL FEAR
OF CHANGE

RESISTANCE
WITHOUT THE EXALTED
PERSPECTIVES
OF HIGHER AWARENESS,
THERE IS A NATURAL
FEAR AND RESISTANCE
TO ACCEPTING LIFE
JUST AS IT IS

**FEAR
OF THE UNKNOWN**
WITHOUT
AN AUTHENTIC FEELING
OF TRUSTING IN *LIFE*,
THERE IS
A NATURAL FEAR
OF THE UNKNOWN

SUFFERING

I relax into what is - the present moment - and accept that my life is unfolding perfectly.

Due to the spin of the Earth and the force of gravity, all rivers exhibit a natural current
　　That keeps them steadily flowing toward some distant ocean or large body of water.

If you throw a feather into the moving current of a river and it lands on the water's surface,
　　It will be caught in the flow of the river and travel effortlessly downstream.

Should you decide to jump in and let your body float motionless on the water like a feather,
　　You would obviously advance in the direction of the river's flow.

But, instead, if you tried to swim upstream while the current is strong,
　　You would have to struggle and work very hard against the constant force of the water.

It's much easier to let go of control and surrender in the direction of the current
　　Than to fight against the natural flow of the river.

The idea of jumping into a river and deciding to swim with - or against - the current
　　Is representative of how we choose to respond - or react - to the many events of our life.

We can expand our peace of mind by consciously surrendering and relaxing into what is,
　　Whereas suffering is felt when we resist life's experiences just as they are.

Suffering comes from resisting what is actually happening right now in our life,
　　From resisting how things really are,
　　　　In other words - resisting life as it appears in this moment.

For some people, there is an obsessive desire for life to be different than it is,
　　To have it be the way it used to be in **the past,** or the way it could be in **the future**
　　　　And, thus, they live in an illusory reality that is other than **the present moment.**

Suffering comes from our **attachment** to desiring a personal agenda or specific form of reality
　　And also from defending a dysfunctional self-image that does not serve us.

Furthermore, suffering is caused from a fear of death that we've acquired during our life
　　Erroneously believing we will be annihilated forever, or cease to exist,
　　　　A belief that arises from the **ignorance** of not knowing our *Eternal Nature.*

As we consciously cultivate a greater awareness of what our life is truly about,
　　Life offers us new choices that can lead to sublime experiences of inner freedom.

When we intentionally dive through the threshold of expanded awareness
　　And plunge into the waters of greater understanding of what really matters,
　　　　There comes a time of *grace* when we recognize how to effortlessly flow
　　　　　　Down *"the River of Life"* as it merges with *the Ocean of Limitless Love.*

The ultimate goal of our *awakening journey* is much more than learning "to flow with the *River*",
　　It is ultimately "becoming the *River* itself".

Circle of Suffering

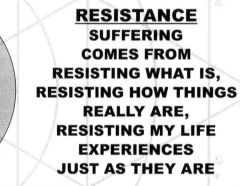

ATTACHMENTS
SUFFERING
COMES FROM
BEING ATTACHED
TO MY DESIRES
AND FROM DEFENDING
A DYSFUNCTIONAL
SELF-IMAGE THAT
DOES NOT SERVE ME

IGNORANCE
SUFFERING
COMES FROM A FEAR
OF DEATH, BELIEVING
I WILL CEASE TO EXIST,
A BELIEF THAT ARISES
FROM THE IGNORANCE
OF NOT KNOWING
MY *ETERNAL NATURE*

RESISTANCE
SUFFERING
COMES FROM
RESISTING WHAT IS,
RESISTING HOW THINGS
REALLY ARE,
RESISTING MY LIFE
EXPERIENCES
JUST AS THEY ARE

PAST AND FUTURE
SUFFERING
COMES FROM LIVING
WITH A LACK
OF PRESENCE
CREATED BY FOCUSING
MY THOUGHTS
ON PAST RESENTMENTS
OR FEAR OF THE FUTURE

SPHERES OF CONTROL

In this moment I have control of my choices, actions, intentions, and how I focus my attention.

Philosophers have debated for thousands of years
    How the various aspects of "order and chaos" influence our everyday lives.

Modern chaos theory (arising out of advanced physics) has demonstrated mathematically
    That *a general system in chaos* has a natural impulse, or yearning,
        To resolve itself into one of order and greater harmony.

When we listen to certain daily news programs
    We are reminded that life on Earth is currently involved in all kinds of chaotic events,
        Such as war, terrorism, domestic violence, accidents, and natural catastrophes.

Now just imagine that you somehow travel to the Moon and then look back at the Earth
    Where, from this distant vantage, you can't see chaos, but see a larger sphere of order
        As you gaze at a faraway world which appears to be spinning perfectly in space.

From the Moon if you see a huge meteor hit Earth, it follows that chaos is observed once more,
    Until you move yourself yet again and, imaginarily, travel to a remote star and look back,
        Where you view our entire Solar System including Earth, turning in perfect order,
            And this same huge meteor now becomes part of the system's perfection.

The farther out you might journey into the Universe away from our home planet
    And the bigger perspectives you observe, the more *the spheres of order* get larger.

Based on our perspective, our personal level of control in respect to the phenomenal world
    Also has a specific relationship to the numerous *spheres of order and chaos.*

From a very large **universal perspective, we have no control over the cosmic events**
    Of supernovas, massive solar storms, or falling meteors that could ravage our planet.

From a **planetary perspective, we have no control over the global environmental events**
    Of earthquakes, volcanoes, storms, or hurricanes that could occur on Earth at any time.

In general, we have no control over the thoughts and choices of others, acted out pathologies,
    Or cruel military dominance, for **we cannot control the choices of other people.**

But fortunately, **we do have the power to control our own choices, actions, intentions,**
    And where we focus our attention throughout each day.

Life constantly invites us to cultivate a spiritual perspective and greater self-responsibility
    So as to exercise control of our mind and heart via the power of our individual will.

Over time as our perspectives of reality expand, as we learn more of what life is truly about,
    And as we dedicate ourselves to daily practices that support our interior cultivation,
        We can learn to develop greater awareness of our individual **sphere of control**
        So we may responsibly use the power of our will to do our part
            In contributing to a more compassionate and peaceful world.

Circle of Spheres of Control
(In Relation to Order and Chaos)

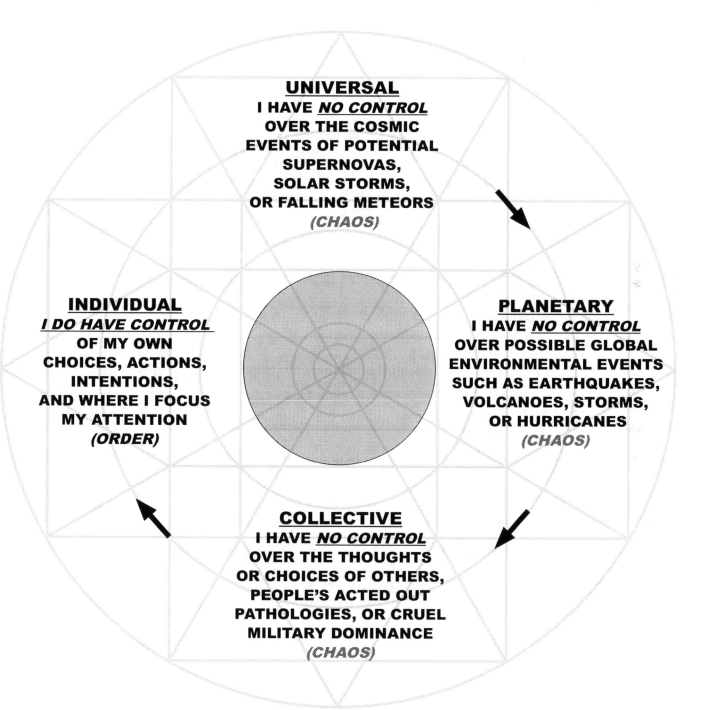

UNIVERSAL
I HAVE *NO CONTROL*
OVER THE COSMIC
EVENTS OF POTENTIAL
SUPERNOVAS,
SOLAR STORMS,
OR FALLING METEORS
(CHAOS)

PLANETARY
I HAVE *NO CONTROL*
OVER POSSIBLE GLOBAL
ENVIRONMENTAL EVENTS
SUCH AS EARTHQUAKES,
VOLCANOES, STORMS,
OR HURRICANES
(CHAOS)

INDIVIDUAL
I DO HAVE CONTROL
OF MY OWN
CHOICES, ACTIONS,
INTENTIONS,
AND WHERE I FOCUS
MY ATTENTION
(ORDER)

COLLECTIVE
I HAVE *NO CONTROL*
OVER THE THOUGHTS
OR CHOICES OF OTHERS,
PEOPLE'S ACTED OUT
PATHOLOGIES, OR CRUEL
MILITARY DOMINANCE
(CHAOS)

IX

BODY AWARENESS PRACTICES

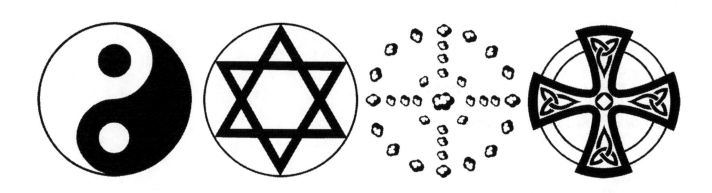

AFFIRMATIONS FOR CONSCIOUS LIVING

I consciously shape my future with new possibilities using my intentions and elevated emotions.

The words we speak have power, and the thoughts we hold within our mind
    With conscious awareness, clear intentions, and elevated emotions
        Have immense power to shape our future.

On the following page is *an affirmation circle* that uses a series of word phrases
    To assist us in manifesting a radiant body, a compassionate heart, a tranquil mind,
        And a sustained alignment with *the Source of Life*.

These affirmative phrases are designed to connect adjacent phrases into one sentence,
    And the affirmations are most effective when spoken out loud.

For example, the individual phrases join in this way:
"The better aligned I am with the Source of Life,
    The better thoughts I choose."

"The better thoughts I choose,
    The better I feel a love for life."

"The better I feel a love for life,
    The better health I experience."

"The better health I experience,
    The better aligned I am with the Source of Life."

These affirmations can support us to live more consciously, with greater mindfulness,
    And recognize the natural interconnections of body, heart, mind, and *Spirit*.

These affirmative phrases can also be spoken in the opposite, or counter-clockwise direction,
    Which, as well, will create a powerful effect.

For example:
"The better aligned I am with the Source of Life,
    The better health I experience."

"The better health I experience,
    The better I feel a love for life."

"The better I feel a love for life,
    The better thoughts I choose."

"The better thoughts I choose,
    The better aligned I am with the Source of Life."

You can also begin this *affirmation circle* at any point within the circle in either direction,
    And as you speak these words with passion and enthusiasm,
        Realize that you are consciously shaping your future world with new possibilities.

Circle of Affirmations for Conscious Living
(A Transformative Practice)

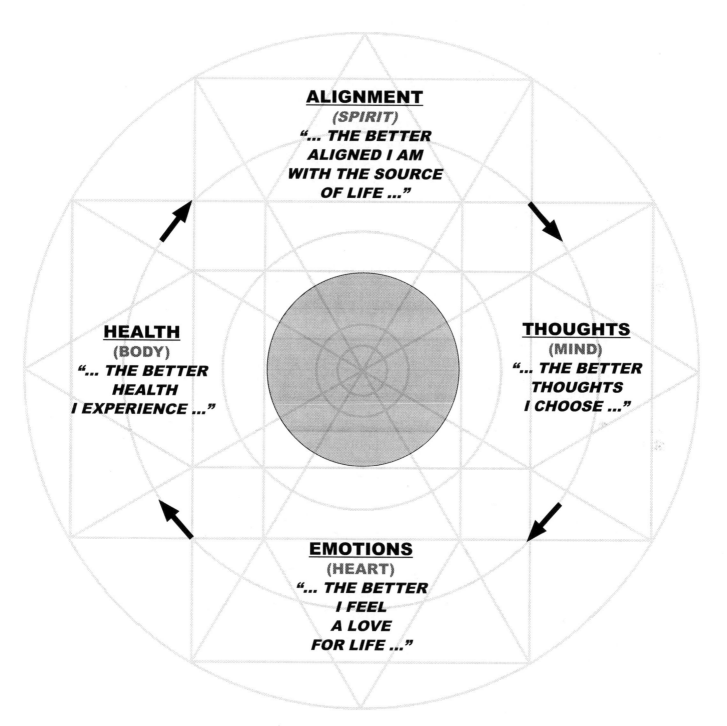

ALIGNMENT
(SPIRIT)
"... THE BETTER
ALIGNED I AM
WITH THE SOURCE
OF LIFE ..."

HEALTH
(BODY)
"... THE BETTER
HEALTH
I EXPERIENCE ..."

THOUGHTS
(MIND)
"... THE BETTER
THOUGHTS
I CHOOSE ..."

EMOTIONS
(HEART)
"... THE BETTER
I FEEL
A LOVE
FOR LIFE ..."

LONGEVITY

Today I choose to share my creative gifts and talents in intentional ways that serve others.

There are certain indigenous tribes around the world that are known for their longevity,
In other words - there are many members of these various native groups
Who have been blessed to live long and vigorous lives.

Some of these indigenous groups live in high mountainous regions
And live healthy lives that exceed 100 years, occasionally reaching up to 120 or more.

Numerous scientists have traveled to these different regions of the world
To seek an explanation regarding why the people of these cultures live so long.

From their research, scientists have postulated that some of the groups live longer
Because of the unique type of structured mineral water they drink daily,
While for other groups in other areas of the planet,
It may be some specific food or local herb they eat frequently
Which is full of health-producing antioxidants and nutrients,
And for others, it's their stress-free attitudes and lifestyles.

Yet if we want to live longer, while also experiencing a vibrant and healthy life,
We usually can't just pick up and suddenly relocate to these exotic regions of the world,
And it can be expensive to import their pure water or herbs for us to drink or eat.

But since we do have control over our own choices and actions within our personal lives,
We can choose to discipline ourselves so as to engage in a few simple activities
That will enhance our **longevity** wherever we are living.

In relation to our body, we can cultivate longevity by controlling our food intake
And being mindful to **eat smaller portions of food at each meal**.

It has been shown scientifically that when we eat just what we need to nourish ourselves,
Which is usually much less than what we've been trained to eat in an affluent society,
We burn up a smaller amount of energy for digestion of food
And create less toxins in our body from unconscious habits of over-eating.

There are also studies which reveal that those who are able to **find more humor** in their lives,
And laugh a lot, have a propensity to live longer healthier lives.

We have all heard about the detrimental effects of excessive stress on wellness,
And we will most likely live a happier life if we **reduce our stress by living simply**.

Finally, the eastern yogis tell us those who mindfully **breathe slowly and inhale deeply**
Will gain many vital years of living from the inherent power within deep breathing.

Not everyone wants to live for 120 years, but those who discover a natural passion for life
And the blessed treasure of using their life to serve others
Usually tend to seek longevity so they can have many years of vibrant living
To share the creative gifts and talents they yearn to give.

Circle of Longevity
(Transformative Practices)

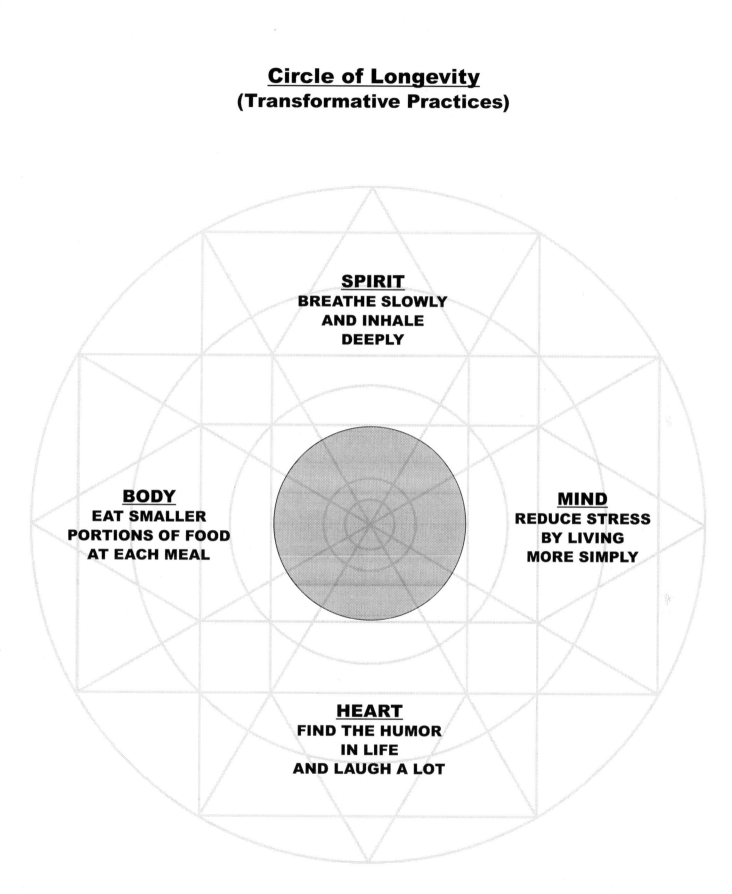

SPIRIT
BREATHE SLOWLY
AND INHALE
DEEPLY

BODY
EAT SMALLER
PORTIONS OF FOOD
AT EACH MEAL

MIND
REDUCE STRESS
BY LIVING
MORE SIMPLY

HEART
FIND THE HUMOR
IN LIFE
AND LAUGH A LOT

THE GIFTS OF CONSCIOUS BREATHING

I frequently stop to breathe deeply so I may anchor myself in the gift of the present moment.

If you are sitting in an audience listening to a talk at a business conference or spiritual retreat,
　　Or even if you are at home enjoying a self-help audio program,
　　　　The speaker may invite you to personally participate in the event
　　　　　　By asking you *"to take a deep breath"*.

If you then choose to follow his or her suggestion *"to consciously breathe deeply"*
　　You will, most likely, immediately feel more calm and relaxed,
　　　　And may also experience a greater awareness
　　　　　　Of being more present to what is happening around you.

Conscious breathing is a simple way for us to become more mindfully aware
　　That we can intentionally place our complete attention in the present moment.

For it's in the present moment that we feel at ease with each life experience just as it is,
　　And it's "the place within us" where we feel fully alive.

When we habitually focus our attention on our resentments of the past - or fears of the future
　　By moving our attention away from what is, we place self-created stress on our life.

Yet it's only when we have the awareness to live in the present moment
　　Where we truly experience feelings of being <u>safe</u>, <u>loved</u>, <u>empowered</u>, and <u>connected</u>.

Taking a slow conscious breath instantly heightens all five of our physical senses,
　　Helps us to feel more relaxed, reduces stress,
　　　　And supports us in achieving a clear state of mind.

Our awareness becomes ever more expanded through the simple act of a full breath
　　As colors appear more vivid, music takes on additional nuances of sound,
　　　　And even our food tastes better.

A full rich breath **nourishes our blood, cleanses our lungs, and energizes our body**
　　By supplying more oxygen to all of our cells.

Conscious breathing is like "candy to the *Soul"*
　　For we yearn to feel the energy and connection
　　　　That takes place within our body when we receive this essential nourishment.

Conscious breathing also helps us **fully align with**
　　The ever-present field of sublime silence, the creative womb of our inner realm.

As a powerful, yet easy, transformative exercise, we can choose to make it a practice
　　To frequently stop for brief moments throughout the day
　　　　In order to take a few deep relaxing breaths.

It is amazing that something so wonderfully simple,
　　Which is available to us at all times, can do so much.

Circle of the Gifts of Conscious Breathing
(A Transformative Practice)

ALIGNMENT
CONSCIOUS BREATHING
HELPS ME
FULLY ALIGN WITH
THE EVER-PRESENT FIELD
OF SUBLIME SILENCE,
THE CREATIVE WOMB
OF MY INNER REALM

ENERGY
CONSCIOUS BREATHING
NOURISHES, CLEANSES,
AND ENERGIZES
MY BODY
BY SUPPLYING
MORE OXYGEN
TO ALL OF MY CELLS

PRESENCE
CONSCIOUS BREATHING
HELPS ME BECOME
MINDFULLY AWARE
TO PLACE
MY COMPLETE
ATTENTION IN
THE PRESENT MOMENT

RELAXATION
CONSCIOUS BREATHING
HEIGHTENS
RELAXATION
AND REDUCES STRESS,
WHICH HELPS ME
ACHIEVE A CLEAR
STATE OF MIND

X

THE EVOLUTIONARY PERSPECTIVE

GIFTS FROM AN EVOLUTIONARY PERSPECTIVE

Embracing an evolutionary perspective awakens a joy in me to develop my unlimited potential.

For centuries coins have been made with different images etched on each surface of the coin,
And these two distinct sides are traditionally called "heads" and "tails".

Of course, we cannot physically look at both sides of a coin at the same time,
For example in one moment, we can only observe the "heads" side
And then we must turn the coin over to examine the other, or "tails" side.

The universal dynamics of our lives also have two primary aspects, or dimensions to it:
1) the exterior aspect (our physical form) and 2) the interior aspect *(our Eternal Nature)*,
In other words, creation and consciousness - or the relative and absolute realms.

Many people see reality from mostly "one side", i.e. from an outer sense of the physical world,
With little or no awareness of its internal, absolute, or consciousness dimension.

And yet, over time, through a process of life experience, self-reflection, and inner growth,
We can gain a more complete understanding of life that includes our interior world
Which ultimately involves having a direct realization of our *True Nature*.

In a similar manner, our exploration of evolution has two sides to it as well, for example,
It includes both the outward facts of science and the inward revelations of spirituality,
Both our unfolding understanding of the natural world and of *the Transcendent*.

When evolutionary theory was first introduced around the year 1850 CE,
The main principles of evolution were embraced from a solely scientific vantage
Based on the Cartesian mechanistic understanding of the Universe at that time.

"The religious side of the coin", which was portrayed by most traditional dogmatic religions,
Stated the creation of the world arose solely from the vast power of a *Supreme Deity*.

Yet a hundred and fifty years later, there are many acclaimed scientists and theologians
Who are now courageously integrating both science and spirituality
With the understanding that a modern concept of evolution can certainly include
The interweaving and merging of an interior *Limitless Transcendent Power*
As *the Intelligent Force* that shapes the exterior evolving Universe.

This expanded perspective of evolution allows us to experience *the dynamics of our lives*
From a place of much greater spiritual awareness - and a richer understanding of life.

An evolutionary perspective inspires us to **live our life responsibly with integrity,**
Transform our unloving tendencies, feel greater compassion for others,
And **awaken a joy to develop our unlimited potential.**

Today with this understanding, people are discovering there's a price to pay for the ignorance
Of not looking at "both sides of the coin"
And that there are many gifts of the heart we can receive
From embracing "the Big Picture perspective of life".

Circle of Gifts From An Evolutionary Perspective

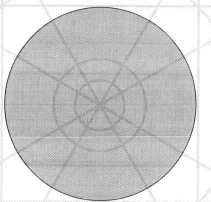

INTEGRITY
REALIZING EVERYTHING IS AN INTEGRAL PART OF A PERPETUALLY EVOLVING UNIVERSE EMPOWERS ME TO ALIGN WITH *LIFE* AND LIVE WITH INTEGRITY
+*GIFT* – *CREATES A VISION OF LIVING WITH INTEGRITY*

DEVELOPMENT
KNOWING THAT ALL OF EVOLVING LIFE HAS A NATURAL IMPULSE TO LEARN INSPIRES ME TO FURTHER DEVELOP MY OWN POTENTIAL
+*GIFT* – *AWAKENS A JOY TO DEVELOP MYSELF*

TRANSFORMATION
EMBRACING "THE BIG PICTURE" PROVIDES ME CLARITY CONCERNING MY THOUGHTS WHICH SUPPORT LIFE - AND THOSE WHICH DO NOT
+*GIFT* – *MOTIVATES ME TO TRANSFORM MYSELF*

COMPASSION
***THE EVOLUTIONARY PERSPECTIVE* HELPS ME FEEL EMPATHY FOR ANOTHER - AND LIVE A COMPASSIONATE LIFE THAT SERVES OTHERS**
+*GIFT* – *CULTIVATES IN ME COMPASSIONATE SERVICE*

INDIVIDUAL LINES OF PERSONAL DEVELOPMENT

Today I consciously develop the areas of my life that polish "the diamond of my Soul".

If a person planted several pots of miniature red roses using soils of different nutrient value
>And then placed the flower pots outside in various areas of their yard,
>>There would, most likely, be differences in the way the individual plants grew.

Some of the roses grown in richer soil would, probably, develop stronger plants,
>The ones that were grown in the direct light of the Sun would, maybe, be taller,
>>And the ones placed in the shade grown in unfertilized soil might be stunted.

The smaller less-developed plants would, almost certainly, grow better
>If they acquired more nutrients, or were moved to a place which received more sunlight.

Each of us has many *individual areas of personal growth* that we're cultivating during our life,
>Or in psychological terms, this has also been referred to as our **lines of development**,
>>Meaning that some of our life skills and abilities are more developed than others.

Like the wide spectrum of colors produced from all the different hues of a rainbow,
>Some of "our individual colors" are bright, while others are still dim and harder to see.

Of course, there are **physical**, **emotional**, **mental**, and **spiritual** branches of personal growth,
>And each of these branches has its distinctive *lines of development* for us to advance.

Some examples of **the developmental lines for the physical body** are the <u>kinesthetic line</u>,
>Which represents the state of our musculature and our available body movement,
>>The <u>sexuality line</u>, which is the healthy expression of our natural sexual impulses,
>>>And our <u>needs line</u>, the ability to appropriately fulfill our personal needs.

A few of **the lines for the heart** are the <u>emotional line</u>, an authentic access to our feelings,
>The <u>aesthetic line</u>, which is our growing awareness and appreciation of beauty and art,
>>And our <u>interpersonal line</u>, the way we learn to socially relate and act with others.

And there is a <u>cognitive line</u>, <u>moral line</u>, and <u>values line</u> for the development of our **mind**,
>And a <u>self-identity line</u>, <u>spiritual line</u>, and <u>creativity line</u> for our **spiritual awareness**.

Every instrument within an orchestra produces a novel set of sonic frequencies and harmonics
>Which allows each individual instrument to generate its own different sound or timbre
>>Depending on which harmonics are dominant for that specific instrument.

Like the various instruments within an orchestra, we are all unique beings with unique talents,
>And we each have certain *lines of development* (or certain areas of personal growth)
>>Which are dominant and more progressed in some areas than in others.

Yet just like the potted miniature roses that, sometimes, lack nutrients
>Or need to be placed in the nourishing sunlight in order to flourish,
>>We can learn to be aware of which areas of our life require our willful focus
>>>So we may develop a larger spectrum of our creative potential
>>>>And consciously polish "the diamond of our *Soul*".

Circle of Individual Lines of Personal Development
(Various Examples Regarding Specific Areas of Inner Growth)

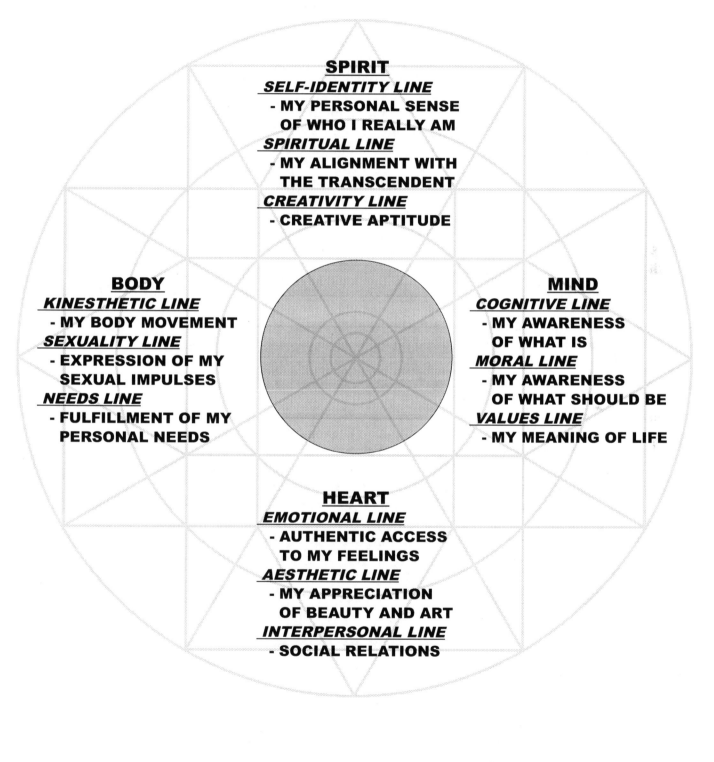

SPIRIT
SELF-IDENTITY LINE
- MY PERSONAL SENSE
OF WHO I REALLY AM
SPIRITUAL LINE
- MY ALIGNMENT WITH
THE TRANSCENDENT
CREATIVITY LINE
- CREATIVE APTITUDE

BODY
KINESTHETIC LINE
- MY BODY MOVEMENT
SEXUALITY LINE
- EXPRESSION OF MY
SEXUAL IMPULSES
NEEDS LINE
- FULFILLMENT OF MY
PERSONAL NEEDS

MIND
COGNITIVE LINE
- MY AWARENESS
OF WHAT IS
MORAL LINE
- MY AWARENESS
OF WHAT SHOULD BE
VALUES LINE
- MY MEANING OF LIFE

HEART
EMOTIONAL LINE
- AUTHENTIC ACCESS
TO MY FEELINGS
AESTHETIC LINE
- MY APPRECIATION
OF BEAUTY AND ART
INTERPERSONAL LINE
- SOCIAL RELATIONS

THE FRACTAL NATURE OF EMERGENT EVOLUTION

The spiritual awakening that's unfolding in me is a natural part of the evolution of the Universe.

The myriad life forms within Nature are abundant with *repeating fractal patterns*
And Nature uses various *fractals* to organically shape countless facets of creation.

Fractals are natural objects or mathematical patterns that repeat themselves at smaller scales
In which a reduced-size copy of the initial pattern is formed in succeeding generations,
Typically producing new emergent variations within each later generation.

There is also a group of *fractal patterns* that repeat themselves identically as they get smaller,
Yet the vast majority of *fractals* repeat their patterns with slight variations each time
Generating new and novel formations at different levels of magnification.

For example, trees grow in *fractal patterns* both above and below the ground
As prominent branches initially stream out from the main trunk,
Then smaller branches repeat a comparable emergent pattern,
And after that, tinier branches produce twigs where leaves sprout forth.

The veins and arteries within the human body form similar *fractal patterns*,
First branching from large passages, next to small blood vessels, then to tiny capillaries.

Other *fractal patterns* that occur in the natural world are not as obvious,
Such as the way amorphous clouds slowly accumulate and form in the sky,
How the ragged rock edges of mountain ranges are structured,
The manner in which the coastlines of countries take shape,
And how the patterns of galaxies and solar systems are created.

Our planet has been shaped by *the fractal nature of emergent evolution* for billions of years
Which *the Natural Intelligence of Life* utilized to form millennia of innovative creativity.

The Earth evolved from a supernova explosion along with the rest of our Solar System,
In time, *awakening* into a living organism where the first forms of life emerged,
And then biological life gradually evolved into the first primitive humans,
Repeating a similar *fractal pattern* of the living Earth.

For millions of years, **the human brain has evolved building intricate cerebral networks**
And complex branches of neural pathways, eventually becoming self-reflective,
Which repeated, once again, this *fractal patterning*.

Many people around the world who are willfully developing their spiritual awareness
Are actively evolving toward a new emergent stage of enlightened awakening.

This expanded and awakened form of human expression
Also repeats the natural *fractal patterning* that takes place in every living organism.

All diverse forms of life are constantly branching out in novel and innovative directions
From their initial roots within "the womb of Mother Earth",
And maybe that's one reason it is, at times, poetically called "The Tree of Life".

Circle of the Fractal Nature of Emergent Evolution
(In Relation to the Awakening Human)

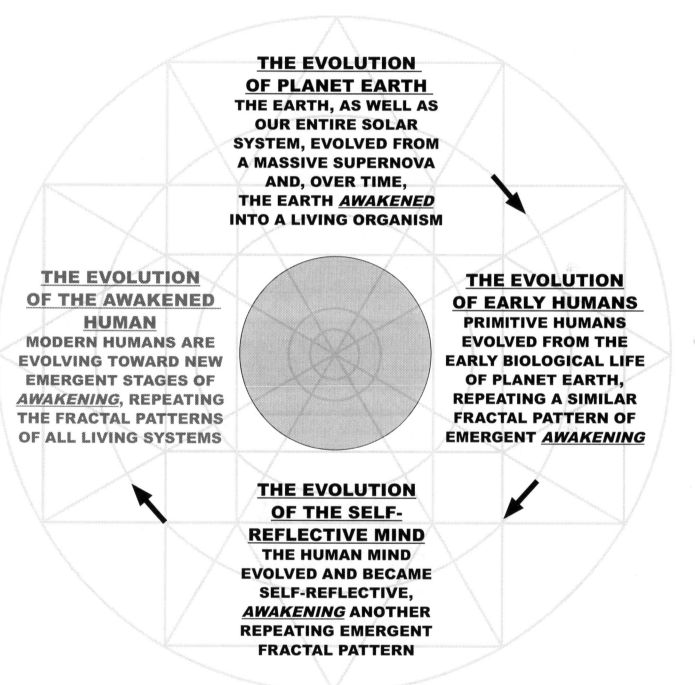

THE EVOLUTION OF PLANET EARTH
THE EARTH, AS WELL AS OUR ENTIRE SOLAR SYSTEM, EVOLVED FROM A MASSIVE SUPERNOVA AND, OVER TIME, THE EARTH *AWAKENED* INTO A LIVING ORGANISM

THE EVOLUTION OF EARLY HUMANS
PRIMITIVE HUMANS EVOLVED FROM THE EARLY BIOLOGICAL LIFE OF PLANET EARTH, REPEATING A SIMILAR FRACTAL PATTERN OF EMERGENT *AWAKENING*

THE EVOLUTION OF THE AWAKENED HUMAN
MODERN HUMANS ARE EVOLVING TOWARD NEW EMERGENT STAGES OF *AWAKENING*, REPEATING THE FRACTAL PATTERNS OF ALL LIVING SYSTEMS

THE EVOLUTION OF THE SELF-REFLECTIVE MIND
THE HUMAN MIND EVOLVED AND BECAME SELF-REFLECTIVE, *AWAKENING* ANOTHER REPEATING EMERGENT FRACTAL PATTERN

117

EVOLUTION OF LIFE AWAKENING

It is my sacred destiny to consciously awaken to, and fully realize, my True Eternal Nature.

Chaotic and disturbing situations can sometimes adversely change the direction of our life,
Yet such events also have the potential to alter our life in positive and meaningful ways.

Each of us have probably heard people speak about their personal experiences
Of encountering a very challenging event in their lives that, over time and with hindsight,
Eventually turned out to be one of the best things that ever happened to them,
But at the actual time it occurred seemed to be incredibly devastating.

Carl Sagan, a well-known astronomer, cosmologist, and astrophysicist,
Made famous the phrase, *"We are stardust"*.

What he was alluding to in this simple statement is that all of the basic chemical elements
Which make up our physical bodies - and which make up all of life on Earth
Were created in the nuclear furnace and intense destruction of a giant star
That, long ago, experienced a massive **supernova explosion**.

It was this chaotic event of an exploding star that thrust these key components into space
Which ultimately allowed life to emerge on Earth birthed from these primary elements.

Could it be possible that *the Impulse of Evolution (the Infinite Intelligence* of the Universe)
Was responding to, and celebrating (poetically speaking), this devastating cosmic event
In the early stages of our own galaxy's development
By creating new innovative expressions of elemental complexity?

From an exploding supernova it required less than a billion years to create a stable central Sun
And a steady rhythmic Solar System consisting of planets, moons, and asteroids,
So that when the conditions were suitable, biological life could *awaken*,
In other words - could evolve into unique forms of life on Earth.

Like the various stages of an unfolding flower (i.e. seed, seedling, stem, bud, and blossom),
There are also many unfolding stages in **the natural evolution of *life awakening***.

Next, *the Evolutionary Impulse* formed **biological life** by taking the billions of years required
To gradually develop the five physical senses (sight, hearing, touch, taste, and smell)
So that self-awareness in advanced animal life forms could eventually evolve.

It then took millions of years for *the Impulse of Evolution* to awaken the expanded possibilities
Within certain **self-aware forms of life**, and to cultivate the novel qualities
Of more advanced intelligence and emotions so the first humans could evolve.

From our anthropological records, it only took thousands of years
For **the first Homo sapiens to develop the self-reflection and self-inquiry**
To experience a direct realization of their *True Eternal Nature*.

Maybe, one day, *the Arrow of Evolution* will create its *future awakenings* ever faster,
Perhaps eventually in, so-to-speak, "the blink of an eye".

Circle of the Evolution of Life Awakening

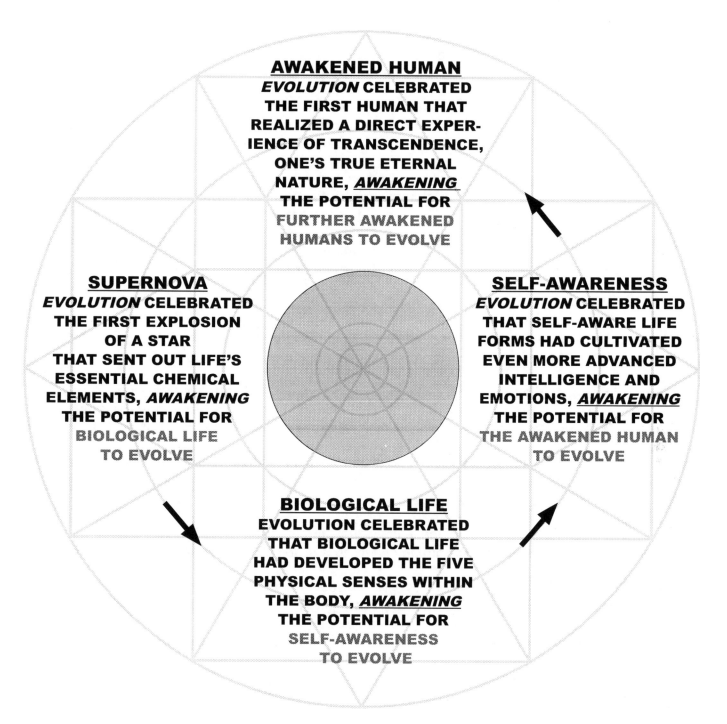

AWAKENED HUMAN
EVOLUTION CELEBRATED
THE FIRST HUMAN THAT
REALIZED A DIRECT EXPER-
IENCE OF TRANSCENDENCE,
ONE'S TRUE ETERNAL
NATURE, *AWAKENING*
THE POTENTIAL FOR
FURTHER AWAKENED
HUMANS TO EVOLVE

SUPERNOVA
EVOLUTION CELEBRATED
THE FIRST EXPLOSION
OF A STAR
THAT SENT OUT LIFE'S
ESSENTIAL CHEMICAL
ELEMENTS, *AWAKENING*
THE POTENTIAL FOR
BIOLOGICAL LIFE
TO EVOLVE

SELF-AWARENESS
EVOLUTION CELEBRATED
THAT SELF-AWARE LIFE
FORMS HAD CULTIVATED
EVEN MORE ADVANCED
INTELLIGENCE AND
EMOTIONS, *AWAKENING*
THE POTENTIAL FOR
THE AWAKENED HUMAN
TO EVOLVE

BIOLOGICAL LIFE
EVOLUTION CELEBRATED
THAT BIOLOGICAL LIFE
HAD DEVELOPED THE FIVE
PHYSICAL SENSES WITHIN
THE BODY, *AWAKENING*
THE POTENTIAL FOR
SELF-AWARENESS
TO EVOLVE

EVOLUTION OF THE PURPOSE OF LIFE

I feel a natural yearning in me to learn, expand beyond my limits, and develop my potential.

Humanity, due to its intrinsic nature, has always tried to reach beyond its known boundaries
By exploring wild frontiers where no person has ever set foot,
Courageously sailing its ships into uncharted oceans,
Climbing and conquering the highest mountain peaks,
And, today, embarking on journeys into the depths of space.

There is a natural yearning within the heart of each person on our planet
To learn, expand beyond one's limits, to develop one's creative potential,
And this innate longing inwardly guides human unfoldment.

At each specific stage of human progress that's attained in one's life,
This guiding impulse to develop is experienced as **life's inner purpose**,
An inherent drive for personal growth that passionately yearns to be fulfilled.

In the early stages of humanity's evolution when human awareness was primitive,
One's purpose was simply **to discover better and more effective ways to survive**.

As the idea of *a Supreme Deity* was first explored in further stages of human development,
One's purpose began to change from merely the focus of physical survival
And transformed into the act of **learning how to be good**
By learning to obey the moral laws "given by an all-powerful God".

In modern times, fueled by the science of evolution and a wealth of scientific evidence,
The focus of one's life purpose has changed to **one who develops higher awareness**
So as to consciously support and contribute to the positive evolution of all of life.

At present, more and more people throughout the world are becoming aware of the simple fact
That every action that's taken - and every choice that's made
Either supports life, or it destroys life - for there is no *in-between or gray area*.

Every adult also experiences each of these individual stages of awareness in their personal life
As a natural part of developing from an *infant* - to a *child* - to a *mature adult*.

When we were infants, our purpose was simply to discover how **to survive** in this new world,
And then when we learned our native language and various cognitive skills,
Our parents and our authority figures taught us
What they believed was supposed **to be good** - and what was *evil*.

As we dedicate ourselves to seeking a greater understanding of what really matters,
Learning to align our awareness with *the Source of Life* and be in service to others,
Our *purpose of life* shifts again into **a passion for developing our awareness**
So we're able to truly contribute to the life-affirming evolution of the Earth.

And as the evolving Universe continues its never-ending expansion,
Could it be that in the natural unfolding of the Cosmos, at some absolute level of reality,
There is possibly no ultimate purpose for life at all - other than **to simply be**?

Circle of the Evolution of the Purpose of Life

**TO AWAKEN
AND TO SIMPLY BE**
IN THE NATURAL
UNFOLDING OF THE
COSMOS, MAYBE THERE IS
NO ULTIMATE PURPOSE
FOR LIFE OTHER THAN
TO AWAKEN TO WHAT IS
TRUE - AND TO SIMPLY BE

**TO DISCOVER
WAYS TO SURVIVE**
AT AN EARLY STAGE
OF ONE'S DEVELOPMENT,
ONE'S PURPOSE
IS SIMPLY TO DISCOVER
BETTER AND MORE
EFFECTIVE WAYS
TO PHYSICALLY SURVIVE

**TO DEVELOP
AWARENESS**
AT THIS NEXT STAGE,
ONE'S PURPOSE SHIFTS
INTO DEVELOPING
AWARENESS OF HOW
TO CONSCIOUSLY
SUPPORT THE POSITIVE
EVOLUTION OF ALL LIFE

**TO LEARN
HOW TO BE GOOD**
AT A FURTHER STAGE,
ONE'S PURPOSE SHIFTS
INTO EXPANDING
ONE'S AWARENESS OF HOW
TO BE GOOD, OR HOW
TO OBEY THE MORAL LAWS
"GIVEN BY GOD"

EVOLUTION OF THE MEANING OF SUFFERING

I choose to perceive my experience of pain as an opportunity to cultivate inner freedom.

Certainly most people are aware that there's much suffering going on in the world
　　As we can observe on the nightly news or, sometimes, experience in our own lives.

Compassion is described as the heartfelt sympathy and concern for the suffering of others
　　As well as the innate desire to be in service to help relieve suffering.

All children quickly learn that the world they live in has experiences of both pleasure and pain,
　　And clearly all self-conscious forms of life encounter pain as a natural part of living.

Yet it's important that we make a definitive distinction between *pain* and *suffering*,
　　For *pain* is the physical or emotional discomfort we sometimes experience
　　　　As a natural facet of our unfolding lives,
　　　　　　And *suffering* is resisting the painful events of life just as they are.

Insects, reptiles, and wild animals surely experience forms of *pain* in their lives,
　　Yet they have no *meaning for suffering*, for they do not have cognitive resistance.

Other than possibly animals in human captivity, it's only we humans who experience *suffering*
　　Since we've developed the capacity to consciously choose to resist life just as it is
　　　　Demanding the painful events of our lives be different than they actually are.

Most of us learned from the people around us to resist undesirable aspects of our life
　　And, thus, resisting pain made us feel we were helpless victims in a fearful world.

For many of us our *suffering,* over time, has become an unconscious dysfunctional habit,
　　Yet this can change as we expand our awareness of what our life is truly about,
　　　　As we initiate a spiritual quest for a greater meaning for our *suffering,*
　　　　　　As we, through *grace,* experience a glimpse of awakening
　　　　　　　　(Or what we can also call *a direct awareness of our True Nature*).

Then from this personal vantage of expanded awareness,
　　We have the possibility to be transformed, to be radically changed
　　　　By recognizing that **our *suffering* has another attribute to it**
　　　　　　As we learn it can become a conscious part for our spiritual growth.

Through the many *cycles of grace* - and through *the fullness of time*,
　　Our *suffering* can guide us to the sacred place within where we experience
　　　　An intense breakdown of the old, where we're invited to ask the deeper questions
　　　　　　That lead us to a profound breakthrough into a new awareness,
　　　　　　　　And where we enter "a sublime portal of awakening".

Here our *suffering* takes on a whole new meaning where we can chose to see it differently,
　　As a blessing in disguise, an opportunity we can use to cultivate inner freedom.

Ultimately, **when we fully awaken spiritually and are completely free from *suffering,***
　　The concept of *suffering* melts away and, once again, ***suffering* has no meaning at all**.

Circle of the Evolution of the Meaning of Suffering

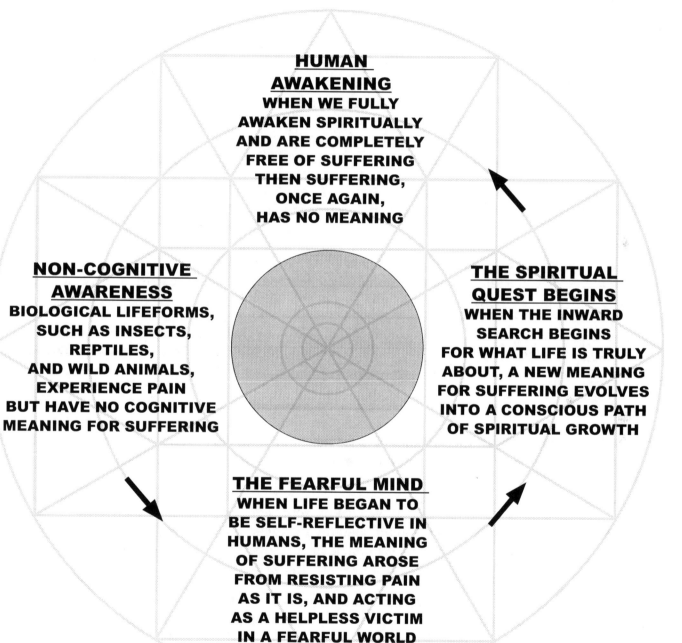

HUMAN AWAKENING
WHEN WE FULLY AWAKEN SPIRITUALLY AND ARE COMPLETELY FREE OF SUFFERING THEN SUFFERING, ONCE AGAIN, HAS NO MEANING

NON-COGNITIVE AWARENESS
BIOLOGICAL LIFEFORMS, SUCH AS INSECTS, REPTILES, AND WILD ANIMALS, EXPERIENCE PAIN BUT HAVE NO COGNITIVE MEANING FOR SUFFERING

THE SPIRITUAL QUEST BEGINS
WHEN THE INWARD SEARCH BEGINS FOR WHAT LIFE IS TRULY ABOUT, A NEW MEANING FOR SUFFERING EVOLVES INTO A CONSCIOUS PATH OF SPIRITUAL GROWTH

THE FEARFUL MIND
WHEN LIFE BEGAN TO BE SELF-REFLECTIVE IN HUMANS, THE MEANING OF SUFFERING AROSE FROM RESISTING PAIN AS IT IS, AND ACTING AS A HELPLESS VICTIM IN A FEARFUL WORLD

EVOLUTION OF ENLIGHTENMENT

It is my destiny, and my obligation to Life, to awaken to higher stages of spiritual awareness.

Long ago when early humans first gazed up and pondered the moonless night sky,
　　Some might have believed the stars were "the eyes of the gods peering down on them".

As eons passed, humans became more "enlightened" about these tiny lights in the heavens
　　By annually observing the gradual movement of stars as the seasons changed.

Over time, there were inspired people who built a series of telescopes that provided knowledge
　　That the planet Earth is an integral part of a massive galaxy filled with billions of stars,
　　　　And eventually humanity became further "enlightened" about the Universe
　　　　　　As larger, more powerful telescopes were constructed
　　　　　　　　Which discovered billions of galaxies throughout the Cosmos.

One day in the future as more advanced telescopes are created,
　　We may be able to see far beyond our Universe into a vast reality we can't yet conceive.

For thousands of years, some of the world's religious traditions
　　Have taught that *spiritual enlightenment* is a final awakened state of consciousness
　　　　One arrives at after lifetimes of effort as if it were the ultimate reward of a holy life
　　　　　　Where one "replaces" the suffering of the world for eternal bliss with God.

Yet due to the developmental insights of certain present-day philosophers and theologians,
　　Many people now understand the idea of *enlightenment* as a natural evolving process
　　　　As well as an obligation to *Life* to awaken to higher stages of spiritual awareness,
　　　　　　And that to be *spiritually enlightened* is the ultimate destiny for all people.

One way to look at **primitive humans** is to observe that "the enlightened ones" at the time
　　Were those who attained the higher knowledge to develop agricultural tribes or villages,
　　　　While "the unenlightened" were those still living with basic survival skills
　　　　　　And only capable to draw on the most primitive awareness.

In more **modern times**, during a period which was actually referred to as *The Enlightenment*,
　　"The enlightened" were those who attained an advanced level of moral conduct,
　　　　While "the unenlightened" were those less developed groups of people
　　　　　　Who still displayed little awareness for moral values of right and wrong.

Today as many **awaken** spiritually, "the enlightened" are those who have transformed the ego,
　　Are free of attachment and suffering, and respond to life's events with inner freedom,
　　　　While "the unenlightened" are those still imprisoned by fear and attachment.

As we look into **future times**, it may be the people who are "the unenlightened of our future"
　　Are those at a stage of spiritual awareness which we currently define as "enlightened",
　　　　Yet "the actual enlightened of tomorrow" are the love-centered visionary pioneers
　　　　　　Who have gone far beyond what we can presently conceive is possible.

If we were to explore what *enlightenment* is through "the telescope of expanded awareness",
　　We might observe that our human journey of *spiritual awakening* may truly be limitless.

Circle of the Evolution of Enlightenment

FUTURE HUMANS
UNENLIGHTENED: THOSE
AT A SPIRITUAL STAGE
WE CURRENTLY DEFINE
AS "ENLIGHTENED"
ENLIGHTENED: THOSE
WHO HAVE ADVANCED
FAR BEYOND WHAT WE
PRESENTLY CONCEIVE

PRIMITIVE HUMANS
UNENLIGHTENED: THOSE
WHO STILL USED THE
MOST PRIMITIVE
SURVIVAL SKILLS
ENLIGHTENED: THOSE
WHO DEVELOPED
AGRICULTURAL TRIBES
OR VILLAGES

AWAKENED HUMANS
UNENLIGHTENED: THOSE
IMPRISONED BY FEAR
AND ATTACHMENT
ENLIGHTENED: THOSE
WHO UNCONDITIONALLY
LOVE ALL OF LIFE, FREE
OF ATTACHMENT

MODERN HUMANS
UNENLIGHTENED: THOSE
WITH NO AWARENESS
FOR MORAL VALUES
OF RIGHT AND WRONG
ENLIGHTENED: THOSE
WHO HAVE ATTAINED
A HIGH MORAL LEVEL
OF SOCIAL CONDUCT

XI

ARCHETYPES OF CONSCIOUS CONTRIBUTION

SPHERES OF CONTRIBUTION

Today I use my creative gifts and talents to help build a more glorious world.

When the tiny seed of an oak tree finds its way into moist fertile soil
   Where the seed is adequately nourished and cradled at the appropriate temperature,
      Then in the proper season, an oak tree will begin to sprout forth.

When an old oak tree that has died falls to the ground after its long productive life,
   It makes a loud crashing sound which may startle the birds and other forest creatures.

When a bird in the forest loses one of its wing feathers because it's suddenly frightened,
   The feather will slowly descend to the ground with the gentle help of gravity.

And when a bird's feather lies on the ground for a long time,
   It eventually decomposes and provides nutrients to the soil of the forest
      So that new oak trees can grow, as part of the grand cycle of ever-unfolding life.

Nature is continually demonstrating that in the physical world of *cause and effect* -
   When one initiating *cause* transpires, it naturally produces a resultant *effect*.

Similarly in our personal lives, our individual experiences of *cause and effect*
   (Such as how the thoughts we think and the choices we make directly affect our life)
      Follows a similar pattern that parallels the larger world of Nature.

As our awareness grows from all that we learn from our many life experiences *(cause)*,
   Then our inward expansion is mirrored as our outer expressions in the world *(effect)*.

And likewise, as our inner development expands through consistent daily practice,
   Then so too does *our expanding development (cause)* become out-pictured in our life
      As *our transformation and healing* which is expressed outwardly *(effect)*.

Also, in its proper season, when a certain stage of our spiritual freedom has been awakened,
   So does our conscious contribution and service to others naturally awaken in us as well.

As we consciously develop our awareness and open our heart
   Based on what we learn from our life experiences and daily transformative practices,
      Our personal spheres of contribution blossom larger and larger as well
         As a consequence *(effect)* of our dedicated inner growth *(cause)*.

The Spheres of Contribution grow like the phases of a sprouting seed placed in fertile soil,
   Shifting from primarily **taking care of one's personal wellbeing and happiness**
      To then learning how to **serve the needs of one's immediate family or tribe**,
         To then **contributing to the positive growth of community and nation**,
         And, in time, to **embracing the development of all humanity**
            By using one's creative gifts to help build a better world.

As "the seeds of higher awareness and greater care for the wellbeing of others"
   Are intentionally planted within "the inner garden of our *heart*",
      Then, naturally, the Tree of Life grows larger and more compassionate branches.

Circle of the Spheres of Contribution

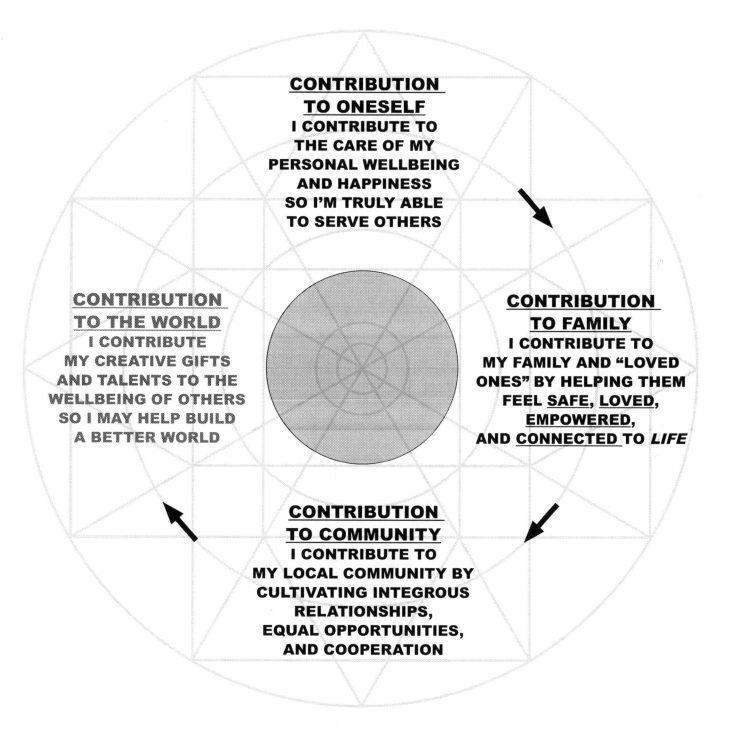

CONTRIBUTION TO ONESELF
I CONTRIBUTE TO THE CARE OF MY PERSONAL WELLBEING AND HAPPINESS SO I'M TRULY ABLE TO SERVE OTHERS

CONTRIBUTION TO FAMILY
I CONTRIBUTE TO MY FAMILY AND "LOVED ONES" BY HELPING THEM FEEL SAFE, LOVED, EMPOWERED, AND CONNECTED TO LIFE

CONTRIBUTION TO THE WORLD
I CONTRIBUTE MY CREATIVE GIFTS AND TALENTS TO THE WELLBEING OF OTHERS SO I MAY HELP BUILD A BETTER WORLD

CONTRIBUTION TO COMMUNITY
I CONTRIBUTE TO MY LOCAL COMMUNITY BY CULTIVATING INTEGROUS RELATIONSHIPS, EQUAL OPPORTUNITIES, AND COOPERATION

CONTRIBUTION TO THE WORLD

I use my creative imagination, together with others, to find novel ways to create a better world.

There is a quote from the famous physicist, Albert Einstein, who stated,
"Imagination is more powerful than knowledge".

Everything we, as humans, have ever built, fabricated, or consciously brought into form
Through the power of our hands - or by the sweat of our brows
Was first conceived in someone's imagination.

The human gift of imagination provides understanding to knowledge
And is a fundamental faculty that enables us to use the power of our mind
To co-create with others, a more cooperative and sustainable planet.

Through the innate power of unlimited imagination, all people with their vast creativity
Can find innovative ways to contribute their creative gifts to help build a better world.

So if we are to envision and bring into physical form a more enlightened and peaceful world,
Then we, certainly, can use our individual and collective imagination to help shape it.

Most people would probably agree that we can all imagine a future
In which **children are brought up within supportive families and environments**
Where they experience health, empowerment, and a feeling of being loved.

We can also envision a tomorrow where these children grow up in sustainable communities
Which are **prosperous and economically stable,**
Where these communities encourage every child to receive an education
And offer ample opportunities to express their unique creative talents.

We can picture each child learning to **expand his or her awareness of what really matters**
Using "The Great Story of an intelligently evolving Universe"
In which every form of life is seen as an integral and important part of the whole,
A story that can bring together (through understanding and compassion)
The people from various cultures, nations, and religions.

Furthermore, we are surely able to imagine that the caretakers and leaders of this planet
Will, one day, understand the **spiritual and moral responsibility**
To help fairly distribute and balance the world's available resources
Between the people and countries that are blessed with abundance
With those that, temporarily, are not.

Obviously with the current state of our world,
Accomplishing these goals quickly is not an easy task.

Yet when children grow up with an opportunity to be healthy, prosperous, and educated,
Embrace reality from an expanded view and perspective of what their life is truly about,
And feel the support of our planet's conscious caretakers,
These children of the world will, more likely, become **awakened leaders**
Who will compassionately guide the global endeavors of tomorrow.

Circle of Contribution to the World

THE GREAT STORY
I USE *THE EVOLUTIONARY PERSPECTIVE*
AS AN INCLUSIVE
WORLDVIEW THAT HELPS
PROMOTE GREATER
UNDERSTANDING
BETWEEN ALL CULTURES,
NATIONS, AND RELIGIONS

ENLIGHTENED LEADERSHIP
I SUPPORT
CONSCIOUS NETWORKS
OF AWAKENED
LEADERSHIP THAT CAN
COMPASSIONATELY
GUIDE EVERY AREA
OF HUMAN ENDEAVOR

GLOBAL EMPOWERMENT
I SUPPORT INTEGRAL
SYSTEMS OF:
+*HEALTH*
+*PROSPERITY*
+*EDUCATION*
+*AWAKENING*
- FOR ALL PEOPLE

NATURAL ECONOMY OF RESOURCES
I SUPPORT THE FAIR
DISTRIBUTION
OF RESOURCES
BETWEEN THE PEOPLE
AND COUNTRIES
THAT HAVE MUCH
WITH THOSE THAT DO NOT

SPHERES OF ENLIGHTENED LEADERSHIP

Today I surrender my personal will so I may be guided by the Infinite Intelligence within me.

Within the natural world, many of the more evolved forms of animals that live in groups
 Determine their structure of leadership through a dramatic demonstration of strength.

For example, a pack of wolves or a band of gorillas recognize their leaders
 Based on the most powerful males of the group battling together in a savage ritual fight
  That resolves which of them is the strongest.

In a similar manner, primitive humans would also determine who their leaders were
 By the strongest male of the tribe trying to vanquish the others for control.

In time, this archaic manner of leadership which ruled native tribes for eons, changed form
 Into the strong monarchial leaders "who were favored by their supernatural deities"
  And eventually became the reign of royal families and patriarchal dynasties.

Around 500 BCE in a region we know as Greece, a number of advanced cities flourished
 Where a new concept of leadership began to emerge.

Within the minds of the progressive elite, the first forms of democracy were birthed
 Creating a novel innovative system of how to govern one another.

This democratic exploration of governance has been slowly developing for over 2500 years,
 Yet, today, as people around the world gain greater cultural and social maturity,
  Many are becoming aware that true leadership requires other specific qualities.

Enlightened leadership is not only about making the best laws to govern its cities and nations
 But must also embrace the people's natural yearning to **search for a larger meaning**,
  It must include their **quest for learning the truth of what life is really about**,
   Plus it must address their innate longing for **greater creative expression**
    As well as their people's inherent obligation to **care for the Earth**.

At this time there is a natural yearning to perceive leadership from a higher level of awareness
 In which we all must engage the personal responsibility to learn to be *a visionary leader*.

We are currently living in an unprecedented era in which *Life* is constantly inviting us
 To courageously embrace our destiny as a conscious awakened leader
  So ultimately we can live together in a world blessed with *awakened leadership*.

Humanity has been on a long unfolding journey of collectively discovering how to govern itself
 Through a process of leadership that gradually progressed from power by the strongest,
  To rigid control by religious royalty, to democratic agreement by the people,
   To, maybe one day, every person learning to be *a responsible leader*.

As we consciously educate ourselves - as well as our children - regarding what really matters,
 We may eventually create a future based around what we can call *universal leadership*
  In which each one of us learns to surrender our personal will and egoic agenda
   To the ever-present guidance of *the Infinite Intelligence* within us.

Circle of Spheres of Enlightened Leadership
(The Primary Themes of Leadership and Integral Education)

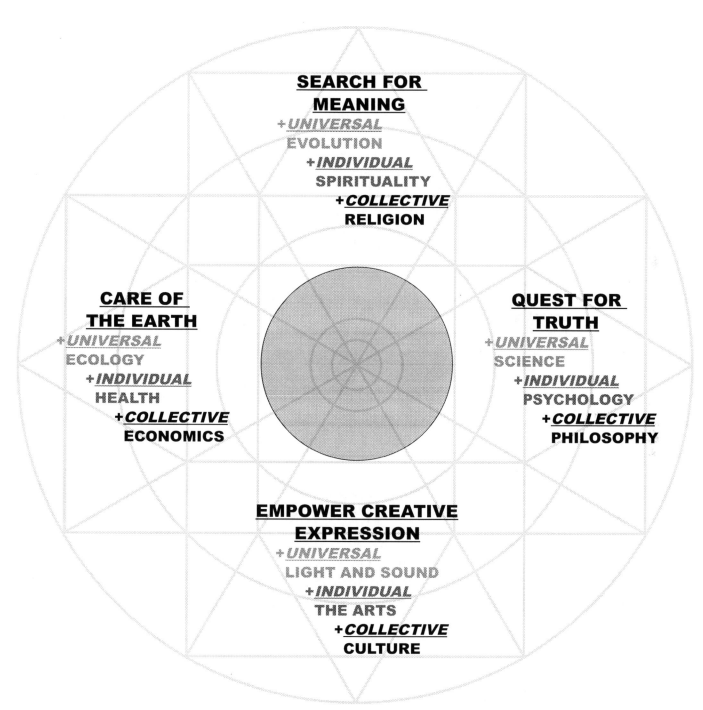

SEARCH FOR MEANING
+*UNIVERSAL* EVOLUTION
+*INDIVIDUAL* SPIRITUALITY
+*COLLECTIVE* RELIGION

CARE OF THE EARTH
+*UNIVERSAL* ECOLOGY
+*INDIVIDUAL* HEALTH
+*COLLECTIVE* ECONOMICS

QUEST FOR TRUTH
+*UNIVERSAL* SCIENCE
+*INDIVIDUAL* PSYCHOLOGY
+*COLLECTIVE* PHILOSOPHY

EMPOWER CREATIVE EXPRESSION
+*UNIVERSAL* LIGHT AND SOUND
+*INDIVIDUAL* THE ARTS
+*COLLECTIVE* CULTURE

NATURAL ECONOMY OF RESOURCES

Today I cultivate a natural state of balance within myself so I may better serve the good of all.

Each day water vapor from evaporating lakes, rivers, and oceans rises toward the heavens
> To slowly form large clouds of moisture that hang in the sky,
>> And as the gathering moisture inside a cloud builds up sufficient pressure,
>>> It eventually finds release in a downpour of rain.

Two adjoining tectonic plates within the crust of the Earth continually push against each other
> As they build up massive pressure in the substrata below the ground
>> That must, one day, be discharged in an earthquake.

Constantly changing weather patterns will produce both high and low pressure systems,
> And as adjacent systems build, they can develop into storms, tornados, or hurricanes.

There is *a natural economy* that continuously operates within the Earth's global environment
> Which keeps all of Nature in balance and harmony
>> When the forces of life, sometimes, generate extreme stresses or pressures.

Similar dynamics are taking place in our national and global financial economies
> Which can also generate "financial storms and quakes"
>> If not systematically checked or kept in a state of balance.

When one group of people accumulates an excessive amount of resources or finances
> Compared to another group that has very little
>> And these groups have not yet developed *a world-centered consciousness*,
>>> Then the possibility of chaotic pressures of imbalance can occur.

If these pressures are not released and resolved with conscious awareness and cooperation,
> Then eventually "a financial or social storm may emerge".

Just like within Nature, we humans are also in a perpetual process of maintaining balance,
> And if we desire to be a positive force for cultivating balance within our world,
>> We must first embrace the responsibility to uphold balance within ourselves.

Recently there has been a movement occurring in which some of the world's wealthier people
> Are finding the altruistic awareness and compassion to take action,
>> And do what they can to responsibly assist the poorer people of the world.

Some **for-profit businesses** are now being structured by conscious visionary CEO's
> In ways that create more jobs and prosperity to help the world's poverty stricken people.

And effective **humanitarian organizations** and creative financial innovations like **micro-credit**
> Are providing social and monetary assistance to needy individuals all around the planet.

Yet one of the most practical and benevolent ways
> To bring balance to the financial storms of our world is, still, for each one of us,
>> In whatever way we can, with whatever large or small resources we have,
>>> To think of ourselves, and act, as **philanthropists** guided by our *hearts*.

Circle of the Natural Economy of Resources

PHILANTHROPISTS
THE WEALTHIER PEOPLE
OF THE WORLD
WITH THE AWARENESS
AND COMPASSION
TO RESPONSIBLY ASSIST
THE POORER PEOPLE
OF THE WORLD

MICRO-CREDIT
BANKS AND INTERNET
SERVICES THAT
ASSIST INDIVIDUALS
BY MAKING SMALL
LOANS TO PEOPLE
IN NEED ANYWHERE
IN THE WORLD

BUSINESS SECTOR
CONSCIOUS FOR-PROFIT
BUSINESSES THAT
ARE STRUCTURED
TO CREATE JOBS AND
PROSPERITY TO HELP
THE WORLD'S POVERTY
STRICKEN PEOPLE

**HUMANITARIAN
ORGANIZATIONS**
HUMANITARIAN
ORGANIZATIONS THAT
EFFECTIVELY PROVIDE
HEALTHCARE AND SOCIAL
HELP TO IMPOVERISHED
AREAS OF THE WORLD

SPIRITUAL PHILANTHROPIST

As I give to others I am giving to myself as well, for we're all interconnected as one global family.

When you gaze up at a clear blue sky during the daytime hours,
> You know that the Sun is radiating its constant stream of nourishing light to our planet
>> Which provides one of the necessary ingredients for life forms to flourish.

The numerous green forests that populate the globe
> Are spotted with trees which continually produce oxygen
>> Spawning an atmospheric cocoon that surrounds the Earth
>>> And supplying this key element most species of animals need to live.

And we, as humans, are abundantly blessed with the natural diversity
> Of the various fruits and vegetables growing throughout the four corners of the world
>> Propagated from a vast array of flowering plants.

The sunlight, trees, and flowering plants are all "in service" to the constant unfolding of Nature,
> And we can use these images to furnish us
>> With three metaphorical examples of *the philanthropic nature of life.*

From observing the natural world, we can see there's an innate impulse within each form of life
> That essentially yearns to give of itself, "to be in service to life" so to speak,
>> And strives to contribute to the evolution of more diverse creative expressions.

Certainly we can observe this natural longing to give and to share
> In the parental instincts of most female mammals within the animal kingdom
>> As we observe a mother instinctually nurturing and serving her offspring.

In a certain way of thinking, the nurturance of a caring mother is a philanthropic quality,
> For **as our hearts overflow with appreciation, compassion, and love for others,**
>> **We, in a manner of speaking, become *philanthropists for the higher good*.**

Therefore a *spiritual philanthropist* (from this expanded meaning of the word)
> **Is one who shares a portion of one's abundance with others who are in need**
>> **That arises from an inborn sense of natural obligation to a greater cause.**

From this vantage, a *spiritual philanthropist* is also **a person who consciously chooses**
> **To serve the wellbeing of others** - and who has discovered that **giving to others**
>> Is giving to oneself as well, for we're all interconnected as one global family.

In time as we develop our awareness, learn to transcend beyond our self-centered concerns,
> Discover that there's a natural obligation to be empathetic towards the needs of others,
>> And learn to become an integral part of a much larger collective purpose,
>>> Then the natural yearning to contribute our creative gifts
>>>> And express *our innate philanthropic nature* emerges in us as well.

When we gaze up at a clear blue sky and cradle this expanded awareness within our heart,
> *Life's* daily invitation continually beckons us *to shine our light like the radiant Sun*
>> *And to share our abundance so that all of life's creatures may flourish.*

Circle of the Spiritual Philanthropist
(From an Expanded Sense of Meaning)

GIVING
SP. PHILANTHROPIST –
**ONE WHO
HAS EXPERIENTIALLY
DISCOVERED THAT
GIVING TO OTHERS
IS ACTUALLY GIVING
TO ONESELF AS WELL**

SHARING
SP. PHILANTHROPIST –
**ONE WHO
JOYOUSLY SHARES
A PORTION
OF ONE'S ABUNDANCE
WITH OTHERS
WHO ARE IN NEED**

SERVICE
SP. PHILANTHROPIST –
**ONE WHO
CONSCIOUSLY CHOOSES
TO BE IN SERVICE
TO THE WELLBEING
OF OTHERS
AT ANY LEVEL OF GIVING**

COMPASSION
SP. PHILANTHROPIST –
**ONE WHOSE
EMPATHETIC HEART
OVERFLOWS
WITH APPRECIATION,
COMPASSION,
AND LOVE FOR OTHERS**

EMPOWERING THE CHILDREN OF THE WORLD

Today I make responsible and integrous choices that empower the people in my life.

A master gardener knows that to effectively shape a fruit tree
    Into a form which will provide the most productive harvest,
        He or she must begin to prune the tree when it's very young.

Over many years of precise and intentional pruning of a fruit tree,
    It gradually develops into a shape the gardener originally envisioned.

Similarly, circus animal trainers recognize that it's possible, yet challenging,
    To teach a full-grown wild tiger to obey some basic commands,
        But it's actually much easier to teach a tiger those same commands
            When it's still young, for it learns so must faster during its early years.

There's a well known saying, *"It's hard to teach an old dog new tricks"*,
    And animal trainers realize they may have to wait much longer while the animal grows
        To get the particular result they're looking for,
            Yet the final outcome is, usually, so much better in the end.

In today's world that requires governance and enforcement to maintain social harmony,
    It's important for the leaders of each nation to establish benevolent laws and policies
        That form progressive agreements of social order and positive change.

But authentic political and social change is difficult and slow to attain
    When people are attached to loveless worldviews and habitually set in their old ways.

As we learn to effectively **educate the children of the world** with new expansive worldviews,
    Then the next generation of community and world leaders will make policy decisions
        Based on more inclusive perspectives and an awareness of what really matters,
            Which has the obvious benefit to accelerate constructive global change.

Yet generally, in order for children to be educated effectively, they must come from families
    With **adequate prosperity and sustainable lifestyles**, so they can attend schools.

And of course, for families around the world to have successful lives and sustainable lifestyles,
    They must experience satisfactory health and wellbeing.

So in order to authentically empower the education of the world's children,
    We must first empower families with knowledge of local and regional health practices
        Which can open the door for them to greater prosperity.

As we empower, and help promote, the development of sustainable productive lifestyles,
    This can, over time, have the benefit of opening the door to higher education.

Furthermore, as we learn to become conscious caretakers of "the garden of the Earth"
    And thoughtfully prune and nurture "the growth of our children's potential"
        With the empowering actions of **global health**, **prosperity**, and **education**,
            It will open the door of our future to **a more awakened world**.

Circle of Empowering the Children of the World

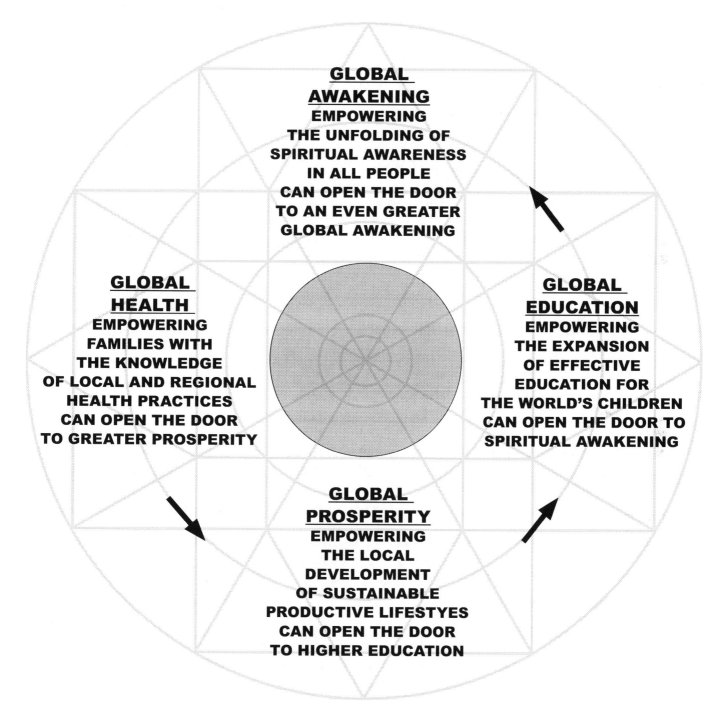

GLOBAL AWAKENING
EMPOWERING THE UNFOLDING OF SPIRITUAL AWARENESS IN ALL PEOPLE CAN OPEN THE DOOR TO AN EVEN GREATER GLOBAL AWAKENING

GLOBAL HEALTH
EMPOWERING FAMILIES WITH THE KNOWLEDGE OF LOCAL AND REGIONAL HEALTH PRACTICES CAN OPEN THE DOOR TO GREATER PROSPERITY

GLOBAL EDUCATION
EMPOWERING THE EXPANSION OF EFFECTIVE EDUCATION FOR THE WORLD'S CHILDREN CAN OPEN THE DOOR TO SPIRITUAL AWAKENING

GLOBAL PROSPERITY
EMPOWERING THE LOCAL DEVELOPMENT OF SUSTAINABLE PRODUCTIVE LIFESTYES CAN OPEN THE DOOR TO HIGHER EDUCATION

ARCHETYPES OF CONSCIOUS CONTRIBUTION

I consciously live my life in a way that serves, and contributes to, the wellbeing of others.

Modern highways are spotted with numerous types of traffic signs
　　Which communicate all kinds of important information to passing drivers.

Hundreds of years ago during the horse-and-buggy era, there were very few road signs
　　And the signs that did exist were mostly used to display the names of nearby cities
　　　　With arrows pointing the traveler in the direction of the city's location.

If you wanted to reach a particular town or city,
　　You would travel in the direction where the sign pointed.

Of course, it would not benefit your journey to cling to the signpost
　　Or grab the sign for yourself and carry it with you,
　　　　For the function of road signs is to guide you to your destination.

In a similar fashion, an archetype is a symbolic tool, a visionary blueprint, a personal signpost
　　That we can use to creatively envision the benevolent qualities
　　　　We desire to embody and express within our day-to-day life.

The concept of *a visionary archetype* can be utilized in our life as a representational image
　　That "points us" in a direction toward the potential of what we can become.

Certain archetypal images can be used as temporary stepping-stones
　　To assist us in traversing to "the other side of possibility",
　　　　Yet these images are not meant for us to cling to in any way,
　　　　　　But are to be employed to help catapult us forward toward our goals.

The Archetypes of Conscious Contribution, which are listed on the following page
　　As the Visionary Healer, Visionary Storyteller, Visionary Teacher, and Visionary Leader,
　　　　Can be thought of as symbolic signposts along the journey of our life
　　　　　　That point us toward a life of meaningful service and contribution.

These four archetypes can be incorporated in a daily transformative practice
　　To help us creatively imagine qualities and characteristics of the person we desire to be
　　　　And to consciously live our life in a way that serves the wellbeing of others.

They can assist us to journey down the rocky road of transforming our shadow aspects
　　Which then leads us to an experience of greater compassion and empathy.

The Archetypes of Conscious Contribution are visionary representations
　　Which are not meant to be held onto forever,
　　　　But are to be shed when more valuable pointers appear on our path.

There are always numerous roads that can take us to our destination
　　And many illuminating signposts along the routes we choose to travel,
　　　　Yet what's most important is that we keep moving forward along our journey
　　　　　　To *the next awakening* where the signs of the heart have always pointed.

Circle of Archetypes of Conscious Contribution

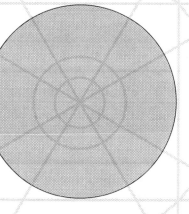

VISIONARY LEADER
IT IS THE PART OF ME THAT HELPS OTHERS EXPAND THEIR AWARENESS OF HOW TO BE A TRUE LEADER - AND TO EMBRACE LIFE AND ITS CHALLENGES FROM A MORE INCLUSIVE PERSPECTIVE AND VISION

VISIONARY HEALER
IT IS THE PART OF ME THAT HELPS OTHERS ATTUNE THEIR MIND, HEART, AND BODY WITH THEIR *ETERNAL NATURE* AND ALIGN WITH THE UNLIMITED SOURCE OF ALL HEALING POWER

VISIONARY TEACHER
IT IS THE PART OF ME THAT TEACHES OTHERS THROUGH EXAMPLE TO ALIGN WITH *THE SOURCE OF LIFE*, LEARN WHAT LIFE IS TRULY ABOUT, FOSTER BEAUTY, AND SERVE OTHERS

VISIONARY STORYTELLER
IT IS THE PART OF ME THAT SHARES WITH OTHERS EMPOWERING STORIES WHICH ARE INSPIRED FROM "A BIG PICTURE PERSPECTIVE" SO AS TO EXPAND AWARENESS OF WHAT REALLY MATTERS

VISIONARY HEALER

I surrender everything in my life to the Infinite Presence of Love, the true source of all healing.

A master flute maker has developed the skill to take a hollow piece of wood,
    Precisely cut its length to the appropriate size,
        Capably drill the proper finger holes at the ideal measured locations,
           Expertly carve out the breath hole,
                And, thereby, bu-ild a finely crafted musical instrument.

The exterior surface of the flute can then be decorated and embellished
    With intricate designs or colorful inlays to further enhance its beauty.

And yet this artfully constructed instrument will not fulfill its true destiny
    Until an accomplished musician picks up the flute
        And skillfully sends his or her breath through it
           With an intention to generate melodic waves of musical tones.

We can use this image as a metaphor for *the Life Force energy which flows through us*
    As we envision that our *journey of life* can be likened to building a wooden flute,
        Where *the wood* represents our <u>body</u> that's to be shaped through development,
           The flute maker symbolizes our <u>mind</u> consciously crafting the instrument,
                And our <u>heart</u> is our central connection to *the Master Musician*.

As we learn to harmonize our <u>body</u>, <u>heart</u>, and <u>mind</u> as "one integrated instrument"
    Through our alignment with *Life* - as well as taking proper action to maintain balance,
        The Master Musician (our Eternal Self) directs *Life Force* energy through us
           Playing its exquisite *Divine Music* and radiating its healing *Power of Love*.

A highly developed healer is one who helps others heal themselves
    By assisting them in aligning with the true source of all transformative power.

So as we learn to embody this awareness, we can use the image of **the Visionary Healer**
    To assist us in envisioning *the Breath of Life, the Source of All That Is,*
        Flowing through us in a way that rejuvenates and restores us.

Each of us has the natural innate potential to be "a sacred instrument" that serves *Life*
    By being **an open vessel in every moment**
        For the healing *Light of Limitless Love* to flow through us.

By using the archetypal image of **the Visionary Healer** as a daily transformative practice,
    It can help inspire us to **support others in their healing process by inviting them**
        To surrender to *the Infinite Presence of Love*, the source of all healing.

This archetype is also **one who empowers others by being an everyday example**
    Of how to give the gift of our love and compassion - and to develop higher awareness.

A finely crafted wooden flute is beautiful as it lies alone on a coffee table or bookshelf,
    But its true magnificence comes alive
        When the focused breath of a *Master Musician* fills it with exquisite melodies.

Circle of the Visionary Healer
(An Archetype of Conscious Contribution)

ALIGNMENT
I HELP OTHERS
HEAL THEMSELVES
BY ASSISTING THEM TO
MAINTAIN AN ALIGNMENT
WITH THE TRUE SOURCE
OF ALL TRANSFORMATIVE
AND HEALING POWER

SERVICE
I SERVE OTHERS
IN THEIR HEALING
BY BEING
AN OPEN VESSEL
FOR THE HEALING *LIGHT*
OF LIMITLESS LOVE
TO FLOW THROUGH ME

AN EXAMPLE
I EMPOWER OTHERS
BY BEING AN EXAMPLE
WITHIN MY LIFE OF HOW
TO GIVE THE GIFT OF MY
LOVE AND COMPASSION,
AND TO DEVELOP
HIGHER AWARENESS

SURRENDER
I SUPPORT OTHERS
IN THEIR HEALING
PROCESS BY INVITING
THEM TO SURRENDER TO
THE INFINITE PRESENCE
OF LOVE, THE TRUE
SOURCE OF ALL HEALING

GRACE

I consciously align my awareness with the Source of Life and, thus, I live in a state of grace.

On a still breezeless day an unannounced wind can suddenly arise
    Which, like all wind, is absolutely invisible
        And its presence will seem to mysteriously appear "out of thin air"
            For no apparent reason.

If we use the above portrayal as a metaphor, the surprise wind can be suggestive
    Of something miraculously bursting forth, unexpectedly, and without any warning.

Many of the religious traditions of the world speak of **a divine blessing or unexpected gift**
    That suddenly and miraculously appears from *the Heart of God*, from *the Source of Life*,
        From an unseen *Transcendent Reality*, without any apparent reason.

For centuries, many religions have called this divine blessing - ***grace***,
    And like an abrupt invisible wind, it seems to appear out of nowhere,
        Unannounced, as if it were a surprise gift from the heavenly realms.

From one perspective, *grace* can be thought of as our personal experience of **the miraculous**
    Such as a sudden unexplained healing or miracle occurring in our life,
        Or a startling burst of high creativity
            That comes to us in a flash of exalted revelation.

Grace can also be thought of as **the direct experience of *the Natural Intelligence of Life***
    Suddenly entering our conscious awareness.

Furthermore, an emergent leap in evolution can also be seen as an expression of *grace*
    For it is an unforeseen developmental shift in the apparently linear line of unfolding life.

From *an evolutionary perspective*, there exists an emergent quality within all of life
    In which there are radical breakthrough moments in the arc of evolution
        When brand new species (through slow adaptation) suddenly burst on the scene.

Therefore *grace* can be perceived as **a leap in human consciousness** -
    In that *grace* can be understood as the sudden emergence
        Of higher levels of our development or personal transcendence
            That unfold within our awareness as an elevated stage of awakening.

It is the mysterious explosion of consciousness that catapults human development forward
    Which allows us to see the world, others, and ourselves from an expanded point of view,
        For to recognize and honor it - is to truly call it forth in our life.

An experience of *grace* gives us optimism and hope for the future,
    And is a powerful force that directs us to be better human beings.

Thus we're constantly being invited to take another giant leap of faith in our *awakening journey*
    And to fully relax into who we really are - so we may ultimately experience
        The gift of *living within a state of grace in every moment.*

Circle of Grace

DIVINE BLESSING
GRACE –
THE EMERGENCE
OF A DIVINE BLESSING
THAT UNEXPECTEDLY
APPEARS IN MY LIFE
WITHOUT ANY
APPARENT REASON

**NATURAL
INTELLIGENCE**
GRACE –
THE DIRECT EXPERIENCE
OF *THE NATURAL
INTELLIGENCE OF LIFE*
SUDDENLY ENTERING MY
CONSCIOUS AWARENESS

**A LEAP IN
CONSCIOUSNESS**
GRACE – THE
SUDDEN EMERGENCE
OF HIGHER LEVELS
OF MY DEVELOPMENT
OR TRANSCENDENCE
WITHIN MY AWARENESS

THE MIRACULOUS
GRACE –
THE EMERGENCE
OF SUDDEN
UNEXPLAINED MIRACLES,
OR STARTLING BURSTS
OF HIGH CREATIVITY IN
A FLASH OF REVELATION

MODES OF HEALING

A greater meaning for my life comes from offering kindness, loving fully, and serving others.

Various birds from around the world have evolved distinct shapes, colors, and characteristics,
And even though their diverse avian forms play different roles within the arc of evolution,
We still refer to each creature from this shared evolutionary branch as - *a bird.*

Similarly, *the process of becoming well* also takes on several forms at different moments of life,
Yet these various modes are all aspects of one shared phenomenon we call - *healing.*

One healing mode most people are familiar with is *symptom relief,* a form of basic healing
That arises from the temporary removal or covering of symptoms which produces relief,
But does not directly address the actual source of the imbalance or disease.

To grasp this, we can use the visual image of a handful of iron filings placed on a drum skin
To graphically illustrate *the symptom relief mode* - as well as other **modes of healing**.

Imagine a drum skin is connected to an electric oscillator that sends it harmonious frequencies
Where scattered iron filings, which lie on the drum, then form a pleasing ordered pattern
(We'll use "the pleasing geometric pattern" within the filings to symbolize health),
And later, as discordant frequencies are sent through the same drum skin,
The filings change into a discordant pattern *(representing disease).*

Symptom relief is analogous to obtaining *a drum-size photo* of the original ordered pattern
And covering the discordant pattern of the actual iron filings with this *"pleasing photo"*
So from an outside appearance, there would now be a visible image of "order",
Yet this procedure does not address the actual source of the discord.

The next form of healing is generated from one's own interior **Field of Love** being re-activated
By a spiritual healer, a holy person, a non-physical entity, or a sublime moment of *grace.*

This is like placing the drum, with its discordant pattern of filings, into an electromagnetic field
In which the *electromagnetic field* restores an original pleasing pattern of the iron filings.

Another healing mode can come from releasing unconscious physiological or emotional stress
Using various techniques like bodywork, inner child therapy, acupuncture, or Qigong,
So that **Life Force energy** (or *Chi*) can flow through one's body unobstructed.

Here, the visual image is of an unimpeded *electric current* from the oscillator linked to the drum
Sending it specific frequencies which restore the initial ordered pattern in the iron filings.

There's an added form of healing that comes from **an emergent shift** or **spiritual awakening**
Due to attaining a higher stage of awareness in which previous symptoms cannot exist,
And this mode is similar to a *spontaneous miraculous re-patterning* in the filings
Which again restores the original pleasing pattern *(symbolizing health).*

Of course, we may experience all of the different **modes of healing** at various times in our life,
Yet imagine the frequency in which *emergent healing* could appear within people's lives
In a world that was focused on *kindness, unconditional love,* and *serving others.*

Circle of the Modes of Healing

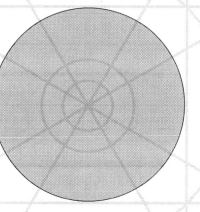

EMERGENCE
HEALING THAT COMES
FROM AN EMERGENT
SHIFT OR AWAKENING
WITHIN ME THAT IS DUE
TO ATTAINING A HIGHER
STAGE OF AWARENESS
IN WHICH PREVIOUS
SYMPTOMS CANNOT EXIST

SYMPTOM RELIEF
THE BASIC HEALING
THAT COMES FROM
THE TEMPORARY
REMOVAL OR COVERING
OF SYMPTOMS
PRODUCING RELIEF,
YET DOES NOT ADDRESS
THE ACTUAL SOURCE
OF THE IMBALANCE

**LIFE FORCE
ENERGY**
HEALING THAT COMES
FROM RELEASING
UNCONSCIOUS
PHYSIOLOGICAL
OR EMOTIONAL STRESS
SO *LIFE FORCE* ENERGY
CAN FLOW THROUGH
MY BODY UNIMPEDED

FIELD OF LOVE
HEALING THAT COMES
FROM MY OWN INNER
WELLSPRING OF *LOVE*
WHICH IS RE-ACTIVATED
BY A SPIRITUAL HEALER,
A HOLY PERSON,
A NON-PHYSICAL ENTITY,
OR A MOMENT OF *GRACE*

EMERGENCE

I feel a natural impulse in me inviting me to cultivate a life of inner freedom and service to others.

The high elevations of the Rocky Mountains in the western United States
Have unique weather patterns that can radically change very quickly.

If you observe the clear blue sky above a mountain peak in the cool hours just after dawn,
Small white clouds will seem to suddenly appear in the sky as if coming from nowhere,
Or as the popular saying goes, *"… from out-of-the-blue"*.

The high-pressure systems over the mountains blend with low-pressure air in a particular way
Which cause new clouds to abruptly emerge into the sky.

**Emergence is the sudden appearance of a new characteristic, or quality of expression,
When, over time, the conditions in the environment have lined up for it to occur.**

The process of emergence can be likened to the novel quality of boiling water
In which a pot of clear motionless water that has been heated for a period of time
Will build up enough energy to generate a sudden response in the water
So as to be agitated from the heat and burst into a pot of bubbling liquid.

**Emergence is the mysterious manifestation of a whole new paradigm of possibility
Arising from the accumulating experiences that create a sudden transformation.**

At one time on Earth eons ago in the early evolution of green vegetation,
There were no flowers in the forests or grasslands that had yet taken form
For the verdant leafy plants of the planet had not yet learned to attain
The expanded level of consciousness required for flowers to be created.

But then, as if in the blink of an eye, the plant kingdom experienced **a leap in consciousness
Which allowed a sudden out-picturing of a brand new form of plant life**,
For as the conditions became just right, the first flower appeared on our planet.

The vast spectrum of unique species that live on Earth, including early humans,
Have evolved because they share this *transforming emergent aspect of Nature.*

Thus, **emergence can also be thought of as an inexplicable, and seemingly miraculous,
Quantum leap of awareness in the linear arc of evolution.**

In today's world, there's an opportunity for another important facet of emergence to take place
In the hearts and minds of people everywhere, as men and women awaken a possibility
Of making the personal inner shift from a self-oriented fear-based awareness
To a higher awareness based on love, compassion, and service to others.

And similar to the billowy clouds that suddenly appear out of nowhere within a clear blue sky,
At one time on Earth long ago, there were no *awakened humans*,
Yet through the natural phenomenon of **emergence**, through the gift of *grace*,
And through a commitment to love now "heating up" all over the planet,
People everywhere are now awakening.

Circle of Emergence

A SUDDEN APPEARANCE
EMERGENCE –
THE SUDDEN APPEARANCE
OF A BRAND NEW
CHARACTERISTIC
OR UNIQUE QUALITY
OF EXPRESSION

A LEAP IN EVOLUTION
EMERGENCE –
AN INEXPLICABLE,
AND SEEMINGLY
MIRACULOUS, QUANTUM
LEAP OF AWARENESS IN
THE ARC OF EVOLUTION

A LEAP IN CONSCIOUSNESS
EMERGENCE –
THE SUDDEN PHYSICAL
OUT-PICTURING
OF A NEW FORM OF LIFE
DUE TO AN INNER LEAP
IN CONSCIOUSNESS

A NEW PARADIGM
EMERGENCE –
THE MYSTERIOUS
MANIFESTATION
OF A NEW PARADIGM
OF POSSIBILITY ARISING
OUT OF ACCUMULATING
EXPERIENCES OVER TIME

"HELIUM BALLOONS" - A METAPHOR FOR EMERGENT AWAKENING

I offer compassion, loving care, and kindness to everyone I meet today.

At some time in your life you've probably watched a helium balloon slowly ascend into the sky
Possibly because a child let go of his or her grip on the string connected to the balloon.

A helium balloon is one that has been filled with helium, an inert gas that's lighter than air,
And thus the balloon must rise pulling and tugging upwards on whoever is holding it.

If someone kept giving a child more helium balloons one by one, forming a large bundle,
The force of the upward tug would get stronger and stronger with each balloon added
Until eventually (if the child held on) the balloons would lift the child into the air.

There is a foundational and mysterious characteristic regarding the intrinsic nature of evolution
That's referred to as the phenomenon of **emergence** - in which, over time,
A species develops a gradual build up of dynamics caused by specific conditions
Leading the species to a sudden surfacing of an entirely new creative form
(But only after the optimal conditions have been generated).

Four billion years ago, the sudden appearance of *life* on Earth became a new emergent form
Because the ideal conditions were just right for this next stage of Earth's *awakening*.

At one time during the Earth's early evolution,
There were no substances like crystals or diamonds that had yet evolved on our planet.

Yet with exactly the right conditions and pressures,
Crystals and diamonds found a novel way to appear on the scene *(to awaken)*
As did a sudden emergence of the first plant, the first animal, and the first human.

Another emergent process unfolding within the minds and hearts of each person on our planet
Is *spiritual awakening* - and many people are now experiencing this type of emergence.

With every thought of love, forgiveness, or compassion - or as we engage in service to others,
We intentionally add to the gradual build up of more energy for our *awakening*.

As we shift our awareness from identifying who we think we are as our separate physical body
And realize we are one with all of life, we build up more energy for our *awakening*.

And as we steadily transform our fearful self-oriented nature with every loving choice we make
And consciously maintain an alignment with *the Source of Life*,
We continue to build up more spiritual energy for our *awakening*.

In the above *helium balloon metaphor* - every spiritual thought is analogous to a helium balloon
Each tugging and pulling us upward towards a higher awareness of who we really are.

And then, one day, there's *an emergent moment* within our life as the conditions are just right
When it only requires one more thought, one more personal choice to offer kindness,
"One more balloon of compassion" to suddenly "lift us off the ground of limitation"
Into an expanded consciousness of spiritual freedom.

Circle of "Helium Balloons"
(A Metaphor for Emergent Awakening)

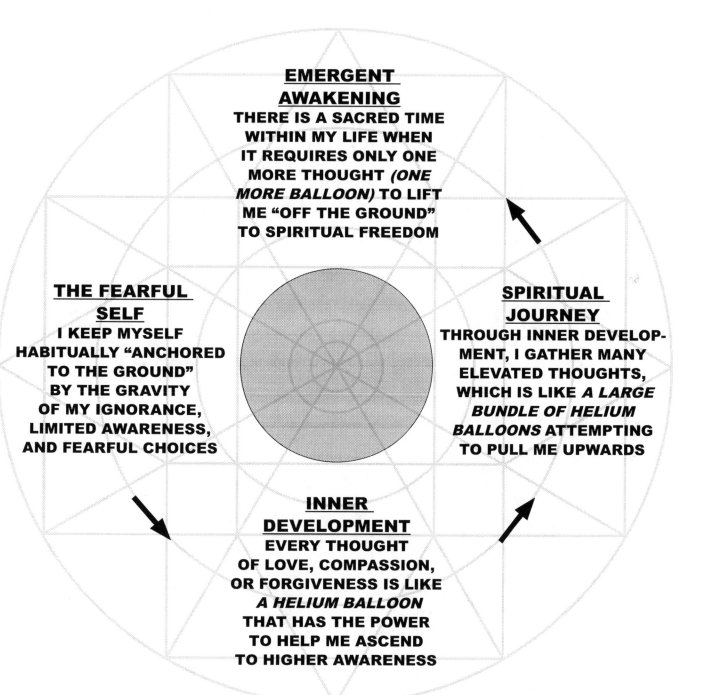

EMERGENT AWAKENING
THERE IS A SACRED TIME WITHIN MY LIFE WHEN IT REQUIRES ONLY ONE MORE THOUGHT *(ONE MORE BALLOON)* TO LIFT ME "OFF THE GROUND" TO SPIRITUAL FREEDOM

THE FEARFUL SELF
I KEEP MYSELF HABITUALLY "ANCHORED TO THE GROUND" BY THE GRAVITY OF MY IGNORANCE, LIMITED AWARENESS, AND FEARFUL CHOICES

SPIRITUAL JOURNEY
THROUGH INNER DEVELOPMENT, I GATHER MANY ELEVATED THOUGHTS, WHICH IS LIKE *A LARGE BUNDLE OF HELIUM BALLOONS* ATTEMPTING TO PULL ME UPWARDS

INNER DEVELOPMENT
EVERY THOUGHT OF LOVE, COMPASSION, OR FORGIVENESS IS LIKE *A HELIUM BALLOON* THAT HAS THE POWER TO HELP ME ASCEND TO HIGHER AWARENESS

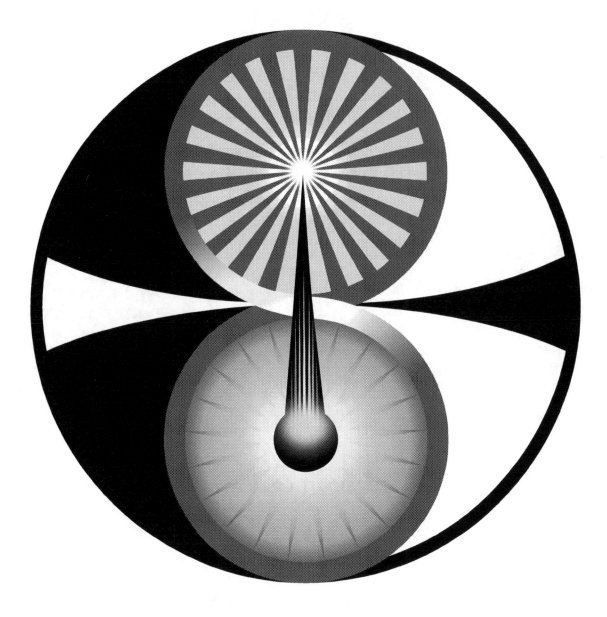

XII

BODY AWARENESS PRACTICES

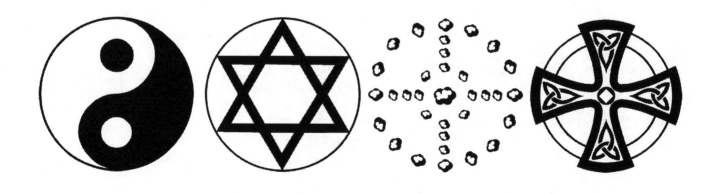

BLESSINGS

I offer simple acts of loving kindness to everyone I meet today.

When a region of land within the natural world, such as a large area of forest,
　　Is experiencing a sustained drought (a long dry period without rainfall),
　　　　One can almost tangibly sense "the joy in the air" - or "elation in the trees",
　　　　When, finally, the rain begins to pour down once again.

The needed moisture is, literally, "a shower of blessings" for the land
　　Restoring the barren earth with vitality
　　　　And giving essential support to the further wellbeing of the trees.

Throughout our lives, most of us experience occasional mood swings, or emotional lows,
　　Certain times when we feel sad, lonely, or depressed.

During "an emotional dry period", it feels good to receive a thoughtful blessing from another
　　In the simple form of **empowering or caring words**
　　　　That are spoken with the intention to uplift our spirits,
　　　　　　Or to receive the gift of **an act of loving kindness**
　　　　　　Given with a desire to brighten our day.

Yet on the other hand, it's also powerful and transformative "for us to be the rain", so to speak,
　　"That showers down upon another" by being the one who offers a blessing to them.

Giving a blessing to a friend, or to anyone, is a way of offering a sacred gift to ourselves,
　　For it can fill us with joy - opening our heart to feel the flow of love
　　　　As it effortlessly streams through our body, heart, and mind
　　　　　　Energizing every cell of our being.

Child psychologists know that if parents want young children to change their negative behavior,
　　It's much better to support and empower them with encouraging words
　　　　Than to only point out what they're doing wrong,
　　　　　　For the latter may generate resistance within them.

Yet it's not only children who respond to this empowering practice,
　　For adults usually respond in the same positive manner.

Each and every person on our planet is like "a garden of possibility"
　　That blossoms much more abundantly and beautifully
　　　　When he or she is nurtured with the support and blessings of those around them.

A blessing can be as simple as sending a benevolent thought to another
　　With the intention of enhancing their wellbeing - or wishing them happiness.

When we abide each day with the awareness and courage of offering blessings to others,
　　We become *a blessing of radiance* ourselves
　　　　Where we consciously sustain an alignment with *the Source of Life*
　　　　And then radiate that loving awareness to the people around us,
　　　　　　Just by our presence.

Circle of Blessings
(A Transformative Practice)

THOUGHT
A BLESSING –
SENDING A BENEVOLENT
THOUGHT
TO ANOTHER PERSON
WITH THE INTENTION
OF ENHANCING
THEIR WELLBEING

ACTION
A BLESSING –
OFFERING AN ACT
OF LOVING KINDNESS
TO ANOTHER
THAT I GIVE
WITH THE DESIRE
TO BRIGHTEN THEIR DAY

WORD
A BLESSING –
SHARING EMPOWERING
OR CARING WORDS
THAT I SPEAK
TO ANOTHER
WITH THE INTENTION
TO UPLIFT THEIR SPIRITS

PRESENCE
A BLESSING –
CONSCIOUSLY SUSTAINING
AN ALIGNMENT WITH *LIFE*,
AND THEN RADIATING
LOVING AWARENESS
TO THOSE AROUND ME
WITH MY PRESENCE

PRAYERS FOR HEALING

Today I cultivate an open portal in my heart for the healing grace of Life to flow through me.

If you have ever been bushwhacking in a thick forest
Finding your way through the trees where it seems no one else has ever walked,
You may have suddenly come upon some narrow deer paths in the woods.

These are thin trails through the forest created by the repetitive travel of many deer
That have been gradually etched into the ground over a period of time.

Similarly, affirmative prayers are like pathways etched into our mind and heart
Which have been intentionally formed through their repetitious use
In time creating new avenues for the blessings of *grace* to flow through us.

Healing is "to make whole", "to bring into balance", and life is always in a natural process
Of moving from order to chaos, then back again to order, so as to constantly evolve.

Each of us is embarked on a life journey toward greater levels of wholeness and freedom,
A spiritual journey that transforms us from living with habits of fear to living consciously,
From a lack of awareness to a crystal clear awareness of who we really are,
A journey that ultimately reveals to us our *True Nature*.

As spiritual travelers on this never-ending path of constant growth and expansion,
We seek effective ways to heal our bodies so as to maintain physical wellbeing,
Keep our hearts open to love, and discover how we can maintain a tranquil mind
So we can continuously receive the blessings and abundance of *Life*.

With practice, we can learn to receive these blessings by simply being an open vessel
For the healing energy of *Limitless Love* "to sound its call through us",
As if we were a wooden flute played by *the Source of Life - the Master Musician*.

We can use the following **prayers** as a transformative practice
To cultivate an open portal within us for *the healing grace of Life* to flow through.

Help me open the pathways of my mind
So I may receive the healing energy of Universal Light and true happiness.

Help me open the gateway to my heart
So I may receive the healing energy of Universal Love and authentic joy.

Help me open the energy centers of my body
So I may receive the healing energy of Universal Power and sacred harmony.

Help me open my entire being
So I may receive limitless healing energy and sublime peace.

Prayers are like "spiritual magnets" which attract to us "the healing melody of the infinite"
So that this "sacred music" can effortlessly and naturally vibrate through us
On the inner pathways we have etched into our mind and heart.

Circle of Prayers for Healing
(A Transformative Practice)

SPIRIT
HELP ME OPEN
MY ENTIRE BEING
SO I MAY RECEIVE
LIMITLESS HEALING
ENERGY
AND SUBLIME PEACE

BODY
HELP ME OPEN THE
ENERGY CENTERS OF MY
BODY SO I MAY RECEIVE
THE HEALING ENERGY
OF *UNIVERSAL POWER*
AND SACRED HARMONY

MIND
HELP ME OPEN THE
PATHWAYS OF MY MIND
SO I MAY RECEIVE
THE HEALING ENERGY
OF *UNIVERSAL LIGHT*
AND TRUE HAPPINESS

HEART
HELP ME OPEN THE
GATEWAY TO MY HEART
SO I MAY RECEIVE
THE HEALING ENERGY
OF *UNIVERSAL LOVE*
AND AUTHENTIC JOY

HARMONY WITH NATURE

I create balance with all the gifts I receive from Nature by what I give back in equal measure.

Typically when people go on vacations, their hearts are full of anticipation
    About all the new and exciting adventures they may experience,
        And they allow themselves time to delight in such things as a relaxing sunset,
            Or enjoy a refreshing hike through lush forests,
                Or take in the rich beauty of majestic mountains.

A vacation can be a time when people "re-open their eyes"
    And their conscious awareness to the magnificent glories and wonders of Nature.

Yet when they return home to the routine lives of their careers and everyday responsibilities,
    Some people get quickly reabsorbed into their "modern concrete jungles"
        As they unconsciously lose their newly found connection with Nature.

In today's world, if a person makes choices and takes actions that directly impact other people
    From a complete lack of awareness of our intrinsic interconnectedness with Nature,
        Then imbalances and destructive consequences that affect others can occur.

If "a person of power" reacts like an immature child, unaware of our place in the Circle of Life
    And makes business or political choices based on selfishness, greed, or ignorance,
        Then environmental degradation, pollution, harm to others,
            Or a misuse of natural resources can take place.

There is a natural impulse within each of us always inviting us to further develop ourselves
    And to transform our unconscious nature into a more mature conscious self.

This yearning is also continually informing us about how **we are an integral part of Nature**
    And how we are constantly evolving (as humans have evolved for millions of years)
        As an interconnected branch of the Tree of Life.

Furthermore, *the Natural Intelligence of Life* is always directing us
    To **maintain a conscious alignment with Nature** - and with all of its creatures
        By being aware to synchronize our lives with the rhythms and cycles of the Earth,
            Recognizing as we expand our awareness of what our life is truly about,
                This alignment can help benevolently guide our everyday choices.

Life is perpetually inviting us to live in a manner
    In which **we create balance with all of the gifts we receive from Nature**
        By what we give back to Nature in equal measure.

Nature is a very powerful teacher and can help guide our actions and choices
    If we're able to respond to its wealth of insightful messengers and visual poetry.

Then, whether we go on a summer vacation - or whether we simply experience our daily lives,
    The rich sunsets, the lush forests, the majesty of mountains - even our houseplants,
        Will seem "to whisper a sublime poetry from the heart of Nature"
            Reminding us we are each integrally connected to every aspect of life.

Circle of Harmony with Nature
(Transformative Practices)

ALIGNMENT
I CONSCIOUSLY
SYNCHRONIZE
AND ALIGN MY LIFE
WITH THE CYCLES
AND RHYTHMS
OF NATURE

BALANCE
I CREATE BALANCE
WITH ALL THE GIFTS
I RECEIVE FROM NATURE
BY WHAT I GIVE BACK
TO NATURE
IN EQUAL MEASURE

INTEGRATION
I FEEL AND EXPERIENCE
THAT I AM
AN INTEGRAL PART
OF A CONSTANTLY
EVOLVING
NATURAL WORLD

GUIDANCE
I RECOGNIZE THAT
MY CHOICES ARE BEING
GUIDED FROM WITHIN
AS I RESPOND TO
NATURE'S INSIGHTFUL
MESSENGERS
AND VISUAL POETRY

XIII

ARCHETYPES OF LIFE MASTERY

ARCHETYPES OF LIFE MASTERY

Today I use my creative imagination to help me become the person I desire to be.

Many people learn to play a musical instrument in a casual way, such as a guitar or piano,
    But few people choose to spend the considerable time and energy required
        To become an accomplished *master* of these skills.

To be an actual *master* of the piano demands the commitment and dedication
    That goes far beyond the musical interests of the average person.

To attain mastery, a committed piano student must connect with an inner passion and drive
    That motivates them to devote the daily hours and years of practice needed
        So, eventually, playing the piano becomes a natural extension of their body.

Nowadays, an important tool that some eminent music teachers use in their practice sessions
    To help their dedicated students succeed with their piano techniques
        Is *the focused power of imagination*
            In which students passionately envision playing music with great mastery.

The students are taught to focus their thoughts with laser-like concentration
    Using the power of their hearts and minds - and then imagine performing the piano
        With the artistry and proficiency of the timeless masters of music.

With ongoing practice of these internal visualizations that center on developing their potential,
    Students are able to accelerate their external command of the instrument.

We can translate this practice of heartfelt visualization to many aspects of our life,
    But certainly we can use it for our *interior journey of spiritual awakening.*

There are many different transformative exercises we can draw upon
    To assist us in awakening our inner being to higher levels of development and mastery.

Yet again, a very powerful and valuable tool
    That's always available to us is our imagination,
        For first forming a clear vision within our mind of what we want to create
          Can be as important as the outward actions we take.

We can use imagination "to see ourselves in our mind's eye"
    Embodying the essential qualities that are required for cultivating the good in life.

One way to accomplish this is by **visualizing certain Archetypes of Life Mastery,**
    Such as the Enlightened King or Queen, the Spiritual Magician,
        The Mystical Lover, or the Peaceful Warrior,
            All of which represent various qualities of mastery and excellence.

Through the daily application of these transformative exercises
    We can practice visualizing the person we desire to be,
        Envisioning ourselves living authentically with a passion for life,
           And imagining the creative gifts we intend to contribute to the world.

Circle of Archetypes of Life Mastery

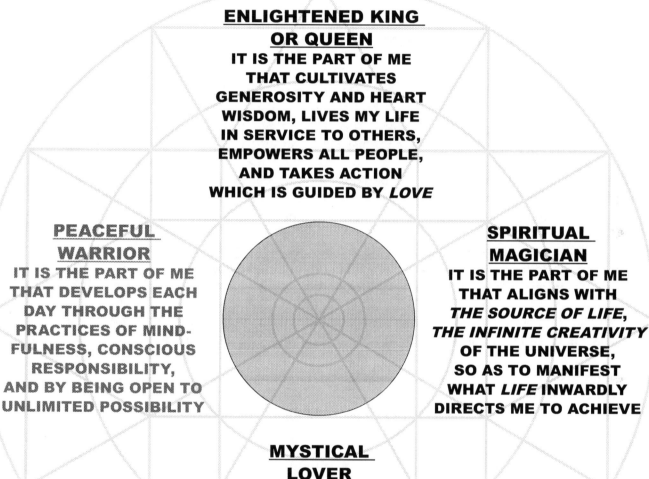

**ENLIGHTENED KING
OR QUEEN**
IT IS THE PART OF ME
THAT CULTIVATES
GENEROSITY AND HEART
WISDOM, LIVES MY LIFE
IN SERVICE TO OTHERS,
EMPOWERS ALL PEOPLE,
AND TAKES ACTION
WHICH IS GUIDED BY *LOVE*

**PEACEFUL
WARRIOR**
IT IS THE PART OF ME
THAT DEVELOPS EACH
DAY THROUGH THE
PRACTICES OF MIND-
FULNESS, CONSCIOUS
RESPONSIBILITY,
AND BY BEING OPEN TO
UNLIMITED POSSIBILITY

**SPIRITUAL
MAGICIAN**
IT IS THE PART OF ME
THAT ALIGNS WITH
*THE SOURCE OF LIFE,
THE INFINITE CREATIVITY*
OF THE UNIVERSE,
SO AS TO MANIFEST
WHAT *LIFE* INWARDLY
DIRECTS ME TO ACHIEVE

**MYSTICAL
LOVER**
IT IS THE PART OF ME
THAT LIVES
AUTHENTICALLY WITH
A PASSION FOR LIFE,
IS FLEXIBLE TO CHANGE,
QUESTIONS EVERYTHING,
AND CARES FOR THE
WELLBEING OF OTHERS

PEACEFUL WARRIOR

Today I embrace every experience of my life with courage, responsibility, and integrity.

For many people, the iconic word "warrior" can conjure up thoughts of courage and bravery,
Yet it can also evoke violent images of a person who battles for control over another.

It may bring up mental pictures of a horde of soldiers who ruthlessly attempt to kill their enemy
With either swords, guns, bombs, or a host of menacing weapons
In order to savagely acquire power over their opponent's dominion.

At this moment, there are numerous places in the world where this kind of warrior
Is still involved in malevolent conquest over the natural rights of others.

For millennia, violence and savagery have seemed to play a part of the history of humanity
Serving as a reckless survival mechanism through the sundry stages of our evolution.

Yet today, a lot of people within the developed nations are finding more evolved means,
Such as diplomacy, education, conflict resolution, relieving poverty, and compassion,
To attempt to resolve the world's numerous challenges.

This is taking place because conscious individuals are shifting away from "the outer warrior"
Which, up to modern times, has been focused on external power,
To an awareness of "the inner warrior", focused on authentic or spiritual power.

In every aspect of life there is an outer component to reality (e.g. Universe, environment, body)
As well as an inner component (e.g. *Consciousness, Source, Infinite Intelligence*).

"The inner warrior" is the courageous part within each of us
That is consciously "willing to battle" our old entrenched thoughts of fear and limitation
Which habitually imprison us and hold us back from being all we can be.

It's also the aspect in us that uses awareness to transform our habitual unloving nature
And reach for something more elevated which has yet to be expressed in this world.

This visionary and spiritual quality of "the inner warrior" can be called **the Peaceful Warrior**,
The natural aspect in us that desires to develop our awareness through **mindfulness**
So we may fully live in the present moment and maintain an alignment with *Life*.

Furthermore, **the Peaceful Warrior** is "the hero within" that embraces
Every experience which arises in our life with **courage, responsibility, and integrity**.

"The inner warrior" is the part of us which is **open to unlimited possibilities for our life**
Recognizing that every moment has the potential to be extraordinary.

And to attain these qualities, we can mindfully engage in daily transformative practices
So as to cultivate higher consciousness and **excellence in everything we do**.

The Peaceful Warrior is the awakened awareness within us that holds high *the sword of truth*
Helping to manifest the way for the eventual emergence of a more enlightened world.

Circle of the Peaceful Warrior
(An Archetype of Life Mastery)

MINDFULNESS
I CONSCIOUSLY DEVELOP
MY SPIRITUAL AWARENESS
THROUGH THE PRACTICE
OF MINDFULNESS
WHICH HELPS ME
FULLY LIVE IN
THE PRESENT MOMENT

EXCELLENCE
I ENGAGE IN DAILY
TRANSFORMATIVE
PRACTICES
THAT CULTIVATE IN ME
HIGHER CONSCIOUSNESS
AND EXCELLENCE
IN EVERYTHING I DO

**CONSCIOUS
RESPONSIBILITY**
I EMBRACE
EVERY EXPERIENCE
THAT ARISES IN MY LIFE
WITH COURAGE,
RESPONSIBILITY,
AND INTEGRITY

**UNLIMITED
POSSIBILITY**
I RECOGNIZE
UNLIMITED POSSIBILITIES
FOR MY LIFE
AND THAT EVERY MOMENT
HAS THE POTENTIAL
TO BE EXTRAORDINARY

COURAGE

I am aligned with the Source of Life as I courageously walk into an unknown future.

Within most of the world's competent armies, soldiers are methodically trained
  To surrender their individual desires, intentions, and feelings
    In a disciplined attempt to teach them to relinquish all personal control
      So they can perform the necessary actions required in the heat of battle.

Instead of characteristically paying attention to their personal desires,
  They are taught to solely rely on the commands of their captain, or commanding officer
    Who, via extensive training, becomes their only sanctioned voice of authority.

These soldiers must learn to quickly respond in the middle of conflict with immediate resolve
  Without thinking or concern for their own needs, so as to develop a warrior's courage
    And perform the brave acts that will serve the needs of the larger collective.

On the other hand, our *inner warrior* or Peaceful Warrior, the visionary aspect within us
  That, each day, courageously "battles" our thoughts of self-imposed fear and limitation
    Must also be trained to consciously respond
      To the voice of *the Inner Captain* (*the Infinite Intelligence* within us),
        Which is always the natural yearning within our heart guiding us
          Toward a life of wellbeing and peace of mind.

Over time, we must learn to consistently listen to the commands of this inner voice
  Rather than the fearful voice of our self-oriented nature
    That habitually holds on to our unloving modes of reacting to life
      Out of fear, needing approval from others, or loss of control.

Our *inner warrior* constantly invites us to discover deeper levels of **courage**
  So we can confidently step into "the battles of life " with the egoic aspects of ourselves.

It also invites us to recognize **a willingness to bravely confront and embrace our fears**
  And to **trust in *Life* so we can stride boldly into *the realm of the unknown*.**

To be authentically courageous demands a commitment and faith to move forward
  Without a need for certainty or guarantee of the outcome,
    And it demands an inner strength to valiantly face our fears head on
      As we discover the truth of who we really are.

The voice of *the Inner Captain* may not be as loud, resounding, or easy to discern
  As the boisterous commands shouted by a brawny captain in the armies of the world.

To hear the voice of *the Inner Captain* (the ever-present guidance of *Universal Intelligence*)
  We must enter the sublime canyons of silence within us
    So as to stop all activity and become still,
      The place where we are truly one with *the Infinite Presence of Love*.

When we're aligned with *Life, we can* courageously walk into a future full of the unknown,
  Yet feel completely protected in a field of absolute safety.

Circle of Courage

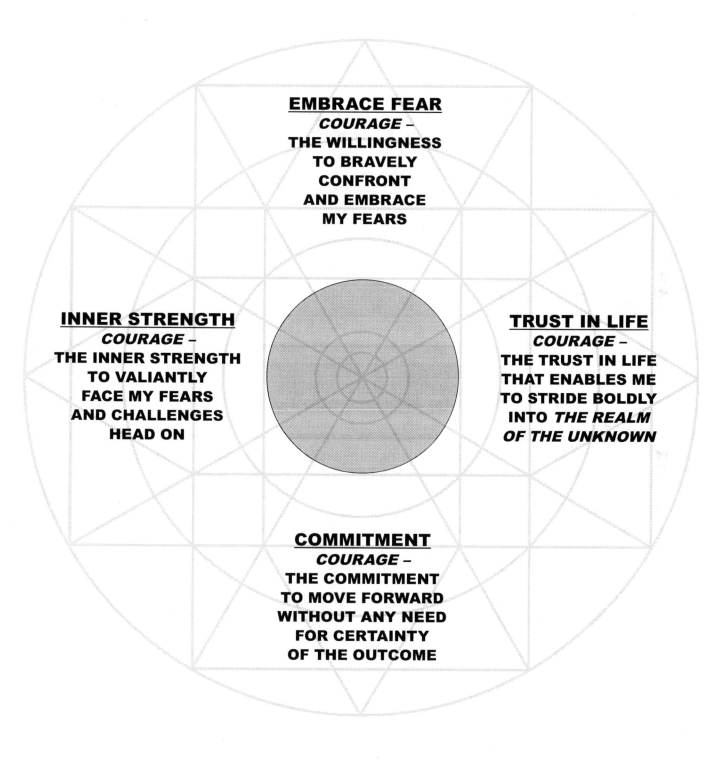

EMBRACE FEAR
COURAGE –
**THE WILLINGNESS
TO BRAVELY
CONFRONT
AND EMBRACE
MY FEARS**

INNER STRENGTH
COURAGE –
**THE INNER STRENGTH
TO VALIANTLY
FACE MY FEARS
AND CHALLENGES
HEAD ON**

TRUST IN LIFE
COURAGE –
**THE TRUST IN LIFE
THAT ENABLES ME
TO STRIDE BOLDLY
INTO *THE REALM*
*OF THE UNKNOWN***

COMMITMENT
COURAGE –
**THE COMMITMENT
TO MOVE FORWARD
WITHOUT ANY NEED
FOR CERTAINTY
OF THE OUTCOME**

CONSCIOUS RESPONSIBILITY

I am responsible for my peace of mind - and I consciously meet every situation with integrity.

A trendy contemporary definition of the word "responsibility" is simply "one's ability to respond"
    To whatever situations, challenges, or opportunities may arise in one's life.

If you were to watch an Aikido or martial arts master in action,
    You would see that the master is able to respond to whatever aggressive movement
        Is directed towards him or her by an opponent,
            And then, because of the master's knowledge and experience,
                He or she is able to use the opponent's energy to an advantage.

Aikido masters spend many years of extensive training
    Learning to be consciously aware of *Chi*, the natural *Life Force* flowing within all beings.

This *Life Force energy* is also present and flowing within every situation or challenge in our life,
    And, like an Aikido master, we can learn to respond to our personal challenges
        In the most harmonious and graceful manner.

In contrast to how many people view the word "responsibility"
    (Which is, typically, as a duty one must perform, or a need to answer one's obligations),
        Conscious responsibility, on the other hand, is a more refined expression
        Which points us to our ability to consciously respond to life
            From a much higher level of awareness and spiritual perspective
                From which we choose responsibility for our peace of mind
                And meet every situation with integrity.

Conscious responsibility can be thought of as demonstrating the heart wisdom
    To take responsible and appropriate actions based on our inner guidance
        (In other words - based on the natural guiding impulse within us
        That yearns to develop a life of high moral principles).

Living with integrity and gaining larger perspectives of what our life is truly about,
    Combined with the intuitive knowing that comes from following our inner guidance,
        Enables us to respond to the challenging events of life with courage.

Furthermore, conscious responsibility is the heightened awareness to respond to life
    By contributing our creative gifts to the beneficial evolution of the world.

Most importantly, **conscious responsibility can be seen as an innate altruistic yearning**
    To serve the wellbeing of others, recognizing the essential Unity within all of life.

The primary foundation that supports our capacity to express conscious responsibility
    Is living in the present moment - and maintaining an alignment with *the Source of Life*.

This ongoing alignment with *Life* can be seen as analogous
    To a garden hose that's connected to the source of its water supply,
        And, of course, when this connection is maintained and the flow is unimpeded,
        It's always available to effortlessly nourish "the garden of our life".

Circle of Conscious Responsibility

HEART WISDOM
CONSCIOUS RESPONSIBILITY – THE WISDOM IN ME TO TAKE RESPONSIBLE AND APPROPRIATE ACTIONS BASED ON MY INNER GUIDANCE

SERVICE
CONSCIOUS RESPONSIBILITY – THE INNATE YEARNING TO SERVE OTHERS AS I RECOGNIZE THE ESSENTIAL UNITY WITHIN ALL OF LIFE

INTEGRITY
CONSCIOUS RESPONSIBILITY – THE NATURAL IMPULSE IN ME THAT DIRECTS ME TO DEVELOP A LIFE OF INTEGRITY AND HIGH MORAL PRINCIPLES

CONTRIBUTION
CONSCIOUS RESPONSIBILITY – THE HEIGHTENED AWARENESS IN ME TO CONTRIBUTE MY GIFTS TO THE BENEFICIAL EVOLUTION OF THE WORLD

UNLIMITED POSSIBILITY

I use my imagination joined with my joyful heart to consciously create the person I desire to be.

When we go to a theater to watch a professional magician perform on stage,
> We can be mesmerized with his or her astonishing feats of magic
>> Which skilled magicians are confidently able to enact right before our eyes.

With the mastery of their craft, they make us believe, at least temporarily,
> That the reality in the theater is much different than what we normally hold to be true,
>> And that, somehow in that moment, the formerly "impossible" is now "possible".

For a brief instant, they open up a whole new world to us, *another paradigm of possibility*,
> By stretching our minds regarding what we currently believe is true.

These trained magicians offer us a momentary gift of perceiving reality in a brand new light
> And from a much broader perspective than the common beliefs of our everyday world.

Within us there's *a Transcendent Impulse* that constantly invites us to learn what really matters,
> To reach for a higher and more expansive vision of what we imagine is possible.

This impulse is a natural yearning that encourages us, so to speak, "to reach for the stars",
> And to strive beyond our present limits of what we think we can become.

Unlimited possibility **is a state of being in which we have faith an event can manifest**
> **Based on an inner certainty that arises from our unwavering beliefs.**

It can be thought of as **an expansive state of awareness**
> **In which the vision of who we imagine ourselves to be - can come true**.

It's making space within our heart and mind for a more benevolent and hopeful future,
> And being courageous enough to surrender to *the realm of all imaginable outcomes*.

Unlimited possibility is a state of being in which infinite options are available to be created,
> And it's recognizing that every moment has the inherent potential to be extraordinary,
>> For from a spiritual perspective of reality "there are no ordinary moments".

It's learning to **consciously live our life from the limitless *realm of the miraculous***,
> A potential everyday reality where anything we can conceive is possible.

In the last hundred years, advanced physics has revealed to us a mysterious quantum realm,
> A sub-atomic world that, to our normal reality, is strange and magical and unfathomable.

Yet it's a science-based reality that is an integral part of our day-to-day world,
> A quantum world in which there's **an infinite potential of possible outcomes**
>> **That can occur based on our consciousness or current level of awareness.**

Could it be that we are all truly "magicians of the heart"
> Working together with every other member of humanity to co-create "a possible future",
>> And *Life* is just waiting to see what we're going "to pull out of our hats"?

Circle of Unlimited Possibility

INFINITE POTENTIAL
UNL. POSSIBILITY –
A STATE OF BEING
IN WHICH THERE IS
AN INFINITE POTENTIAL
OF POSSIBLE OUTCOMES
THAT CAN OCCUR

THE REALM OF THE MIRACULOUS
UNL. POSSIBILITY –
A STATE OF BEING IN
WHICH I CONSCIOUSLY
LIVE AND ACT FROM
THE LIMITLESS *REALM
OF THE MIRACULOUS*

BELIEFS
UNL. POSSIBILITY –
A STATE OF BEING
IN WHICH AN EVENT
CAN MANIFEST BASED ON
AN INNER CERTAINTY
THAT ARISES FROM MY
UNWAVERING BELIEFS

THE POWER OF IMAGINATION
UNL. POSSIBILITY –
A STATE OF BEING IN
WHICH I USE THE POWER
OF MY IMAGINATION
TO CONSCIOUSLY CREATE
THE PERSON I WANT TO BE

171

EXCELLENCE

I live my life as "an expression of art" - and thus, everything I do is a manifestation of beauty.

There are many highly evolved creatures within the natural world
    That are innately directed by their instincts to build amazingly assembled structures.

For example, bees work together in concert to construct their hives
    Which are filled with honeycombs of precise symmetrical patterns,
        And ant colonies carve out intricate underground mazes
            From the primal urgings of their natural drive for survival.

Numerous birds, from massive condors to tiny swallows,
    Fashion nests in trees and on rock ledges to birth their young,
        And beaver families systematically cut down small trees
            To put together their simple "log homes" built along running streams.

In order to create their unique works of natural art,
    All of theses various animals spontaneously follow their inborn instincts.

Humans are the only creatures within all of Nature that intentionally design creative structures
    Which are built from a mind that has evolved beyond merely instinctual impulses.

Over eons, the conditions became just right for humans to evolve a highly developed brain
    That produced symbolic language, which then led to philosophical beliefs and concepts,
        And now today's era of cultural development gives humans further opportunities
            To choose whether to live *an unconscious ordinary life*
                Or whether to consciously cultivate *an elevated path of excellence*.

The word *excellence* is traditionally defined as a particular expression of a person
    That is superior to other people.

Yet, possibly, we can gain more insight into this quality by embracing a more refined definition
    Seeing **excellence** from the perspective of acting from the natural instinct
        That compels life to develop, to be creative, and to express unlimited potential.

From this vantage, **excellence is the result that comes from the discipline and practice**
    Of attaining a specific goal - or performing a service for others.

It can also be thought of as **the result of producing a superb level of creative expression**
    From our choice to passionately develop a cultivated skill or ability.

Just as bees, ants, birds, and beavers are instinctually aligned with "the song of Nature",
    ***Personal excellence* comes as a result of acting from our alignment with *Life*.**

From this sacred alignment, **excellence is the result of courageously following our heart**
    So we may share the unique creativity that we're inwardly inspired to express.

When we consciously choose to maintain this level of attunement, then everything we do
    Is a manifestation of beauty - and our life is "an expression of the highest art".

Circle of Excellence

PRACTICE
EXCELLENCE –
THE RESULT THAT COMES
FROM THE DISCIPLINE
AND PRACTICE OF
ATTAINING A SPECIFIC GOAL
OR PERFORMING
A SERVICE FOR OTHERS

DEVELOPMENT
EXCELLENCE – THE
RESULT OF PRODUCING
A SUPERB LEVEL OF
CREATIVE EXPRESSION
FROM PASSIONATELY
DEVELOPING
A SKILL OR ABILITY

GUIDANCE
EXCELLENCE – THE
RESULT I EXPERIENCE
WHEN I COURAGEOUSLY
FOLLOW MY HEART
SO I MAY SHARE THE
UNIQUE CREATIVITY I'M
INSPIRED TO EXPRESS

ALIGNMENT
EXCELLENCE –
THE RESULT OF ACTING
FROM AN ALIGNMENT WITH
LIFE IN WHICH EVERYTHING
I DO IS A MANIFESTATION
OF BEAUTY - AND "MY LIFE
IS AN EXPRESSION OF ART"

NATURAL CONFIDENCE

I experience natural confidence as I feel safe, loved, empowered, and connected to all of life.

If you were to take a large glass of pure clear water
    And slowly pour grains of salt into the glass
        While constantly stirring the container with a spoon,
            At first, all of the salt will be totally absorbed in the water.

But as you continue to mix in additional salt you will, eventually, reach a saturation point
    In which the grains of salt cannot be absorbed by the water any longer
        And, at this juncture, crystals of salt will start forming at the bottom of the glass.

When it reaches this turning point, the water molecules will have made an energetic shift
    From *a state of absorption* to *a state of saturation*
        Where the water responds to the added salt in a different way than it did before.

In a similar way, each one of us is like "a vessel of potential", "a chalice of possibility",
    In which *the natural impulse to be ever more free* is constantly "being poured into us".

There is *a Transcendent Impulse* within us that's always inviting us to reach for inner freedom,
    A soulful yearning to experience the freedom of genuine confidence,
        The natural confidence of feeling <u>safe</u>, of feeling <u>loved</u>, of feeling <u>empowered</u>,
            And of feeling <u>connected</u> to all of life.

In the above metaphor, the continual stream of salt pouring into a glass of water
    Can symbolize the ongoing flow of our inner development and spiritual expansion
        That has been taking place over the entire span of our life.

At a certain point, when we cultivate just enough conscious growth and expanded awareness,
    We become *filled and saturated* in such a manner that something within us emerges
        And, with *grace*, we shift to an experience of inner freedom and true confidence.

We then undergo a transformation from the anxious concerns of our fears and limitations
    To a confident feeling of absolute safety as we trust in *the Source of All That Is*
    And fully accept that our life is unfolding perfectly.

With greater understanding, we transform from loneliness and separation to **feeling loved,**
    And release everything within us that impedes this love.

With expanded awareness, we move from self-doubt to **a confident feeling of empowerment**
    As we gain clarity regarding what our life is truly about - and what really matters,
        And as we learn to live with greater empathy and compassion for others.

And we **feel connected to others from the profound realization that our *Eternal Nature***
    Is the same *Eternal Nature* that's within all people.

Each of us is a unique "vessel of life" in which "grains of higher awareness keep pouring in",
    Until we "absorb" just enough understanding - and experience just enough compassion,
        Where we ultimately reach *a saturation point*, an inner shift into spiritual freedom.

Circle of Natural Confidence
(In Relation to Core Emotional Needs)

**CONFIDENCE
AS CONNECTION**
I FEEL CONNECTED TO
OTHERS AS I REALIZE
MY *ETERNAL NATURE*
IS THE SAME *ETERNAL
NATURE* THAT'S
WITHIN ALL PEOPLE

**CONFIDENCE
AS SAFETY**
I FEEL SAFE
AS I TRUST IN *THE
SOURCE OF ALL THAT* IS
- AND FULLY ACCEPT
THAT MY LIFE IS
UNFOLDING PERFECTLY

**CONFIDENCE
AS EMPOWERMENT**
I FEEL EMPOWERED
AS I GAIN CLARITY
REGARDING WHAT
MY LIFE IS TRULY ABOUT
AND WHAT REALLY
MATTERS

**CONFIDENCE
AS LOVE**
I FEEL LOVED
UNCONDITIONALLY
BY *LIFE*
- AND RELEASE
EVERYTHING IN ME
THAT IMPEDES THIS LOVE

ABSOLUTE SAFETY

Today I align with the Infinite Presence of Love and feel safe within the protective arms of Life.

It's very natural for all of us to want to feel safe and secure in every aspect of our lives,
> In other words - to experience the feeling that we are shielded from harm
>> And live in a world which is protected from danger.

Like ships securely docked and anchored in the harbor,
> We yearn to feel the safety which comes from being protected within our surroundings
>> And the relaxation of being able to trust the people that affect our lives.

Yet ships are not designed to sit quietly in the harbor
> But are meant to venture out and safely sail "the open seas of possibility".

Now let's take a moment to ask ourselves if there's such a thing as *true security* in this world,
> Or is the idea of *safety* just an illusion, something we've conjured up in our minds?

In the outer world of form, our physical bodies are constantly vulnerable to certain dangers
> And subjected to things like the surprise attacks of innocuous viruses and diseases,
>> The shocking blows of unexpected accidents,
>>> And the sudden misfortunes of natural catastrophes
>>>> Such as earthquakes, tornadoes, wildfires, or floods.

Apparently from the perspective of the world, *safety of the body* continually comes and goes
> Depending on the external situations and momentary conditions of our physical reality,
>> Many of which we seem to have little or no control.

Yet there is another intrinsic facet of *security* that we can call **absolute safety**,
> Which is **the feeling we experience arising from a realization of our *True Nature*,**
>> **The part of us that's eternal, unbounded, and can never be harmed.**

The direct realization of our *Eternal Nature* allows us to feel a depth of internal safety
> That does not come and go with the changes of outer events,
>> But always remains steadfast as the core of who we really are.

Nothing that takes place in the <u>external</u> world of physical phenomena
> Can affect this <u>internal</u> unchanging dimension of our being.

As far as our physical bodies are concerned, we can sometimes feel *a relative level of safety*
> In limited circumstances within this phenomenal world of form,
>> But we can never actually know what may happen in the next moment.

Yet **absolute safety** can be experienced within our heart
> **When our awareness is consciously aligned with *the Infinite Presence of Love*.**

What would it feel like to live with a profound experience of *never-ending safety*
> In which we're like "a ship in the protective arms of an eternal sanctuary",
>> No matter if we're fully secure in "the harbor of inner silence"
>>> Or out upon "the many oceans of life" that we courageously sail each day?

Circle of Absolute Safety

REALIZATION
ABSOLUTE SAFETY –
THE FEELING
I EXPERIENCE
THAT ARISES FROM
A DIRECT REALIZATION
OF MY *ETERNAL*
UNBOUNDED NATURE

SUBLIME KNOWING
ABSOLUTE SAFETY –
THE FEELING
OF PROTECTION
I EXPERIENCE
FROM LIVING IN A WORLD
IN WHICH I KNOW
WHO I REALLY AM

ALIGNMENT
ABSOLUTE SAFETY –
THE FEELING
I EXPERIENCE
WHEN MY AWARENESS
IS TRULY ALIGNED WITH
THE INFINITE
PRESENCE OF LOVE

TRUST IN LIFE
ABSOLUTE SAFETY –
THE FEELING OF
WELLBEING THAT COMES
FROM BEING AT EASE
IN MY SURROUNDINGS
AS I FULLY TRUST IN
THE PERFECTION OF *LIFE*

XIV

BODY AWARENESS PRACTICES

BODY AWARENESS

I use the awareness within my body to consciously experience more aliveness and presence.

The steady invisible force of the Earth's gravity is keeping you
    (And every other solid object around you) from floating away into space.

So as *an awareness exercise*, take a moment to feel the effects of this powerful force on you
    By becoming consciously aware of the part of your body (e.g. feet, buttocks, back, etc.)
        That is supporting your weight right now,
            Whether you're in a chair, a bed, or standing on the floor or ground.

Before this exercise, you were most likely not actively aware of this specific area of your body
    Until you intentionally chose to bring your attention to that area with your mental focus,
        Which then enabled you to feel the physical sensations caused by gravity.

Modern physicists have affirmed that, from a quantum perspective of reality,
    A single photon of light (which has the potential of acting as both a *particle* and a *wave)*
        Only becomes a *particle* when an observer places his or her attention on it.

It is the observer's focused attention on the light that "collapses it" into *particles of energy*,
    Or stated another way, *the transformation of any form of energy follows consciousness.*

In other words - whatever we place our attention on becomes *energized with possibility*
    And, thus, willfully expanding our conscious awareness can support our transformation.

Now, try another simple *awareness exercise* by bringing your awareness
    To an area of your body where you are experiencing pain or discomfort,
        Either strong or subtle, and simply witness the pain without judgment.

By witnessing the pain without judging it, or without "creating a story of good or bad around it",
    You help *Life Force energy*, or *Chi*, to flow into that area to transform the imbalance.

So now bring your awareness to where your body is tense or contracted
    And visualize relaxation being sent to that specific area.

In the same way, when we focus our awareness and witness the tension without judgment,
    Healing energy can move into those areas to balance and support our wellbeing.

Another *exercise* that can be helpful is to become aware of how you are breathing
    And notice whether it is deep or shallow, then consciously breathe naturally
        With an intention to circulate *Life Force energy* throughout your body.

Finally, at any time during the day, you can heighten your normal physical sensations
    By purposefully placing your attention on what your body is sensing,
        Such as the sounds, sights, smells, or the temperature around you.

Since our body is a laboratory for experimentation - and since *energy follows consciousness*,
    We can use the above *exercises* to discover whether our expanded **body awareness**
        Will produce in us a feeling of more aliveness and a greater sense of presence.

Circle of Body Awareness
(Transformative Practices)

NOTICE THE BREATH
BE CONSCIOUSLY AWARE
OF YOUR BREATH,
AND NOTICE IF IT IS DEEP
OR SHALLOW IN ORDER TO
CIRCULATE AN OPTIMUM
FLOW OF YOUR VITAL
LIFE FORCE ENERGY

FEEL SENSATIONS
BE CONSCIOUSLY AWARE
TO HEIGHTEN THE
PHYSICAL SENSATIONS
THAT ARE AROUND YOU,
SUCH AS SOUNDS,
SIGHTS, SMELLS,
OR TEMPERATURE

OBSERVE TENSION
BE CONSCIOUSLY
AWARE OF ANY PLACES
WHERE YOUR BODY IS
TENSE OR CONTRACTED
AND VISUALIZE
RELAXATION BEING
SENT TO THOSE AREAS

WITNESS PAIN
BE CONSCIOUSLY AWARE
OF THE AREAS WITHIN
YOUR BODY IN WHICH
YOU EXPERIENCE PAIN
OR DISCOMFORT,
AND SIMPLY WITNESS THE
PAIN WITHOUT JUDGMENT

CONSCIOUS DREAMING

My evening dreams provide insight into informing my daily choices and developing my potential.

Sometimes when people visit beautiful botanical gardens or metropolitan parks,
    They may find themselves walking by a large ornately crafted water fountain.

Many people enjoy throwing coins into these fountains as a way of making a secret wish
    Focusing their thoughts on something they'd like to have come true in their lives.

This modern folk ritual rose out of an older traditional rite of throwing a coin, or a special object,
    Into a deep well where the coin fell into the darkness of the subterranean earth,
        And where a wish might then be magically transformed into reality.

For these people, it was believed that the wishing well led directly to "the belly of the gods",
    Or to the mysterious part of existence that could benevolently alter the physical world.

Each night when we close our eyes to go to sleep,
    We enter a *portal* that can take us to an altered dimension of consciousness
        Where we have an opportunity to experience **the magical realm of our dreams**.

As we silently slip into this realm of dream images, we encounter a mesmerizing world
    Of colorful imaginative fantasy, or ominous nightmares, or unbounded possibilities,
        Where anything may happen - and where wishes can be transformed into reality.

If we choose to, we may use our evening dream states to access a wealth of knowledge
    By, immediately before we go to sleep,
        Creating a specific intention in our mind for our nightly dream journey
            Which may take the form of a simple question - or a spiritual inquiry.

Just like when we throw a coin into a deep well with an intention of receiving a personal wish,
    We can make an intention, focus on a desire, or ask a question prior to sleeping,
        And gently slip it into the inward darkness within the dimension of our dreams
            As we consciously surrender it to *the Infinite Intelligence* of the Universe,
                Believing our desire or inquiry will find its way to our waking world.

Sometimes dreams can be prophetic and used to envision future possibilities,
    Or to discover clues of how certain life events might potentially unfold.

Our dreams can also be used to help balance and heal
    The emotional disturbances and upsets we experience within our waking lives.

Furthermore, they can be utilized as a transformative practice
    To develop a specific skill, ability, or field of knowledge we want to cultivate,
        To solve problems, or to conceive of brand new ways of doing things.

Every evening when we go to sleep and fall into our dream world,
    We enter *a portal of potential* - and cross *a threshold of possibility*
        Where we can "throw our coin of intention" that's aligned with *the Source of Life*,
            And then let go, trusting our dream will come true in divine perfect timing.

Circle of Conscious Dreaming
(A Transformative Practice)

DEVELOPMENT
I CAN CHOOSE TO USE
MY EVENING DREAMS
TO CALL FORTH
THE DEVELOPMENT
OF A SPECIFIC SKILL,
ABILITY, OR FIELD
OF KNOWLEDGE

FUTURE VISION
I CAN CHOOSE TO USE
MY EVENING DREAMS
TO ENVISION FUTURE
POSSIBILITIES OF HOW
CERTAIN LIFE EVENTS
MIGHT POTENTIALLY
UNFOLD

PROBLEM SOLVING
I CAN CHOOSE TO USE
MY EVENING DREAMS
AS A MEANS
TO SOLVE PROBLEMS,
OR TO CONCEIVE
OF BRAND NEW WAYS
OF DOING THINGS

HEALING
I CAN CHOOSE TO USE
MY EVENING DREAMS
TO HELP BALANCE
AND HEAL THE EMOTIONAL
DISTURBANCES
I EXPERIENCE
IN MY WAKING LIFE

BALANCE OF DAILY ACTIVITY

I maintain a healthy balance in my life regarding my work, my play, my studies, and my prayers.

In elementary school, we learned the Earth orbits around the Sun
    As it travels through space on its annual cyclic journey,
        And that this constant rotational movement is the origin of the four seasons.

Furthermore, we were taught to see this complete yearly cycle as one whole system
    And we discovered how each season contributes to an overall balance of life on Earth.

We also learned that the path of the Moon as it orbits the Earth has four individual phases,
    Specifically the new moon, the full moon, plus the waning and waxing moons,
        And that each lunar phase is part of an integrated wholeness.

Now take a moment to consider how you use your time each day (your normal daily activities)
    And think of these daily activities as "your daily seasons", or "your phases of the day",
        As a way to help you maintain a **greater awareness of balance in your life**.

Imagine each new day consists of "four symbolic seasons", or "four phases of the day",
    Which are the <u>physical</u>, <u>emotional</u>, <u>mental</u>, and <u>spiritual</u> components of your being
        And picture all four of these components requiring nourishment and attention
            In order to truly support a healthy well-balanced life.

Our <u>physical component</u> requires *work*, what we can call our personal offerings of service
    Or what we can also define as the outward creative contributions we offer to others
        That helps us, and society, move forward into greater progress and fulfillment.

This includes the career we choose, the fervent manifestations of our individual creativity,
    Volunteer work, and even the energy output we use to stay physically healthy.

In <u>the area of our emotional lives</u>, it benefits us to spend time each day in *play* or recreation,
    Which can include periods of fun and discovery, as well as deep relaxation and rest
        In order to sustain an experience of overall wellbeing.

There is also a natural longing in us to develop our minds and focus our creative imagination,
    Thus it benefits us to use <u>our mental faculties</u> to *study* and cultivate our cognitive skills.

And, finally, there is <u>the spiritual aspect of our being</u> that intuitively yearns to align with *Life*
    And be nourished by various forms of *prayer*, contemplation, and inner silence.

The full cycle of each day consists of twenty-four hours
    Of which, on average, we sleep about eight of those, leaving sixteen hours remaining.

If we wanted to, we could divide the sixteen by four and try to experience four hours each day
    Of **work**, four of **play**, four also of **study**, and four of what we will generally call **prayer**.

We are always in a dynamic process of co-creating our concept of *our ideal perfect world*
    And therefore in every moment, we can exercise our conscious awareness
        To do the best we can each day to balance our **work, play, studies, and prayer**.

Circle of the Balance of Daily Activity
(I do the best I can each day to balance my ...)

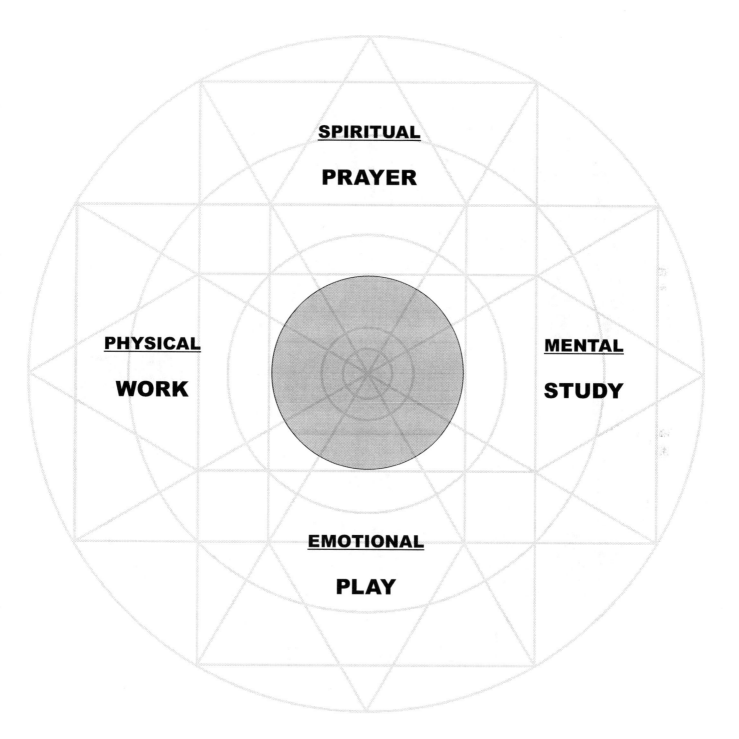

SPIRITUAL

PRAYER

PHYSICAL

WORK

MENTAL

STUDY

EMOTIONAL

PLAY

XV

NAVIGATING THE JOURNEY OF THE GREAT CIRCLE

TRANSCENDENCE

The Source of Life is always inviting me to cultivate my next higher stage of spiritual awareness.

Young children are usually mesmerized by the seeming "magic" they witness
　　When they play with or experience a simple magnet.

Of course, a magnet contains a mysterious force that science calls *magnetism*
　　Which generates an invisible field around it
　　　　And draws objects to it by some "unseen universal wizardry".

A magnet creates a field of energy that's intangible and can't be observed with the naked eye,
　　Yet this invisible field produces a force that can attract to itself bits of metal in its vicinity.

The central core of the spinning Earth also generates a huge magnetic field,
　　As does the interior core of the Sun.

And at the center of our Milky Way Galaxy,
　　There is a massive *black hole* that relentlessly draws stars and celestial bodies to it
　　　　With its incomprehensibly monstrous field of attraction.

Yet the ultimate *Universal Field* that's continuously "pulling on each of us in every moment"
　　Is *the Infinite Intelligence* of the Universe, *the Impulse of Evolution* within the Cosmos,
　　　　The Source of Life which is eternal and unbounded.

Some progressive philosophers, teachers, and scientists have called this *Universal Impulse*,
　　The Unified Field, or even more simply - *The Field*,
　　　　The timeless, dimensionless *Source* from which all of creation emerges.

Each of us is always "being pulled" by the attractive power of this *Field* **to perpetually learn**
　　And to constantly expand our conscious awareness of what our life is truly about,
　　　　For learning and spiritual awakening are part of the central purpose of our life.

This natural impulse in us to learn and develop ourselves is also called *transcendence*
　　And it's the innate longing that's continuously urging us
　　　　To transcend, or stretch beyond, our current experience of life
　　　　　　So as **to develop** higher expressions of our unlimited potential.

Transcendence is *the Transcendent Impulse* in us that yearns **to expand** our consciousness
　　Toward new horizons of possibility,
　　　　And reach for, and **awaken to**, higher stages of spiritual awareness.

For many of us, *transcendence* is most directly accessed
　　When we enter the pristine realm of inner silence
　　　　And quiet the stream of thoughts within our mind
　　　　　　So we can more easily feel the ever-present "tug of this natural force".

Each one of us, in a manner of speaking, is "a child of the Universe"
　　That's being constantly invited to dive into this vast ocean of sublime stillness
　　　　So we may be irresistibly drawn into the magnetism of its *Limitless Love*.

Transcendence
(Evolving Consciousness)

TO LEARN
TRANSCENDENCE –
THE NATURAL IMPULSE
AND INNATE DESIRE
WITHIN ME TO LEARN
AND EXPAND
MY AWARENESS OF WHAT
MY LIFE IS TRULY ABOUT

TO DEVELOP
TRANSCENDENCE –
THE NATURAL IMPULSE
TO GO BEYOND MY
CURRENT EXPERIENCES
SO AS TO DEVELOP
HIGHER EXPRESSIONS
OF MY POTENTIAL

TO EXPAND
TRANSCENDENCE –
THE NATURAL IMPULSE
WITHIN ME THAT
YEARNS TO EXPAND
MY CONSCIOUSNESS
INTO NEW HORIZONS
OF POSSIBILITY

TO AWAKEN
TRANSCENDENCE –
THE NATURAL IMPULSE
WITHIN ME
THAT REACHES FOR,
AND AWAKENS TO,
HIGHER STAGES
OF SPIRITUAL AWARENESS

189

TRANSCENDENT IMPULSES OF CONSCIOUSNESS

Experiencing silence is a sublime way to align my awareness with my Eternal Nature.

You have probably had the experience of waiting for a plane to depart at a large busy airport
And found yourself engrossed in a passionate conversation with a friend
In which you were not consciously aware of all the various sounds around you.

Because you were deep in conversation, for a brief time you didn't hear
The chatter of other people talking in your vicinity, or young children playing nearby,
Or the noisy departure of airplanes taking off outside the terminal.

When we are intently focusing our attention in one specific area,
We typically close off our attention and awareness to other activities around us.

Similarly, when we're placing our attention only in the outer material world of form,
We tend not to hear "the songs of our natural impulses", or *transcendent impulses*,
That are perpetually "singing within us" (in other words, directing us from within).

When we take time to be inwardly silent by quieting the chatter of our minds,
Removing ourselves, for a few moments, from the bustle of the world,
We can more easily become aware of these **impulses of consciousness**
Which are always present within us to help inform and direct our lives.

As we quiet our mind, we attune to an innate **impulse of transcendence**
That's always inviting us to transcend beyond our current experiences of life
And reach for higher stages of spiritual awareness.

Within the stillness, we also align with **the impulse to embrace, and commune with,**
More expansive aspects of our current stage of awareness,
So we can more effectively use our creative gifts and talents to serve others.

As we become ever more mindful, we experience an intrinsic **impulse of diversity**
That's always present within to help guide us in exploring and manifesting
Our unique and diverse forms of creative expression.

And as we still our thoughts, we attune with the most natural **impulse of Oneness**
That's constantly inviting us to be aware of our Unity with *All That Is*.

Experiencing silence is a sublime way to align our awareness with our *Eternal Nature*
And this alignment assists us in serving the positive progression of the world.

For when we become increasingly mindful
Of these **transcendent impulses of consciousness** working through us every day
And stay consciously connected with *the Source of Life*,
We more easily feel *the Infinite Intelligence* of the Universe
Guiding our mind and heart in everything we do.

And thus each day, we can witness *Life's* unlimited expressions of creativity
Effortlessly manifesting through us as true *artists of life.*

Circle of the Transcendent Impulses of Consciousness

THE IMPULSE OF ONENESS

THE NATURAL IMPULSE WITHIN ME THAT INVITES ME TO BE AWARE OF MY ONENESS WITH EVERY EXPRESSION OF LIFE - AND OUR UNITY WITH *ALL THAT IS*

THE IMPULSE OF DIVERSITY

THE NATURAL IMPULSE WITHIN ME THAT GUIDES ME TO EXPLORE AND MANIFEST MY UNIQUE AND DIVERSE FORMS OF CREATIVE EXPRESSION

THE IMPULSE OF TRANSCENDENCE

THE NATURAL IMPULSE TO TRANSCEND BEYOND MY CURRENT EXPERIENCES OF LIFE AND REACH FOR HIGHER STAGES OF SPIRITUAL AWARENESS

THE IMPULSE OF COMMUNION

THE NATURAL IMPULSE WITHIN ME TO EMBRACE, AND COMMUNE WITH, MORE EXPANSIVE ASPECTS OF MY CURRENT STAGE OF AWARENESS

INTERIOR EVOLUTIONARY IMPULSE

Life is always inviting me to expand my awareness so I may learn to love more fully.

When you examine a common tree, you can observe it consists of many individual segments
Starting with a wooden trunk rising out of the ground,
Then a series of large branches emerging from the central trunk,
Numerous smaller branches and twigs that grow out of bigger branches,
And, for much of the year, the twigs are blanketed with leaves.

Of course, this depicts only the outward part of the tree, for it also has a hidden or inward part,
Which contains its intricate unseen system of roots growing below the ground.

Everything in Nature has "two sides of the coin", so to speak,
An outward component (material creation), as well as an inward one (consciousness).

Every animal, plant, and all of the myriad forms of the natural world
Embody this dual quality of interior and exterior dimensions of reality
Which is an essential and foundational principle of Nature.

As humans, we have both a highly evolved <u>outward</u> physical reality
And an <u>inward</u> invisible reality we refer to using the words "heart", "mind", or *"Spirit"*.

The Evolutionary Impulse (the Infinitely Intelligent Power that fashions the entire Universe)
Also has both an <u>interior</u> component, which is **evolving consciousness**,
And an <u>exterior</u> component, which is **evolving creativity**. (see June 8th)

This <u>inward</u> component can be referred to as **transcendence**, **development**, or **awakening**,
While its <u>outward</u> compliment can be defined as manifestation, healing, or contribution.

The Interior Evolutionary Impulse is *the Universal Intelligence*
That perpetually guides and directs the evolution of all forms of life
Toward higher, more ordered, and more cooperative stages of **consciousness**.

It can be thought of as *the Transcendent Impulse* within all facets of life
That continuously moves toward more expanded levels of awareness.

And it's the inward yearning that resides deep within the heart and mind of every person
As **a natural desire to develop** oneself so as to manifest one's greater potential.

This interior evolutionary force is the innate tug that lives within us,
Which constantly attempts to fulfill the inherent longing to discover who we really are.

It is the intrinsic call in us to evolve beyond the habitual hold of our fear-oriented nature
And **awaken to our *True Nature***, in order that we may learn to love unconditionally.

Our natural human yearning to transcend beyond our current limits
And expand into new horizons of possibility
Forms the foundation and "inner roots for the Tree of Life" so we can branch out,
Grow boldly toward "the endless sky" and, one day, "touch the stars".

Circle of *the Interior Evolutionary Impulse*
(Evolving Consciousness)

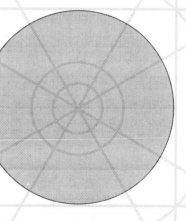

CONSCIOUSNESS
INTERIOR EV. IMPULSE –
THE UNIVERSAL IMPULSE
OF INFINITE
INTELLIGENCE THAT
GUIDES THE EVOLUTION
OF ALL FORMS OF LIFE
TOWARD HIGHER STAGES
OF CONSCIOUSNESS

AWAKENING
INTERIOR EV. IMPULSE –
THE INNATE IMPULSE
WITHIN ME TO EVOLVE
BEYOND MY FEAR-BASED
NATURE AND AWAKEN
TO MY *TRUE NATURE,*
IN ORDER TO LEARN TO
LOVE UNCONDITIONALLY

TRANSCENDENCE
INTERIOR EV. IMPULSE –
THE EVOLUTIONARY
IMPULSE WITHIN ME
AND ALL OF LIFE
THAT MOVES TOWARD
HIGHER AND MORE
EXPANDED LEVELS
OF AWARENESS

INNER DEVELOPMENT
INTERIOR EV. IMPULSE –
THE NATURAL IMPULSE
IN ME THAT DIRECTS ME
TO REACH FOR HIGHER
STAGES OF AWARENESS,
DEVELOP MY POTENTIAL,
AND DISCOVER
WHO I REALLY AM

MODES OF INNER DEVELOPMENT

I feel a natural yearning in me that constantly invites me to love and accept myself just as I am.

If you could somehow in a moment - observe a child growing through the first decade of its life,
You could then witness each developmental stage the child faced over those ten years.

For example, initially an infant develops its early awareness solely from its inborn impulses
By which it instinctually knows how to find its first nourishment from its mother's breasts
And how to spontaneously explore and sense its nearby surroundings.

During another stage of growth, the child learns how to mimic the movements it perceives
From the daily actions of its mother - and from observing members of its family.

As the child matures, its inner development is quickened by what it discovers from others,
Like friends, teachers, TV celebrities, who share their ideas about "how reality works".

The child may then enter a stage where it's motivated by his or her unique interests
And starts to develop them through various self-studies or by learning specific skills.

Throughout time, humans have sought ever-better ways to learn, or **modes of development**,
Thus for early humans, similar to when we were infants, the first means of development
Was directed solely by their **instincts** - which guided their physical survival.

Many eons ago, this instinctual impulse served our ancestors to overcome numerous dangers,
Yet now, this same innate impulse is serving each of us as well - by inwardly inviting us
To cultivate higher stages of awareness - and develop our creative potential.

And similar to the intelligent impulse that guides the developmental stages of a growing child,
This same natural impulse is also guiding all people to cultivate their inner development
By seeking higher knowledge, achieving new skills, learning different trades,
Or **working to tangibly improve** at something through devoted practice.

Yet today, many of us are beginning to explore another unconventional mode of development
Which comes from aligning our personal consciousness with *collective awareness fields*
(Fields of higher awareness) so as to consciously access higher knowledge.

A field of awakened awareness can be thought of as "a morphic field of energy"
That acts as a "container" holding the collective knowledge of all awakened individuals.

This unique form of *awareness field* initially came into being from the accumulated awareness
Of every awakened human on Earth who lives now - or who has previously lived.

There comes a decisive time *when we learn to fully love and accept ourselves just as we are*,
And, by doing so, the result of this radical acceptance is we begin to radically trust
That our inner development is always guided from within us by *the Source of Life*.

If we truly listen, *Life* will lead us to an experience of inner freedom, a stage of **life mastery**
That eventually emerges within us from our constant practice of awakened awareness,
A stage where we must, once again, humbly learn to be as innocent as a child.

Circle of the Modes of Inner Development
(In Relation to the Stages of a Human Lifetime)

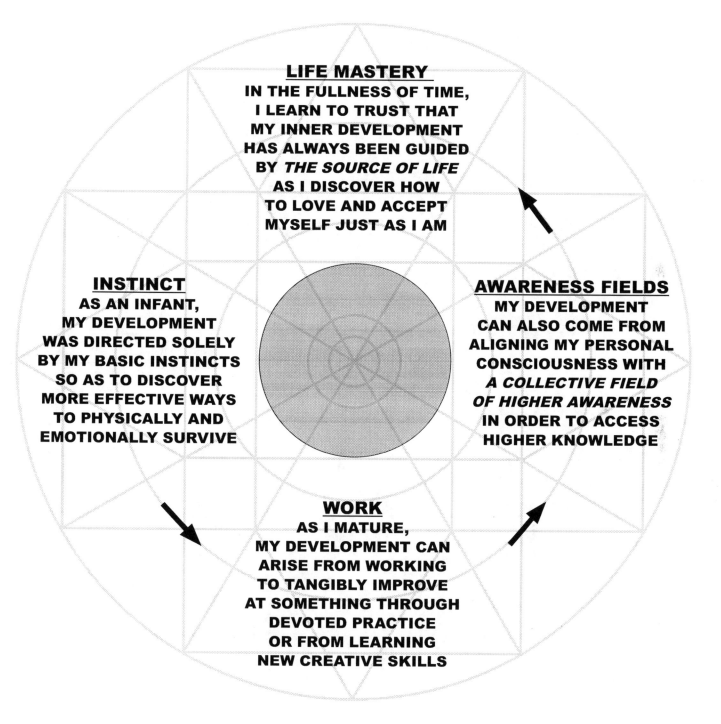

LIFE MASTERY
IN THE FULLNESS OF TIME,
I LEARN TO TRUST THAT
MY INNER DEVELOPMENT
HAS ALWAYS BEEN GUIDED
BY *THE SOURCE OF LIFE*
AS I DISCOVER HOW
TO LOVE AND ACCEPT
MYSELF JUST AS I AM

INSTINCT
AS AN INFANT,
MY DEVELOPMENT
WAS DIRECTED SOLELY
BY MY BASIC INSTINCTS
SO AS TO DISCOVER
MORE EFFECTIVE WAYS
TO PHYSICALLY AND
EMOTIONALLY SURVIVE

AWARENESS FIELDS
MY DEVELOPMENT
CAN ALSO COME FROM
ALIGNING MY PERSONAL
CONSCIOUSNESS WITH
*A COLLECTIVE FIELD
OF HIGHER AWARENESS*
IN ORDER TO ACCESS
HIGHER KNOWLEDGE

WORK
AS I MATURE,
MY DEVELOPMENT CAN
ARISE FROM WORKING
TO TANGIBLY IMPROVE
AT SOMETHING THROUGH
DEVOTED PRACTICE
OR FROM LEARNING
NEW CREATIVE SKILLS

XVI

THE ART OF TRANSFORMATION AND HEALING

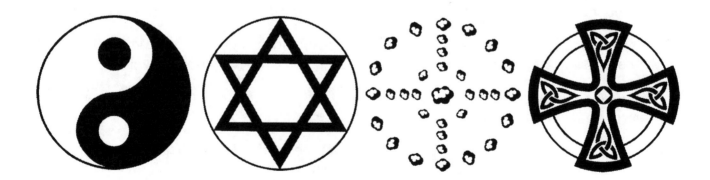

THE GREAT CIRCLE OF DEVELOPMENT AND TRANSFORMATION

As I expand my awareness of what is true, I cultivate in me greater transformation and healing.

All of Nature's diverse creatures living upon or below the surface of the Earth
Require some form of nourishing food to sustain them.

There are many single-celled organisms that take in nutrients from the water surrounding them
And these soluble nutrients are absorbed through their cell walls.

Highly developed plants get their nutrients both directly from the Sun through photosynthesis
And from the various minerals in the ground brought up by their intricate root systems.

Some animals only eat food that comes from plant sources,
While the nutrient needs of other animals necessitate the protein of flesh.

The external nourishment necessary for each of these creatures must, in some fashion,
Pass through an internal system of the organism
Where the food is digested and transformed into an altered pattern of energy
And then utilized for its ongoing development.

As well as solid food, which is *the outer component of nourishment* used by physical forms,
Every creature on Earth is also "nourished", so to speak, by *an inner component*.

From one vantage, *the inner component of nourishment* for all organisms can be thought of
As the instinctual impulse of *Natural Intelligence* that directs its **inner development**
Which is then expressed as the organism's **outer transformation** in the world.

During eons of evolution, humans have become the only creatures we know of
That have the conscious ability to be self-aware of its forms of *inner nourishment*.

As human beings, our *inner nourishment* comes from the expansion of inner development
Derived from our life experiences - as well as self-reflection and transformative practice.

As our inner being develops and expands, our conscious growth is then mirrored in our body
And expressed outwardly as personal transformation - or various forms of healing.

By shifting from a life that's shaped by our fearful choices - to a life that's nourished by *Love*,
This inward shift is reflected in our outer world as expressions of wellbeing or healing.

As we continue to develop through expanding our awareness, keeping our heart open,
And staying aligned with *the Source of Life*, we cultivate ever-greater transformation.

Along our unfolding journey of life, we "sit at the banquet table of unbounded possibilities"
In which our "Banquet Host", *the Infinite Presence of Love,* is perpetually inviting us
To feast upon "the most nourishing foods we can possibly receive".

This *inner nourishment* gives us the wisdom to learn, to create, to align, and to serve,
And helps provide us with the vitality and courage required
For "the hero's journey" we must embark on each day.

The Great Circle of Development and Transformation
(The Transformative Dynamics of Healing)

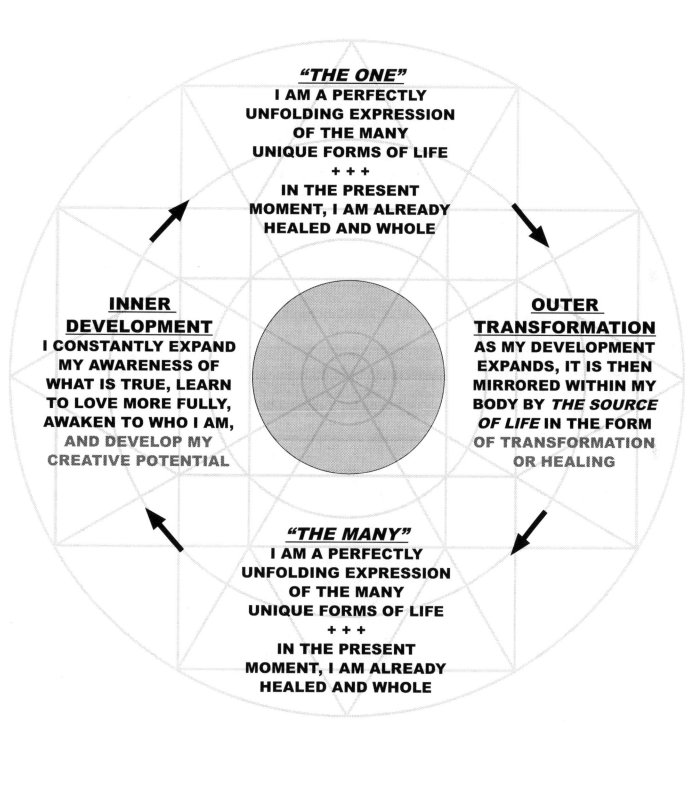

"THE ONE"
I AM A PERFECTLY
UNFOLDING EXPRESSION
OF THE MANY
UNIQUE FORMS OF LIFE
+ + +
IN THE PRESENT
MOMENT, I AM ALREADY
HEALED AND WHOLE

**INNER
DEVELOPMENT**
I CONSTANTLY EXPAND
MY AWARENESS OF
WHAT IS TRUE, LEARN
TO LOVE MORE FULLY,
AWAKEN TO WHO I AM,
AND DEVELOP MY
CREATIVE POTENTIAL

**OUTER
TRANSFORMATION**
AS MY DEVELOPMENT
EXPANDS, IT IS THEN
MIRRORED WITHIN MY
BODY BY *THE SOURCE
OF LIFE* IN THE FORM
OF TRANSFORMATION
OR HEALING

"THE MANY"
I AM A PERFECTLY
UNFOLDING EXPRESSION
OF THE MANY
UNIQUE FORMS OF LIFE
+ + +
IN THE PRESENT
MOMENT, I AM ALREADY
HEALED AND WHOLE

THE GREAT CIRCLE OF THE SPHERES OF CONSCIOUSNESS AND FIELDS OF CREATION

As I learn what my life is truly about, my heart naturally opens to greater love and compassion.

If you were to look at the primordial development of the Earth based on scientific knowledge,
    You could observe that during the first half-a-billion years of our planet's evolution
        Various elemental forms of **matter** (i.e. earth, water, gases) were all that existed.

Around four billion years ago, the first forms of **life** emerged as single-celled organisms,
    And then two billion years later, myriad life forms appeared as oxygen became plentiful.

The arrival of a third expression, the self-reflective conscious **mind**, was manifested into being
    Approximately one hundred thousand years ago through the cognition of early humans.

Recognizing these three principal phases of Earth's evolving history **(matter, life, and mind)**
    Can help us be aware of three aspects of our current human evolutionary development
        Which, at this present time, are also unfolding naturally within our personal life
            Via the health of our <u>body</u>, feelings of our <u>heart</u>, and choices of our <u>mind</u>.

The Great Circle of the Spheres of Consciousness and the Fields of Creation
    Is a Contemplation Circle that describes a simple foundational concept of our reality:
        The evolution of creation outwardly mirrors evolving consciousness.

If you could "dive inside" an actual molecule in order to examine the way it's constructed,
    You would see it consists of several chemical elements that are made up of atoms,
        And atoms are made of smaller protons, neutrons, and fields of electrons,
            And even these so-called particles of energy can be further sub-divided.

In a similar manner, if you desire to deepen your understanding of *evolving consciousness*,
    You can examine it by "diving in" and observing its distinct *sectors* or *spheres of time*:
        The Sphere of Matter, the Sphere of Life, and **the Sphere of Mind**.

Each *sphere* defines a phase of evolutionary time, or developmental stage of consciousness,
    Starting at the very beginning of the Universe and continuing until the present moment.

From the central axiom - *the evolution of creation outwardly mirrors evolving consciousness* -
    We can augment our awareness of the unfolding dynamics of reality by recognizing
        That these **Spheres of Consciousness** are then mirrored as form into the world
            Via a creative process of **the Fields of Creation** which further sub-divides
                As **the Field of Light**, **the Field of Love**, and **the Field of Power**.

One way to describe this dynamic process is that **the Source of All That Is ("The One")**
    Mirrors **the three Spheres of Consciousness (matter, life, and mind)** into our world
        As beneficial aspects or outer expressions of our life via **the Fields of Creation**,
            Which then appear as our creative gifts and contributions *("The Many")*.

For most of recorded history, greater knowledge and understanding of what life is truly about
    Has assisted we humans in better preparing "the fertile soil of our minds and hearts"
        For "the flowers of greater compassion to blossom in the garden of our lives".

The Great Circle of the Spheres of Consciousness and Fields of Creation

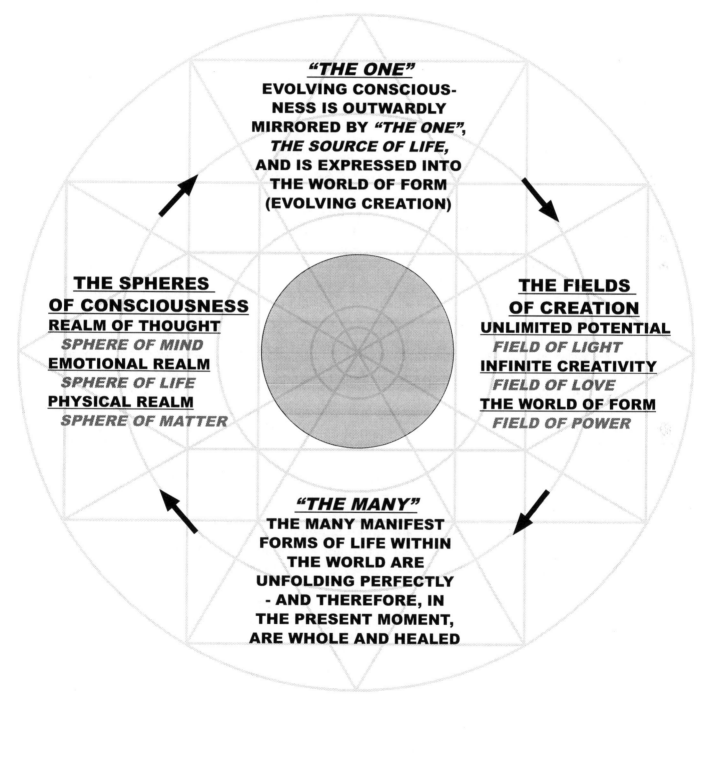

"THE ONE"
EVOLVING CONSCIOUS-
NESS IS OUTWARDLY
MIRRORED BY *"THE ONE"*,
THE SOURCE OF LIFE,
AND IS EXPRESSED INTO
THE WORLD OF FORM
(EVOLVING CREATION)

THE SPHERES
OF CONSCIOUSNESS
REALM OF THOUGHT
SPHERE OF MIND
EMOTIONAL REALM
SPHERE OF LIFE
PHYSICAL REALM
SPHERE OF MATTER

THE FIELDS
OF CREATION
UNLIMITED POTENTIAL
FIELD OF LIGHT
INFINITE CREATIVITY
FIELD OF LOVE
THE WORLD OF FORM
FIELD OF POWER

"THE MANY"
THE MANY MANIFEST
FORMS OF LIFE WITHIN
THE WORLD ARE
UNFOLDING PERFECTLY
- AND THEREFORE, IN
THE PRESENT MOMENT,
ARE WHOLE AND HEALED

SPHERES OF CONSCIOUSNESS

Everything I perceive is made of universal energy that emerges from The Unified Field.

Every time you use a computer to send emails, or organize your finances, or import photos,
You utilize a specific internal digital program that controls a distinct computer function.

To describe it simply, a typical computer program is "an invisible system of instructions"
Which has been designed to control a sequence of intended outcomes.

It can be thought of as "an unseen sphere of information" or "an intangible set of directions",
Which are the internal commands that give shape to what is on your computer screen
Depending on information you give the computer and the program you are using.

Most people cannot directly perceive this hidden sphere of information inside the computer,
But, via the screen, you can absolutely monitor and examine its outer manifestations.

Thus a computer can be a useful metaphor for grasping how certain realms of consciousness
Are shaped into physical reality by an invisible and intangible *Natural Intelligence*.

From scientific and philosophical observations regarding the primary dynamics of existence,
It has been observed there are three distinctive waves, or three dimensions of reality,
Which, over long periods of evolutionary time, have emerged within the Universe:
The first wave of **matter**, the second wave of **life**, and the third of **mind**.

These three waves of expression were given form by a ubiquitous *Field of Infinite Intelligence*,
A *Sphere of Universal Consciousness* which acts like a vast cosmic computer program
That generates a limitless number of images on "an infinite computer screen".

Spheres of Consciousness can also be poetically pictured as "the invisible hands of God"
That fashion boundless universal energy into the countless material forms of our world.

Like internal computer programs, **Spheres of Consciousness** cannot be seen with our eyes,
But we can certainly observe in the world, the outward manifestations of their creativity.

The Sphere of Matter (or *the Physiosphere)*, the first nested wave of the physical realm,
Is the consciousness that gives shape to all material structures within the Universe
Such as atoms, molecules, galaxies, stars, planets, mountains, and oceans.

The Sphere of Life (or *the Biosphere),* the second nested wave of the emotional realm,
Is the consciousness that gives shape to all biological life like microbes, plants, animals,
That, over time, have developed varied physical sensations and basic emotions.

The Sphere of Mind (or *the Noosphere),* the third nested wave describing the intelligent mind,
Is the consciousness that gives shape to both the individual and collective mind
Within all intelligent life forms, which have evolved advanced thought processes.

All manifestations of the three **Spheres of Consciousness** are comprised of *universal energy*
Emerging from **the Sphere of Unity** (also called *the Unisphere* or *The Unified Field)*
And "God only knows" how long until the next sphere of consciousness appears.

Circle of the Spheres of Consciousness
(The Nested Waves of Evolving Consciousness)

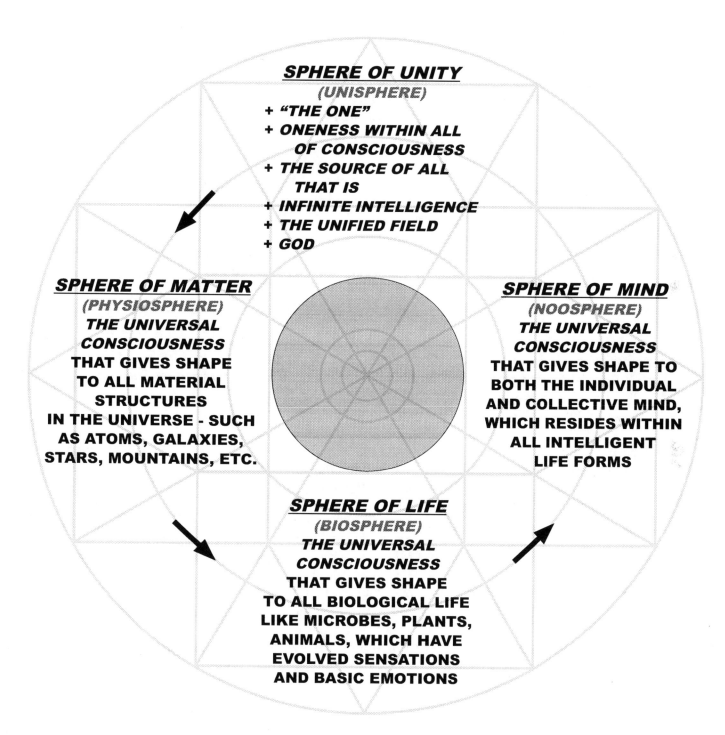

SPHERE OF UNITY
(UNISPHERE)
+ *"THE ONE"*
+ *ONENESS WITHIN ALL OF CONSCIOUSNESS*
+ *THE SOURCE OF ALL THAT IS*
+ *INFINITE INTELLIGENCE*
+ *THE UNIFIED FIELD*
+ *GOD*

SPHERE OF MATTER
(PHYSIOSPHERE)
THE UNIVERSAL CONSCIOUSNESS THAT GIVES SHAPE TO ALL MATERIAL STRUCTURES IN THE UNIVERSE - SUCH AS ATOMS, GALAXIES, STARS, MOUNTAINS, ETC.

SPHERE OF MIND
(NOOSPHERE)
THE UNIVERSAL CONSCIOUSNESS THAT GIVES SHAPE TO BOTH THE INDIVIDUAL AND COLLECTIVE MIND, WHICH RESIDES WITHIN ALL INTELLIGENT LIFE FORMS

SPHERE OF LIFE
(BIOSPHERE)
THE UNIVERSAL CONSCIOUSNESS THAT GIVES SHAPE TO ALL BIOLOGICAL LIFE LIKE MICROBES, PLANTS, ANIMALS, WHICH HAVE EVOLVED SENSATIONS AND BASIC EMOTIONS

OUTER EXPRESSIONS OF CONSCIOUSNESS

Everything in the world, as well as my body, is made of light vibrating at different frequencies.

Modern scientists have produced many highly sensitive instruments that demonstrate
There is a range of frequencies in our Universe called *the electromagnetic spectrum*
Which is the sum of all frequencies of electromagnetic radiation, or simply *"light"*.

The visible band of frequencies that enables us to perceive and experience the physical world
Is a very tiny portion of the full spectrum of electromagnetic radiation
Of which the majority of this spectrum is either above or below the visible range.

Below the thin band of visible frequencies are bands of infrared, microwaves, and radio waves,
And lower still on the spectrum are a series of sound frequencies that vibrate our ears.

Above the range of visible light, there are many additional bands of high frequency *light*
Such as ultra-violet, X-rays, and Gamma rays.

In the future, as scientists construct more sensitive electromagnetic instruments,
We may find that this spectrum of *light* produces even higher frequencies without end.

Some metaphysicians have declared that everything in the Universe, from galaxies to atoms,
Is made of *light* (electromagnetic radiation) that is vibrating at different frequencies.

Many affirm that consciousness is an ultra-high frequency made up of "the vibration of *Love*"
Which then, at lower frequencies, takes shape as multiple layers of phenomenal form
That are expressed as various vibrational forms of reality within the Universe
And then, ultimately, as physical matter at lower frequencies.

The Spheres of Universal Intelligence, or what can be called **the Spheres of Consciousness**,
Which include **Matter** *(Physiosphere)*, **Life** *(Biosphere)*, and **Mind** *(Noosphere)*,
Give shape and form to <u>physical</u>, <u>emotional</u>, and <u>thought realms</u>, respectively,
At different frequencies of manifested expression.

The three **Spheres of Consciousness** are then out-pictured in the phenomenal world of form
As the innumerable manifestations of <u>physical matter</u>, <u>biological life</u>, or <u>intelligent life</u>.

As far as we currently know, consciousness embodies its most complex and ordered forms
Within humanity through the expressions of our **bodies**, our **hearts**, and our **minds**.

It has been speculated that all information within the physical realm is held in the <u>human body</u>,
All information within the emotional realm of our planet is held in the <u>human heart</u>,
And all information of universal intelligence is embodied in the <u>human mind</u>.

We humans appear to be the most complex creatures on Earth that we're currently aware of,
Yet we're only "one small band of frequency within the infinite spectrum of existence".

If we had eyes which could prophetically see into the future as humanity continues to evolve,
We might behold that **in the future, the outer expressions of human consciousness
Will, most likely, be *light years* beyond our current human capacities.**

Circle of the Outer Expressions of Consciousness
(As Embodied Within Humanity)

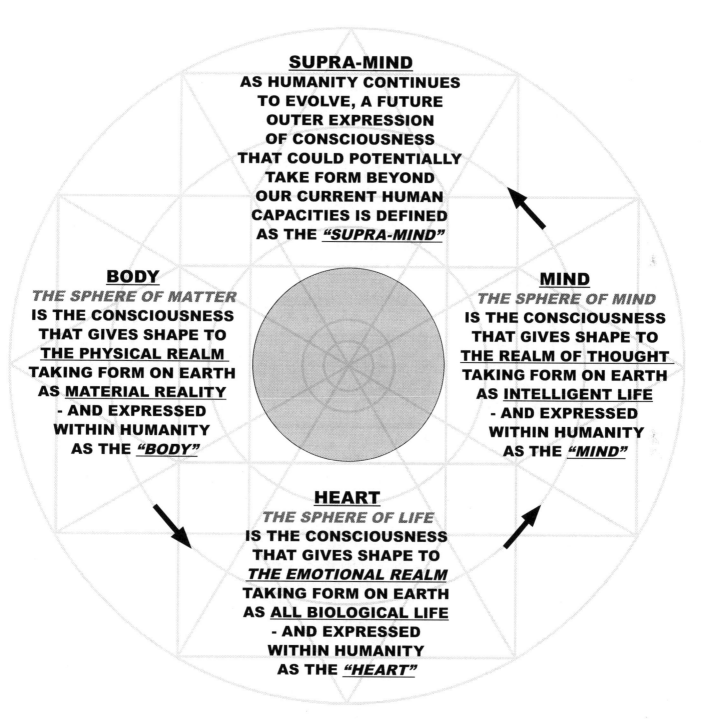

SUPRA-MIND
AS HUMANITY CONTINUES
TO EVOLVE, A FUTURE
OUTER EXPRESSION
OF CONSCIOUSNESS
THAT COULD POTENTIALLY
TAKE FORM BEYOND
OUR CURRENT HUMAN
CAPACITIES IS DEFINED
AS THE *"SUPRA-MIND"*

BODY
THE SPHERE OF MATTER
IS THE CONSCIOUSNESS
THAT GIVES SHAPE TO
THE PHYSICAL REALM
TAKING FORM ON EARTH
AS MATERIAL REALITY
- AND EXPRESSED
WITHIN HUMANITY
AS THE *"BODY"*

MIND
THE SPHERE OF MIND
IS THE CONSCIOUSNESS
THAT GIVES SHAPE TO
THE REALM OF THOUGHT
TAKING FORM ON EARTH
AS INTELLIGENT LIFE
- AND EXPRESSED
WITHIN HUMANITY
AS THE *"MIND"*

HEART
THE SPHERE OF LIFE
IS THE CONSCIOUSNESS
THAT GIVES SHAPE TO
THE EMOTIONAL REALM
TAKING FORM ON EARTH
AS ALL BIOLOGICAL LIFE
- AND EXPRESSED
WITHIN HUMANITY
AS THE *"HEART"*

SPHERES OF BALANCING MODALITIES FOR THE HUMAN BODY

As I align my awareness with the Infinite Presence of Love - my heart wisdom guides my life.

Russian nesting dolls are a series of artfully decorated wooden dolls of diverse sizes
Which have been designed so each doll precisely fits inside the next larger-size doll,
And you probably, at one time in your life, have seen some form of these dolls.

To establish more clarity about nesting dolls - first, a small doll is crafted of wood at the center,
Then a slightly larger replica is made, cut and hollowed, and placed around the first one,
While a bigger third nesting doll is then fashioned and placed over the other two,
And the process continues until there are usually four to ten nesting dolls.

We can use this nested image as a metaphor for the various energy levels of the human body,
Since there are many different visible and invisible expressions of our human design.

Of course, every person has **a physical body** - which is their most dense expression of form
Experienced as solid, tangible, visible, and material in structure
And is the phenomenal manifestation of higher vibrational fields of energy.

Many metaphysicians teach that there are numerous other subtle levels of the human body
And that the next subtle level is **the etheric body**, also called *the vibrational body*,
Which is depicted in sacred art as *the aura* or *halo* around saintly people.

Next, there exists a slightly more subtle invisible body called **the emotional body**,
Which holds our feelings, desires, emotions, and our capacity to express compassion,
And in some esoteric schools, there's an even more subtle **mental body**
Which is our faculty of wisdom and understanding of what truly matters.

Each of these four **bodies** has the inherent potential to express vibrant health and wellness,
Yet they also each have the potential to become out of balance or dis-eased
Through placing attention on fear or attachment.

Yet as we expand our conscious awareness, we find <u>there are specific modalities we can learn
To keep our physical and subtle bodies in proper balance</u>. (See the following circle)

If we think of *Russian nesting dolls* as a symbol for these various levels of the human body
With the smallest innermost doll representing our visible **physical body**,
Then as we add each doll, they can help us visualize more subtle manifestations
Of the different energetic levels we inhabit as human beings.

After **the etheric and emotional bodies**, we add "the doll" that represents our **mental body**
(The faculty within us where vibrant health can emerge
From cultivating the wisdom of the heart that's merged with our compassion),
And it's our heart wisdom that helps heal our etheric and physical bodies,
For as above, so below - as within, so without.

The most exalted form of *"love in action"* that we may currently conceive of could be described
As <u>heart wisdom which guides our life</u> while we caringly <u>serve the wellbeing of others</u>,
Yet there's surely no end to the nested stages of a life that loves unconditionally.

Circle of Spheres of Balancing Modalities
For the Human Body

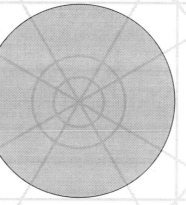

HEART WISDOM
THE MENTAL BODY
CAN BE BROUGHT INTO
BALANCE BY CULTIVATING
HEART WISDOM THROUGH
PRAYER, CONTEMPLATION,
SELF-INQUIRY, EXPANDING
AWARENESS, AND ALIGNING
WITH *THE SOURCE OF LIFE*

MODIFICATION
THE PHYSICAL BODY
CAN BE BROUGHT
INTO BALANCE BY
MODIFYING VARIOUS
ASPECTS OF THE BODY
WITH FOOD, HERBS,
SUPPLEMENTS, REST,
DRUGS, OR SURGERY

COMPASSION
THE EMOTIONAL BODY
CAN BE BROUGHT INTO
BALANCE BY OPENING
THE HEART TO GREATER
COMPASSIONATE ACTION
THROUGH GENEROSITY,
SERVICE, GRATITUDE,
AND FORGIVENESS

PRESENCE
THE ETHERIC BODY
CAN BE BROUGHT
INTO BALANCE BY LIVING
WITH PRESENCE, FULLY
INHABITING THE BODY,
MINDFULNESS, AND USING
CERTAIN BREATH WORK
AND *CHI* PRACTICES

PROGRESSION OF HEALING AWARENESS

Learning what my life is truly about empowers me to choose inner freedom.

If you look up towards the Moon at night and attempt to view the craters of this celestial body,
   You, most likely, will not be able to distinguish them clearly with your ordinary eyesight.

Yet if you were to observe the Moon as you look through a strong pair of binoculars,
   The rocky edges of these lunar craters become much more apparent.

If you then take a bigger step and examine the craters through a small amateur telescope,
   They can be inspected with greater detail and definition.

Furthermore, if you could peer at them through a state-of-the-art 200-inch lens telescope
   Which professional astronomers have constructed on top of a high mountain peak,
      You would be able to see the precise contours of their unique geological features.

As we continue to observe the wonders of Nature with ever better instruments
   Providing us with improved vision and expanded capabilities,
      We shift what we see from limited sight - to enhanced visibility - to precise clarity.

A similar progression of gaining greater clarity can occur in our ever-unfolding *spiritual journey*,
   For as we cultivate heart-centered awareness in regards to what our life is truly about,
      We, through our continuous development, begin to live a more awakened life
         As we mature from living in fear - to peace - to inner freedom.

When we're young, immature, and without a lot of meaningful life experience of the world,
   We can sometimes become angry at the way our life seems to be "unfairly" challenged,
      Blaming the way we feel on the various problems or difficulties we encounter.

As our conscious awareness expands through a steady process of inner development,
   We discover we can choose to be grateful for all that we're learning from our problems.

With growth and understanding, life leads us to the threshold of an awakened consciousness
   Where, ultimately, **gratitude for all experiences of life** arises in our awareness.

We may also have had difficult periods during our life when we felt life was not fair
   Because of various severe personal challenges or crises we had to deal with.

Yet as we become mindful to keep our heart open, see the "Big Picture", and embrace what is,
   We discover that our problems offer us vital opportunities to develop and free ourselves
      Which can eventually lead us to the awakened awareness
         Of **accepting that our life is unfolding perfectly just as it is**.

Should we find ourselves in the midst of intense pain during an early part of our life journey,
   It may be typical to resist the way things are - and feel separate from the rest of reality.

But as we learn to witness our reality and our life experiences through larger and larger lenses,
   It becomes ever clearer to us that we must **fully surrender our personal attachments**
      And, ultimately, become **aware of our Oneness with all of life**.

Circle of the Progression of Healing Awareness
(My Life Maturing from 1) Fear to 2) Peace to 3) Inner Freedom)

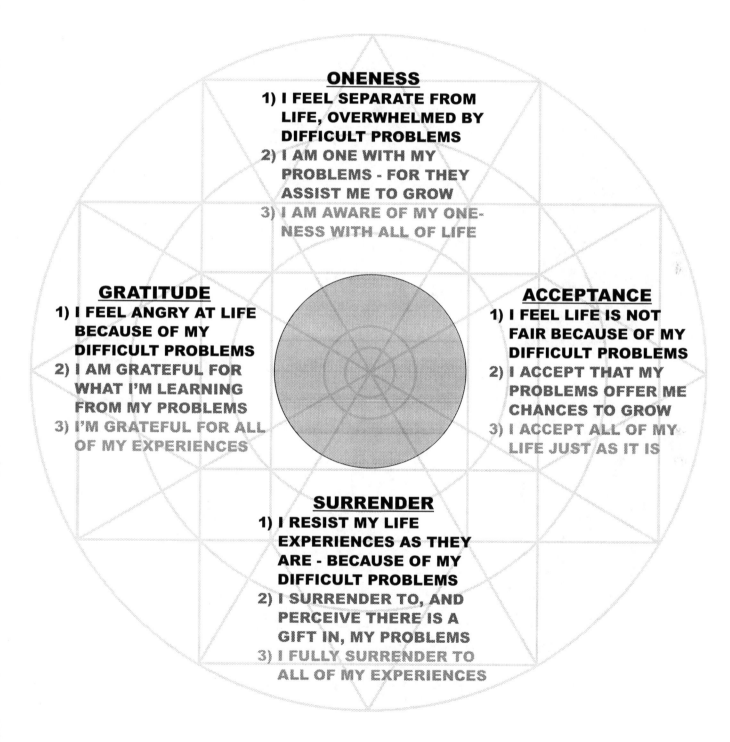

ONENESS
1) I FEEL SEPARATE FROM LIFE, OVERWHELMED BY DIFFICULT PROBLEMS
2) I AM ONE WITH MY PROBLEMS - FOR THEY ASSIST ME TO GROW
3) I AM AWARE OF MY ONE-NESS WITH ALL OF LIFE

GRATITUDE
1) I FEEL ANGRY AT LIFE BECAUSE OF MY DIFFICULT PROBLEMS
2) I AM GRATEFUL FOR WHAT I'M LEARNING FROM MY PROBLEMS
3) I'M GRATEFUL FOR ALL OF MY EXPERIENCES

ACCEPTANCE
1) I FEEL LIFE IS NOT FAIR BECAUSE OF MY DIFFICULT PROBLEMS
2) I ACCEPT THAT MY PROBLEMS OFFER ME CHANCES TO GROW
3) I ACCEPT ALL OF MY LIFE JUST AS IT IS

SURRENDER
1) I RESIST MY LIFE EXPERIENCES AS THEY ARE - BECAUSE OF MY DIFFICULT PROBLEMS
2) I SURRENDER TO, AND PERCEIVE THERE IS A GIFT IN, MY PROBLEMS
3) I FULLY SURRENDER TO ALL OF MY EXPERIENCES

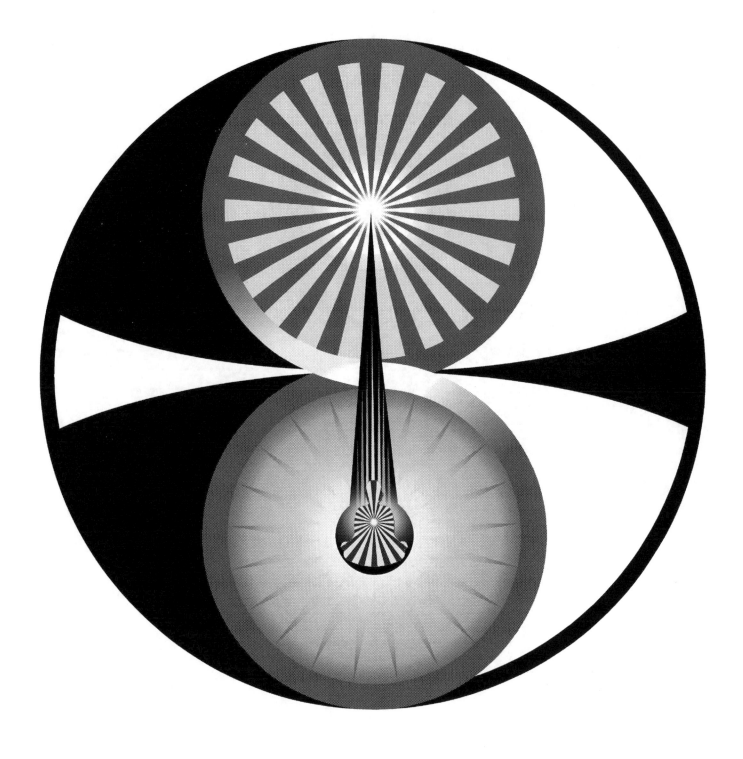

XVII

CONCLUSION - SACRED DESTINY

PRIMARY CHOICES FOR CULTIVATING INNER FREEDOM
Today I choose to align with Life, be grateful, develop my potential, and be of service to others.

Most types of flowers will grow and blossom to some degree
 In soil that has an adequate amount of basic nutrients, sunlight, and moisture.

Yet experienced gardeners know if they want to produce flowers with more vibrant blossoms,
 They can furnish their plants with specific nutrients to boost their natural growth.

For when flowers receive added beneficial nourishment,
 They can more easily develop into their next expression of beauty.

Of course, a gardener could choose to sit back and do absolutely nothing
 By simply watching their flower garden grow on its own without any additional help.

But if a gardener intentionally chooses to enhance the development of the flower's life cycle,
 Then a whole new level of blossoming and beauty can be attained.

The same is true regarding "the inward blossoming of our everyday lives"
 As we, over time, become aware of the natural yearning in us to awaken spiritually.

If we, like the seasoned gardener, decide to enhance the quality of our life experience
 By intentionally choosing to cultivate inner freedom - and learn to love unconditionally,
  Then "the radiant garden that grows within our heart can more fully blossom".

One powerful choice we can make to help encourage this flourishing
 Is to engage in some form of daily **meditation or silence**
  As a practice to keep our awareness aligned with *the Source of Life*.

Furthermore, each day we can choose to embrace **the Pillars of Awakening**, which are:
 1) Be grateful for what we're learning from every experience of our life,
  2) Surrender everything in our life to *a Greater Power* and let go of attachments,
   3) Accept that our life is unfolding perfectly just as it is,
    And 4) deepen our awareness of our Oneness with all of life.

It can also be liberating to expand our conscious awareness of what really matters
 And learn to embrace a more compassionate perspective of what our life is truly about.

An expansive spiritual perspective has the blessing of bringing us to a place within our heart
 Of living with greater empathy and inclusion of others - and all creatures of the Earth,
  As well as inspiring us to **develop our potential** - and realize who we really are.

Finally, an important choice to help cultivate our inner freedom
 Is to choose to contribute our creative gifts to the life-affirming progression of evolution
  And generously **serve the wellbeing of others**.

If we desire for "our garden of life to flourish" so we may experience our next level of possibility
 We can choose to nourish ourselves with the kind of "beneficial nutrients"
  That will help us blossom into our sacred destiny - of living an awakened life.

Circle of Primary Choices For Cultivating Inner Freedom

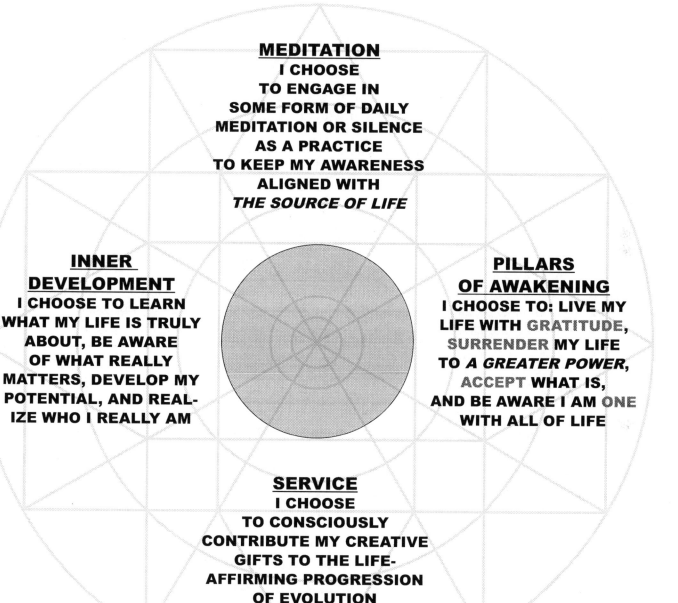

MEDITATION
I CHOOSE
TO ENGAGE IN
SOME FORM OF DAILY
MEDITATION OR SILENCE
AS A PRACTICE
TO KEEP MY AWARENESS
ALIGNED WITH
THE SOURCE OF LIFE

**INNER
DEVELOPMENT**
I CHOOSE TO LEARN
WHAT MY LIFE IS TRULY
ABOUT, BE AWARE
OF WHAT REALLY
MATTERS, DEVELOP MY
POTENTIAL, AND REAL-
IZE WHO I REALLY AM

**PILLARS
OF AWAKENING**
I CHOOSE TO: LIVE MY
LIFE WITH GRATITUDE,
SURRENDER MY LIFE
TO *A GREATER POWER*,
ACCEPT WHAT IS,
AND BE AWARE I AM ONE
WITH ALL OF LIFE

SERVICE
I CHOOSE
TO CONSCIOUSLY
CONTRIBUTE MY CREATIVE
GIFTS TO THE LIFE-
AFFIRMING PROGRESSION
OF EVOLUTION
AND TO SERVE THE
WELLBEING OF OTHERS

"THE BIG QUESTIONS"

I frequently ask the questions that help me expand my awareness of what my life is truly about.

At some moment during your life, you have probably walked outside in the early morning chill
And noticed the alluring sight of a spider web ornamented with glittering dewdrops
That sparkled like tiny diamonds in the golden rays of the Sun.

Spiders patiently sit at the center of their fragile webs, which they weave with delicate strands
Waiting for flying insects to unsuspectingly enter - and be helplessly caught in their lairs.

We can use the image of a web as a metaphor to appreciate how the practice of contemplation
Can be a technique for "gathering insights and revelations in the net of an open mind".

Contemplation is a practice in which we still our mind, ask a question about an idea to explore,
And then witness our thoughts being directed by *Life* into a flow of patterned awareness
That brings us greater clarity about the question - through revelation or intuition.

Each inspired inquiry or question we offer to *Life* can feel like "a vast net of unlimited potential",
A net where various expansive thoughts are gathered into "a container of possibility"
Attracting "the winds of revelation" that we simply behold in our awareness.

"The web of contemplation" is invisibly formed within us to catch soaring intuitions and insights,
And snare ever-expansive perspectives of greater understanding and compassion,
Yet allows "the clouds of illusion", or loveless thinking, to pass right through.

There are numerous types of contemplative practices that are valuable and revelatory,
And one important practice is frequently asking *the perennial questions of life*.

For example, **"Why am I here?"**, **"What really matters?"**, **"What is my life truly about?"**,
And the question **"Who am I?"** that has been asked by countless people for millennia.

When we ask these kinds of questions, it's similar to panning for gold in a mountain stream
Where dirt and mud pass through the sifter, yet *the precious gold* is what remains.

"The Big Questions" are like powerful telescopes that peer into a starry sky,
For they help us gain a greater understanding of life's mysteries and paradoxes.

Every time we ask these questions, it's as if we're gazing into a new corner of the Universe
And just as the vast Cosmos seems to be infinite and unbounded,
The answers or revelations we receive from these questions are also boundless.

As the stunning geometric images of computer generated fractal patterns advance endlessly
Creating more and more exquisite shapes and colors as the visual patterns unfold,
"The so-called answers" to these life-defining questions go on eternally as well
Never ceasing to inform us with greater awareness and understanding.

And as this autumn season comes to completion on the eve of the winter solstice,
Our perpetual questioning of life - and our *infinite awakenings* - continue on and on
As we frequently draw on these "Big Questions" so as to peer into possibility.

Circle of "The Big Questions"
(The Perennial Inquiry of Life)

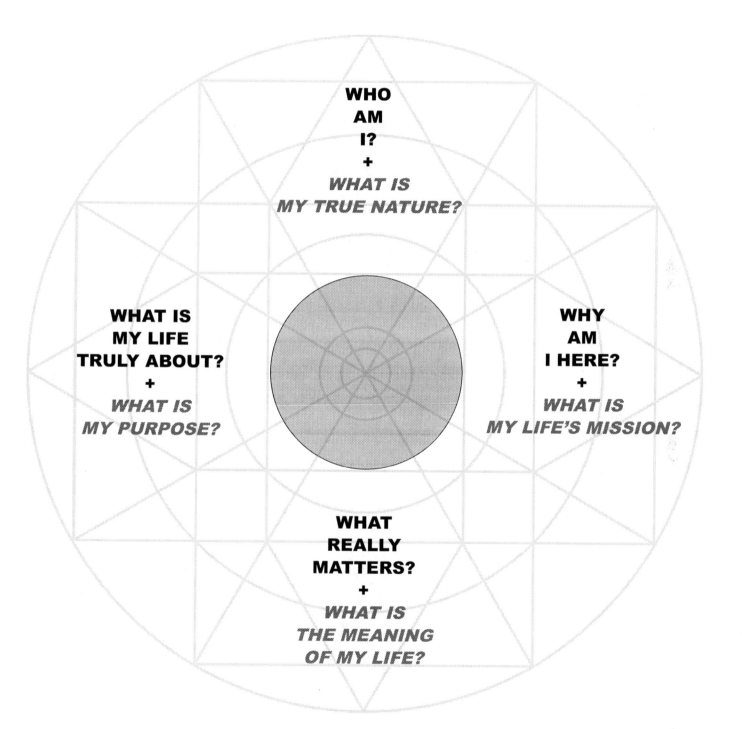

WHO
AM
I?
+
*WHAT IS
MY TRUE NATURE?*

WHAT IS
MY LIFE
TRULY ABOUT?
+
*WHAT IS
MY PURPOSE?*

WHY
AM
I HERE?
+
*WHAT IS
MY LIFE'S MISSION?*

WHAT
REALLY
MATTERS?
+
*WHAT IS
THE MEANING
OF MY LIFE?*

This series of Contemplative Practices continues in

The Winter Volume: December 21 – March 18

The Spring Volume: March 19 – June 19

The Summer Volume: June 20 – September 21

The Great Circle Mantra

My life is unfolding perfectly
Just the way it is
Because all that truly exists
Is *Perfect Love*
Yet I am here
To help the world become more perfect
By living my life
Perfectly guided by Love

Introduction To The Poem - *A Very Fortunate Sailor*

This poem was inspired by one of the Contemplation Circles from the Winter Volume of **Journey of The Great Circle** called "An Ocean Journey - a Metaphor for *the Journey of Awakening*".

This Contemplation Circle explores the idea that life is *a journey of discovery, a journey of self-mastery, a spiritual journey*. It is a transformative journey of ever-expansive learning and inner development in which we, as individuals, naturally ascend or develop through ever-higher stages of awareness.

In this metaphoric story-poem, the journey begins in a stage of awareness in which we believe in the illusion that we are a victim of life's difficulties and afflictions. As a helpless victim in a hostile world, it initially seems we have little or no control over them.

Yet eventually over time our awareness expands, based on what we discover from our diverse life experiences. We learn ever-greater perspectives of who we really are and, thus, begin to take more conscious responsibility for our life. As we do this, the vessel of our heart and mind becomes more evolved and more developed.

Each progressive vessel of experience that we become aware of allows us to move through the adventure of our life with more peace, harmony, and inner freedom. Ultimately we discover there is nowhere to go and nothing to do – only to be the magnificence of who we have always been.

— *Oman Ken*

This poem is an excerpt from Oman Ken's poetry book entitled
"Infinite Awakenings – Philosophical Story Poems Envisioning A More Glorious World".

A Very Fortunate Sailor

Once again - it was the perpetual sunrise of his life
He had faced a similar taste of dawn a thousand times before
For *the Exalted Essence* of his being had fashioned for him
Myriad uncharted oceans where he might carry out his investigations
His epic expeditions to explore the limitless realms of enchantment
The places where the budding flower of his heart
Could blossom into more generous fields of glory
To reveal the jewel of what is genuine and unquestionable
Of that which never changes

Yet - during this precise morning of his endless voyage
His newborn eyes were still blinded
By the abject drudgery and seeming havoc of a hostile world
His heavy heart still thickly veiled
In the unrelenting illusions reigning down
His busy mind still cluttered
With the meaningless pursuits of untamed desires

And then - once more
As he had done so many times before
He drifted without direction upon a vast ocean
Floating on his tiny raft without sail or rudder
Haphazardly being tossed by winds and waves
Mechanically thrown from one ripple to another
Until the long hard day of his life
Came to an unavoidable completion
At the caress of midnight

It required countless arduous eons
Of aimlessly drifting upon his rudimentary crafts - time and time again
Until finally he landed within a promised dawn of his life
In which everything was by some means altered
As if he was now looking out
From a more elevated precipice upon the mountain
Where his novel insights and broadened perspectives
Invited him to embrace a more lucious reality
One that offered him
A superior way to journey forward

The paltry rudderless raft dissolved
  While his *Sublime Essence* sculpted yet another vessel
    A sea-worthy ship erected to navigate an immense ocean
      A finely constructed craft with large sails
        To seize the grandeur of the wind
          And a stable rudder to forge a calculated direction
            Like an arrow thrust towards its target
              Released from the bow of an unruffled heart

It was a range of probing questions about meaning
  His authentic inquiry into purpose
    The passionate search for life's greater story
      That positioned him behind the ship's helm
        Steering this majestic vessel
          Knowingly navigating its course
            Until the day of his life expired
              Into one more portal of midnight's silence

Yet again - sundry eons passed
  Until he found himself at an unparalleled morning of his life
    Where this time - his *Oceanic Heart* knew he was ready
      And thus patterned a majestic schooner
        With multiple masts of colossal sails
          Attached to wooden decks expertly crafted
            And highly ornamented with seasoned artistry

On this voyage he became skilled
  At surrendering his entire ship
    And all longstanding control
      To the benevolent commands of an *Inner Captain*
        To an *Ultimate Force*
          Orchestrating the ceaseless unfolding of the Cosmos
            To the *Intelligence* that ultimately commands all ships
              That persistently explore and chart
                The unending corners of existence

On this schooner - there was nowhere to go
  Yet he reached every distant shore amid perfect timing
    On this regal vessel - there was nothing to do
      Yet the world he sailed was becoming
        A more glorious sanctuary with each fleeting sunset

But just as all ships assemble their allotted time at sea
   And must one day revert to the eventual fate of dry dock
      This schooner too found its way back to the harbor
         From its wealth of revelations upon a boundless ocean
            And disappeared into the next threshold of midnight

It is a very fortunate sailor
   Who one day awakens to that destined dawning of life mastery
      Who recognizes that *Life* perfectly navigates life
         That *"The One"* who truly pilots the schooner
            And the *"Inner Captain"*
               As well as the "Journeyer upon the Ocean"
                  Are now - and have always been - one and the same

Then and there - he watched himself
   Begin to share with others
      The saga of his epic adventure
         Declaring that as every sailor
            First embarks upon their ocean odyssey
               They may initially believe they need to steer the ship
               But in reality - all they need do is enjoy the ride

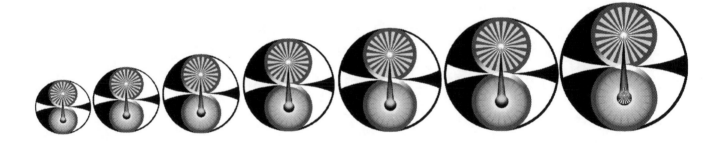

✳ JOURNEY OF *THE GREAT CIRCLE* – GLOSSARY OF TERMS ✳

Being defines the invisible and formless realm of *the Transcendent*. It is the sublime realm of existence in which all that exists is *Transcendent Oneness* - all that exists is *Absolute Perfection* - all that exists is *Unbounded Eternity* - all that exists is *Limitless Love*.

Becoming defines the natural process within any form of life that is developing its potential - which leads to manifesting more diverse creative expressions of itself or its environment. In relation to human beings, *Becoming* is one's *journey of awakening*. It is the *journey of discovery* or *spiritual journey* regarding one's inner development, the expansion of one's awareness, or one's spiritual awakening - which leads to greater contributions of one's creative gifts and talents employed in the service of others. *Becoming* can also be referred to as "one's creative actions and expressions to help make the world a better place".

Biosphere is *the Universal Consciousness* that gives shape to all biological life like microbes, plants, animals, which have evolved physical sensations and basic emotions.

Cause and Effect – The originating cause of everything within the phenomenal Universe is consciousness. The resulting effect from the creative intelligence of consciousness is the manifestations within the world of form (creation).

Consciousness is the invisible *Force of Natural Intelligence* which creates the visible world - the non-physical *Transcendent Power* which creates the physical Universe - an intangible internal *Awareness* which creates a tangible external reality. It is the invisible field of natural intelligence and information of any material or phenomenal structure that determines and gives creative shape to its visible form or pattern. Consciousness is the transcendent interiority of any structure of life which is the animating creative power that brings exterior form to its temporal body.

There is always some facet of consciousness (or natural intelligence) in every form of material expression within the Universe, such as the unique consciousness in every human being, animal, plant, micro-organism, rock, planet, star, galaxy, and beyond.

Consciousness is also the level or ability of a manifested form or structure within the Universe to be aware of, and respond to, experiences in its environment. A plant has a limited ability to respond to its environment. Whereas an animal has a greater, more developed ability. As far as is generally accepted, human beings have the greatest ability to be aware of, and respond to, experiences in their environment, and thus it is said that humans have the most evolved consciousness of all creatures on Earth.

Creation defines the phenomenal embodiment of the material realm. It is all expressions of the Universe - such as galaxies, stars, planets, microorganisms, plants, animals, and humans. Creation is also a word that represents the world of Nature.

In this book, the words Nature, Sun, Moon, Earth, Solar System, Universe, Cosmos are capitalized to represent that at a particular realm of consciousness, they are each a living entity of creation which is to be held in reverence, respect, honor, and is to be seen as sacred.

Emergent Healing is the spontaneous transformation that instantaneously happens within our body, heart, or mind when we experience a radical and profound shift in consciousness. *Emergent healing* is an extraordinary change and sudden balance that occurs in our being when we experience an internal "quantum leap" to a higher stage of awareness.

At these higher stages of awareness where we embody a greater level of wholeness, various forms of disease and imbalance, which we may have encountered previously, can no longer exist within the elevated frequency of *Limitless Love*.

Enlightenment is the sublime embodiment of inner freedom - which is living at a stage of spiritual consciousness where one abides in inner peace no matter what occurs. *Enlightenment* (from the perspective of this book) is not only about one's personal *awakening* or awareness of Oneness with God *(the Transcendent)*, but that any sustained individual alignment with *Ultimate Reality* must also be embodied and grounded within one's physical body and then shared collectively through the personal actions of serving the wellbeing of others.

In some contemporary spiritual groups, the concept of *enlightenment* is now perceived as an ongoing experience of loving others and loving self unconditionally while serving the good within all of life.

Evolution is the creative and natural development within all of life. It is the response within every phenomenon to *the Natural Intelligence* of the Universe which directs each facet of existence to further develop, expand its possibilities, create diversity, and express more of its potential.

The Evolutionary Impulse is *the Natural Intelligence* within the Universe that animates every material form along a path of perpetual creative unfoldment. It is the transcendent organizing principle within all of Creation. It can be thought of as *the Infinite Creativity* within all of existence that intelligently shapes and organizes higher expressions of manifested form such as galaxies, stars, oceans, myriad life forms, and every human being.

The Evolutionary Impulse is (from a religious perspective) the same as *the Universal Force of God* that guides development and manifestation within all forms of the natural world. It is the *Force* that "attracts together" sub-atomic particles, the planets in their solar orbits, all interdependent ecosystems, as well as two lovers who experience romantic passion.

Evolutionary Perspective – see Evolutionary Spirituality

Evolutionary Spirituality is a phrase that describes a "Big Picture Perspective" way of thinking about how our lives develop and transform. Evolutionary spirituality provides us with the gifts of a much larger perspective of reality inspiring us to further develop our higher potential, to motivate us to transform our fear-based self-oriented nature, to create the seeds of greater compassion for all of life, and to take responsible conscious actions toward building a more sustainable future.

Evolutionary spirituality merges both *the Transcendent Power of Consciousness* and the myriad forms of creation. It unifies God with evolution. It is the awareness which embraces a Oneness of an *Infinite and Eternal Intelligence* with an ever-unfolding Universe.

Existence is defined as the totality of the physical and the non-physical, the visible and the invisible, the Immanent and *the Transcendent*. It is the wholeness and merging of consciousness and creation, God and the Universe, Spirit and form, *"The One"* and *"The Many"*, *Being* and *Becoming*.

Fractals are natural objects or mathematical patterns that repeat themselves at smaller scales in which a reduced-size copy of the initial pattern is formed in succeeding generations, typically producing new emergent variations within each later generation.

There is also a group of *fractal patterns* that repeat themselves identically as they get smaller, yet the vast majority of *fractals* repeat their patterns with slight variations each time generating new and novel formations at different levels of magnification.

For example, trees grow in *fractal patterns* both above and below the ground, as well as the veins and arteries within the human body. Other *fractal patterns* that occur in the natural world are not as obvious - such as the way amorphous clouds slowly accumulate and form in the sky, how the ragged rock edges of mountain ranges are structured, the manner in which the coastlines of countries take shape, and how the patterns of galaxies and solar systems are created.

God – see *the Transcendent*

The Great Circle is "a spiritual map of an awakening life" which illustrates that our inner development determines and gives creative shape to how our external reality is expressed in our life. In other words, it portrays the universal dynamics of our inward expansion of consciousness mirrored as our outward creative expression.

There are many examples of traditional iconic images that represent *The Great Circle* - such as the Yin Yang symbol, the Star of David, the medicine wheel, and the sacred cross.

The primary function of **The Great Circle** as a transformative tool is to simply portray a useful collection of words and phrases for the purpose of deeply comprehending the nature of existence. With this awareness we can develop a greater understanding of what our life is truly about and what really matters - and thus, cultivate an unconditional love for each expression of life.

Holiness and Magnificence is another way of describing our *True Eternal Nature*, our *Transcendent Self*, who we really are. In religious language, it is our sacred divinity.

Infinite Awakenings represents the perpetual evolution and constant development that occurs in every phenomenal structure in the Universe - including galaxies, stars, planets, animals, plants, micro-organisms, and humans. "Awakening" describes a natural process of "developing to a higher level of awareness" or "expanding to a more elevated stage of consciousness" or "evolving to a new species". "Infinite" points to the awareness that *Life's* "awakenings" continue on and on without end.

Infinite Intelligence – see *The Transcendent*

The Infinite Presence of Love – see *The Transcendent*

Inner Freedom is when one consciously realizes the perfection that's always unfolding within - and within all of life. Living with this awareness allows the natural states of peace, happiness, joy and harmony to effortlessly arise. It is a life of one who has devotedly learned to love others and all of life unconditionally - and who has gained the joyful awareness of serving the wellbeing of others. In these writings, one who attains this level of mastery is referred to as a **Master of Freedom**.

Therefore, when we are aligned with *the Source of Life* - and gratefully celebrate every experience we have while fully loving and accepting ourselves, as well as every part of life - we are free.

Journey of Awakening is the natural evolutionary journey of ongoing inner development that every person in the world is constantly embarked on (whether he or she is consciously aware of it or not). Over time, this *journey of discovery* becomes conscious and intentional through a process of expanding one's awareness, transforming one's beliefs, discovering how to master a life of inner freedom, and contributing one's creative gifts and talents to the wellbeing of others. This is also referred to as the *spiritual journey* or the *journey of self-mastery*.

Life (when italicized and spelled with a capital) is a word that represents *the Transcendent, the Source of All That Is, the Infinite Intelligence* of the Universe. It is a short way of referring to *the Source of Life*. When "life" is not italicized and capitalized, it represents our human existence in the physical world.

Limitless Love – see *The Transcendent*

"The Many" can be defined in a number of ways, such as the myriad forms of life, the countless expressions of natural creativity on the Earth and throughout the Universe, all that is created, the endless manifestations of creation, etc. In relation to human beings, *"The Many"* is the totality of all humans that exist on the planet. Every person is a unique creative expression of *"The Many".*

Master of Freedom is a visionary archetype that represents our *Fully Awakened Self,* one's *True Eternal Nature* completely experienced and lived within one's physical body. It is the embodied realization of a person who lives a life of inner freedom, loves all of life unconditionally, and serves the good of all with their creative gifts and talents. It is every person's sacred destiny to embody the *Awakened Self* and fully experience their life as a **Master of Freedom.**

Morphogenetic Field is a phrase used in developmental biology and consciousness studies that proposes there is a tangible field of energy that's generated by all things, both physical structures and even mental constructs, which serves to organize the structure's characteristics and patterns.

When we consciously align ourselves to *the morphogenetic field of a specific visionary archetype*, we begin a process of personally resonating to the archetype - and bringing into our awareness the expansive qualities and visionary characteristics which the archetype symbolizes.

Noosphere is *the Universal Consciousness* that gives shape to both the individual and collective mind, which resides within all intelligent life forms.

"The One" – see *The Transcendent*

Oneness is Ultimate Reality in which every form of creation is a unique expression of one *Unity*. It can be described as Infinite Reality in which each expression of life is an integral part of *one unfolding never-ending spiral of Consciousness*. Oneness can be thought of as Quantum Reality in which all of the manifest world of form is made of the same *universal energy (Light)* in constant motion. It can also be described as Transcendent Reality in which the Universe and everything in it is comprised of *one Universal Love*, and many people simply call this *Love* - "God".

Paradox is the perception that two discrete realities which contradict each other both exist at the same time. It is the notion that two expressions of reality which are complete polar opposites can both take place at once.

In the writings of **Journey of The Great Circle**, embracing the existential paradoxes of life is a key to the cultivation of spiritual awakening. Embracing certain paradoxes enables us to merge consciousness with creation - God with the Universe - *Heaven* with Earth.

Physiosphere is *the Universal Consciousness* that gives shape to all material structures in the Universe - such as atoms, galaxies, stars, mountains, etc.

The Source of Life (The Source of All That Is) – see *The Transcendent*

Spiritual Journey – see *Journey of Awakening*

The Transcendent is the *Supreme Ubiquitous Intelligence* that is beyond form. It represents the invisible and formless *Natural Intelligence* throughout the Universe. *The Transcendent* is the sublime organizing principle which fashions everything in the manifested world of the material realm.

For millennia, this *Natural Intelligence* has been referred to in many ways throughout the world (The Thousand Names of the Divine) - such as *the Source of Life, Universal Consciousness, Pure Awareness, God, Allah, Tao, the Creator, the Great Spirit, the Great I Am, the Infinite Presence of Love, the Unbounded Ocean of Being, "The One", Infinite Intelligence, Limitless Love*, and so many more exquisite names for this sublime *Transcendent Power*. In many religious traditions this *Natural Intelligence* is simply referred to as "God".

(Note: Words that represent *"The Transcendent"* within **Journey of The Great Circle** are capitalized and italicized)

The Transcendent Impulse is defined as a constant spiritual yearning that we become aware of in our lifetime. It is the natural impulse to expand our awareness of what our life is truly about, to develop our potential, and to awaken to who we really are (an ascending impulse).

At the same time, it is the constant spiritual yearning of our expanding inner development to manifest ever-new expressions of creativity in our life (a descending impulse). This intrinsic and constant yearning (which is both the longing for spiritual awakening and for spiritual embodiment) that perpetually exists within us and within all forms of life - is called *the Transcendent Impulse*.

True Eternal Nature is the invisible transcendent consciousness of who we really are. It is the part of us that is eternal, unbounded, and limitless. Our *True Nature* is the aspect of who we are that guides and directs our life when we have learned to be aware of it.

There are numerous names for our *True Eternal Nature* - such as *the Higher Self, the Transcendent Self, the Authentic Self, the Essential Self, the Divine Self.* In many religious traditions, it is commonly referred to as the *"Soul"*. Within **Journey of The Great Circle** it is also called our "holiness and magnificence".

The Unbounded Ocean of Being – see *The Transcendent*

The Unified Field is a term, which comes from quantum physics, that's defined as a limitless field of all possibilities that is formless and unbounded from which everything in the entire known Universe has emerged. Many religious traditions speak of this *Field* simply as "God" - or "The Kingdom of God" - or the Divine.

Unisphere is *Universal Consciousness* - which can also be referred to as *"The One", the Oneness within all of Consciousness, the Source of All That Is, Infinite Intelligence, The Unified Field, God.*

Universal Consciousness – see *The Transcendent*

Visionary Archetypes are poetic images of our greater potential or possibility. They represent qualities and virtues on ever-higher levels of human consciousness. Visionary archetypes are symbolic templates that point us to higher stages of inner development and to the qualities and realms of creative expression we strive to achieve. They can be thought of as pictorial representations of superior moral qualities which can empower and motivate us to express something greater in ourselves, a promise of a more positive future for our life.

❊ THE STORY OF AWAKENING WITHIN THE FIRST NARRATIVES ❊

IN THE CONCEPTUAL DESIGN of **Journey of The Great Circle**, there is a poetic interweaving of themes within the first four contemplative narratives of each volume. Together these four narratives reveal "a hidden archetypal story" about every person's *spiritual journey of discovery*.

The first four narratives of the Autumn Volume are:
1) Gifts of Autumn
2) Qualities Within the Seasons of Life
3) The Great Story of Awakening
4) *Journey of Awakening*

The Transcendent Gifts of the Four Seasons

The first narrative of every volume depicts the transcendent gifts of each season, such as "Gifts of Autumn" in this volume. Each season has four qualities listed that describe important interior aspects of our unfolding lives. Every quality has a particular placement either in the north, east, south, or west orientation.

Qualities Within the Seasons of Life

The second narrative within each of the four volumes is called "Qualities Within the Seasons of Life". This narrative lists all the transcendent qualities from the season on the previous page as well as all four qualities from each of the other seasons from the remaining volumes. Therefore, each of the four seasons displays four essential qualities (totaling sixteen individual qualities) that relate to our human developmental journey.

The Great Story of Awakening

The third narrative of each volume is called "The Great Story of Awakening". This narrative explains how the universal archetypal story of our spiritual awakening can be derived from organizing the four transcendent qualities from each of the four seasons into four specific chapters of a "story" that we are calling "The Great Story". These four chapters are the key components of the universal story of an awakening life (The Great Story) - and are listed as:

1) *The Great Circle*
2) Pillars of Awakening
3) Master of Freedom
4) Spheres of Contribution

"The Great Story of Awakening" can be thought of as "the spiritual portrayal of an awakening life" - and is the personal story of our conscious inner development and expansion of our awareness. It is our individual *journey of awakening*, our *journey of self-mastery*, in which we learn to awaken to a higher stage of spiritual consciousness.

The First Chapter: *The Great Circle*

The first chapter of "The Great Story of Awakening" is called **The Great Circle.** This chapter is formulated by gathering the first or top quality of each season from the previous narrative entitled "Qualities Within the Seasons of Life". The chapter of **The Great Circle** includes the following four qualities:

1) From **Winter:**   Align With *"The One"*   - (renewal and alignment)
2) From **Spring:**   Outward Expression   - (creativity and contribution)
3) From **Summer:**   Serve *"The Many"*   - (service to others and cultivating self-care)
4) From **Autumn:**   Inward Expansion   - (development and expanding awareness)

As we explore the daily narratives throughout this book, we will be introduced to the various dynamics at play in the world and in our lives. The first chapter called **The Great Circle** speaks to the natural invitation from *The Transcendent Impulse of Life* to learn what our life is truly about, discover what really matters, and cultivate an awareness of how to live a life of inner freedom.

The Second Chapter: Pillars of Awakening

In the first chapter, **The Great Circle** invites us to explore the Big Questions of *Life* and what our life is truly about. The personal inner development from this pursuit provides us with insights about the next segment of our unfolding story of discovery.

The second chapter, **Pillars of Awakening**, is created by gathering the second set of transcendent qualities from the narrative "Qualities Within the Seasons of Life". This includes the four following qualities:

1) **Winter:**   Oneness
2) **Spring:**   Acceptance
3) **Summer:**   Surrender
4) **Autumn:**   Gratitude

These four qualities are actually different ways to describe self-love and unconditional love - and are the personal attributes we develop using daily transformative practice to consciously transform our suffering into a life of inner freedom.

As an *artist of life*, we practice these spiritual attributes as a way to develop our highest expression of ourselves, as a means to cultivate our creative potential, and as a vehicle to reach for the next horizon of possibility of what we can become. Through our daily practice, we learn to maintain an ongoing alignment with *the Essence of Creation, the Source of Life, the Love of God.* And we reconnect with a natural transcendent yearning within us to feel this alignment in every moment of our life.

The Third Chapter: Master of Freedom

As we develop spiritual maturity and learn to maintain an alignment with *Life*, with *the Source of All That Is* we enter into the third chapter of our *awakening journey*, **Master of Freedom**.

Master of Freedom is the visionary archetypal image of an individual who is a fully integrated awakened being - and who experiences inner freedom, consciously maintains an alignment with *the Source of All That Is,* and uses his or her unique gifts and talents to serve the good of all. The chapter **Master of Freedom** is formulated by gathering the third set of transcendent qualities from the narrative "Qualities Within the Seasons of Life". This includes the qualities:

1) **Winter:**   Awakened Presence
2) **Spring:**   Endless Creativity
3) **Summer:**   Unconditional Love
4) **Autumn:**   Limitless Development

Through dedicated daily transformative practice these four qualities empower us to integrate our inner development into our everyday life as an embodied and anchored experience. These are the qualities of consciously cultivating the mastery of living a life of inner freedom - in other words, living an awakened life. Once this level of spiritual awareness has been realized, it becomes obvious that the most important way to use our creative energy is to offer our unique mission to the world through our personal contributions. Furthermore, we recognize how natural it is to follow the inner guidance of our heart as we share our novel contributions to help create a more glorious world.

The Fourth Chapter: Spheres of Contribution

The fourth chapter of "The Great Story of Awakening" is called **Spheres of Contribution**. As we explore this chapter, we discover ever-greater ways of living in this world and offering our creative gifts and talents. The chapter **Spheres of Contribution** gathers the fourth set of transcendent qualities from the narrative "Qualities Within the Seasons of Life". These include:

1) **Winter:**   Contributions to Oneself
2) **Spring:**   Contributions to Family
3) **Summer:**   Contributions to Community
4) **Autumn:**   Contributions to the World

When we learn to maintain an experience of living our life with peace of mind and inner freedom, the next obvious and intrinsic awareness is for us to serve the wellbeing of others - and to contribute our unique creative gifts and talents.

When these four chapters, *The Great Circle*, **Pillars of Awakening, Master of Freedom,** and **Spheres of Contribution** are placed together sequentially, they form the universal great story of our spiritual awakening, or what has been referred to in this book as **"The Great Story of Awakening"**.

Quadrant Directions	Gifts of Autumn		Qualities Within the Seasons of Life		The Great Story of Awakening
NORTH **Winter**	**Inward Expansion**	* + – x	Align With *"The One"* Oneness Awakened Presence Contributions to Oneself	* * * *	***The Great Circle*** Align With *"The One"* Outward Expression Serve *"The Many"* **Inward Expansion**
EAST **Spring**	**Gratitude**	* + – x	Outward Expression Acceptance Endless Creativity Contributions to Family	+ + + +	**Pillars of Awakening** Oneness Acceptance Surrender **Gratitude**
SOUTH **Summer**	**Limitless Development**	* + – x	Serve *"The Many"* Surrender Unconditional Love Contributions to Community	– – – –	**Master of Freedom** Awakened Presence Endless Creativity Unconditional Love **Limitless Development**
WEST **Autumn**	**Contributions to the World**	* + – x	**Inward Expansion** **Gratitude** **Limitless Development** **Contributions to the World**	x x x x	**Spheres of Contribution** Contributions to Oneself Contributions to Family Contributions to Community **Contributions to the World**

Journey of Awakening

The fourth contemplative narrative found within each volume is entitled *"Journey of Awakening"*. It has been written as another pragmatic version and additional way of understanding the preceding narrative **"The Great Story of Awakening"**.

"Journey of Awakening", with its four stages that describe our *spiritual journey*, form the foundation for our conscious exploration and inner development of self throughout the four volumes of **Journey of The Great Circle**. The four stages are:

1) Development = *The Great Circle*
2) Transformation = Pillars of Awakening
3) Mastery = Master of Freedom
4) Contribution = Spheres of Contribution

✳ THE DANCE, POETRY, AND SONG OF THE FRONT COVER ART ✳

THE FRONT COVER ART of **Journey of *The Great Circle*** is a visual representation of the relationship between three facets of reality: the transcendent aspect of life, one's *Eternal Nature*, and one's physical embodiment. In other words - it is a symbolic representation of the integration of *Spirit*, *Soul*, and body.

We are so much more than we appear to be. Our physical bodies are just a small part of the magnificent totality of who we really are. The realm of our physical body is like an iceberg that appears above the surface of the water. Yet ninety percent of the mass of an iceberg remains invisible underneath the ocean's waters. Similarly a vast part of who we really are remains invisible to our senses, yet it is present in, and determines, every aspect of our life.

Our physical body is obviously visible in the world of form, yet our *True Eternal Nature* and *the Infinite Intelligence within All That Is,* which created everything in the Cosmos, is invisible to our five senses.

The artwork of the front cover symbolically represents this awareness, and gives us a visual metaphor to use to deepen our understanding of it.

The black and white meditator represents our physical body that is embarked on a *journey of discovery* to learn to love all of life unconditionally.

The gold branches and roots of the Tree of Life represent our *True Eternal Nature,* our *Higher Self,* our *Soul,* which is eternal and unbounded - and is the consciousness that is mirrored in our physical body.

The circle around the Tree of Life, as well as the Universe of infinite stars, represent *the Transcendent, the Infinite Intelligence* of the Universe, *the Source of All That Is.*

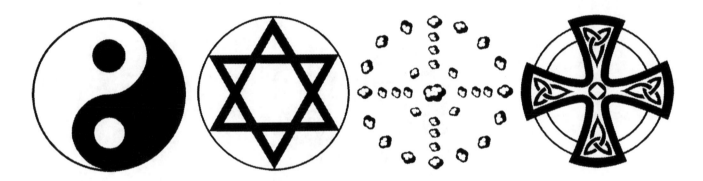

✳ RESOURCES ✳

Braden, Gregg. *The Isaiah Effect + The Divine Matrix*

Brown, Michael. *The Presence Process*

Capra, Fritjof. *The Tao of Physics*

Chopra, Deepak. *The Path of Love + The Seven Spiritual Laws of Success + How To Know God + Quantum Healing*

Cohen, Andrew. *Evolutionary Enlightenment + What Is Enlightenment Magazine*

Davies, Paul. *The Mind of God*

Dispenza, Joe. *Becoming Supernatural + Breaking the Habit of Being Yourself + You Are The Placebo*

Dowd, Michael. *Thank God For Evolution*

Green, Brian. *The Fabric of the Cosmos*

Hawkins, David. *Power Vs. Force + Discovery of the Presence of God + The Eye of the I*

Houston, Jean. *The Possible Human + Life Force + A Mythic Life*

Hubbard, Barbara Marx. *Conscious Evolution*

Katie, Byron. *Loving What Is*

Lipton, Bruce and Steve Bhaerman. *Spontaneous Evolution: Our Positive Future and a Way To Get There From Here*

Mandelbrot, Benoit. *The Fractal Geometry of Nature*

McTaggert, Lynne. *The Field*

Millman, Dan. *Way of the Peaceful Warrior*

Ming-Dao, Deng. *365 Tao Daily Meditations*

Moore, Robert and Douglas Gillette. *King, Warrior, Magician, Lover*

Morter, Sue. *The Energy Codes*

Murphy, Michael. *The Future of the Body*

Patten, Terry. *A New Republic of the Heart*

Ra, Kaia. *The Sophia Code*

Reich, Robert. *The Common Good*

Rudd, Richard. *The Gene Keys*

Swimme, Brian. *Canticle to the Cosmos*

Swimme, Brian and Thomas Berry. *The Universe Story*

Teilhard de Chardin. *The Human Phenomenon*

Tolle, Eckhart. *The Power of Now + A New Earth*

Trott, Susan. *The Holy Man*

Tzu, Lao. *The Way Of Life*

Wilbur, Ken. *The Marriage of Sense and Soul + Sex, Ecology, Spirituality - The Spirit of Evolution*

Williamson, Marianne. *A Return To Love + Enchanted Love + The Healing of America + Everyday Grace*

Yogananda, Paramahansa. *Autobiography of a Yogi*

There is a constant stream of Transcendent Energy,
a Field of Unlimited Creativity,
which surrounds us and permeates within us in every moment.
This Boundless and Transcendent Creativity
is who we really are.

✳ ACKNOWLEDGEMENTS ✳

I THANK THE FOLLOWING PEOPLE for helping me bring this creative project into form.

First, I thank my dear friend, Bob Sizelove, with whom I've shared many adventurous camping trips for over a decade. During one of these camping trips at a place we call "paradise", I received my first Contemplative Circle which became the springboard for **Journey of _The Great Circle_**. For years, Bob and I have discussed the primary themes of this book around a blazing campfire under a star-strung sky. Bob's deep devotion to God and his commitment to ongoing self-development and service has been an inspiring aspect for me in writing this book.

Next, I thank my friend, Jo Norris, for her constant support of my writings. Jo is a progressive and creative catalyst for change and has touched so many people with her loving presence and wisdom. She has touched and inspired me profoundly. Jo has been a supportive angel at many steps during the evolution of this book.

I thank my Beloved partner, Yana DiAngelis, for her unconditional love and perpetual support of seeing the holiness and magnificence within me. Her unwavering recognition of who I really am has been a powerful testament of the unconditional love and compassion that is possible for our glorious world. Her love gave me inner strength during the completion of this project.

I thank my Soul Friend and Anum Cara, Enocha Ranjita Ryan, for years of listening to me read each morning the daily contemplative narrative. She has been such a fervent and constant support of my creativity. Her steady love and the inspiring way she lives her life was so empowering to me in bringing these writings into manifestation.

Furthermore, I thank my dear friend, Maria Cavendish, for her loving support and encouragement all the many years as I spent time contemplating at the creek to bring through this body of work.

I thank my long time friend, Shambhu, who is a masterful guitar recording artist and creative wonder. Shambhu's consistent support and encouragement of all my creative endeavors has been a blessed gift in my life.

And I thank the following editing angels: Maureen Levy for her Amazonian feats, Chaka Ken-Varley, Robert Varley, Kathleen Haverkamp, Rhianne Teija Newluhnd, and those who have given me discerning feedback and assistance in various ways toward the polishing of this work: Shanti Norman, Karl Anthony, Mia Margaret, Charley Thweatt, and Iala Jaggs for showing me a magical place at the creek where I spent over 10 years downloading the inspiration for this book.

As a final note, I thank the following inspiring teachers of philosophical and spiritual viewpoints that have pointed me to embracing larger perspectives of what I believe my life is truly about and what really matters: Marianne Williamson, Jean Houston, Barbara Marx Hubbard, Deepak Chopra, Joe Dispenza, Dr. Sue Morter, Gregg Braden, Alan Cohen, Andrew Harvey, Ken Wilber, Michael Dowd, Brian Swimme, Andrew Cohen, Kaia Ra, and Paramahansa Yogananda.

✳ ABOUT THE AUTHOR ✳

Oman Ken has devoted his life to being a multi-instrumentalist and singer. He lives in a home filled with exotic instruments from around the world, and professionally has focused his musical presentations on the harp, guitar, piano, Native American and ethnic flutes, as well as the gift of his voice. He has performed hundreds of concerts and celebrations across the United States while creating 15 professional recordings of his original vocal and instrumental music.

Oman has also composed three Ritual Theater musicals which he directed and produced in Hawaii, entitled "Genesis: A Ritual of Transformation", "Starwheel: Journey of the Sacred Circle", and "The Mask and the Sword". Furthermore, he has produced myriad multi-media Solstice and Equinox Celebrations with a troupe of 25 people in Houston, Texas and Cincinnati, Ohio.

Oman has presented his transformational workshops: "The Ceremonial Art of Celebration", "Dance Movement as Spiritual Practice", and "The Power Within the Archetypes of the King, Warrior, Magician, and Lover", in various spiritual conferences and retreats around the United States.

After a challenging physical condition made it unfeasible to continue his musical travels, Oman deepened his spiritual quest for inner freedom by spending an abundance of time in Nature contemplating what life is truly about - and what really matters.

The result of his personal investigations was a host of poetic contemplative narratives that became the foundation for this book **Journey of The Great Circle**.

Oman now lives in the majestic Red Rocks of Sedona, Arizona.   JourneyOfTheGreatCircle.com

JOURNEY OF *THE GREAT CIRCLE*
DAILY AFFIRMATION STATEMENTS FOR AUTUMN

(Copy - then cut along the dotted lines to carry an affirmation with you each day)

I - THE DANCE OF THE INFINITE SEASONS

SEPTEMBER 22 or 23   GIFTS OF AUTUMN
Celebrating the seasonal cycles is a way to gain new insights into the true purpose of my life.

SEPTEMBER 22 or 23   QUALITIES WITHIN THE SEASONS OF LIFE
Life is a mirror reflecting back to me all that longs to be developed, released, and transformed.

SEPTEMBER 24   THE GREAT STORY OF AWAKENING
Every morning I align my awareness with the Source of Life - and with what really matters.

SEPTEMBER 25   *JOURNEY OF AWAKENING*
Living my life in service to others is an actual demonstration that I have truly awakened.

SEPTEMBER 26   QUESTIONS THAT EMERGE FROM AN AWAKENED LIFE
Serving others is actually the same as serving myself - for we are all part of one Eternal Self.

SEPTEMBER 27   THE UNITY OF EXISTENCE
I fully accept that my life is unfolding perfectly - and is an integral part of one Unity.

II - THE POETRY OF *THE GREAT CIRCLE*

SEPTEMBER 28   *THE GREAT CIRCLE*
Life is a journey of self-mastery of my outer transformations mirroring my inner development.

SEPTEMBER 29   *THE GREAT CIRCLE* OF GIVING AND RECEIVING
As I give to others I also receive - for giving and receiving are one flow within the Circle of Life.

SEPTEMBER 30   *THE GREAT CIRCLE* OF THE SACRED CROSS

Expanding my awareness of what is true is mirrored within the many expressions of my creativity.

- -

OCTOBER 1   MANY SPIRITUAL PATHS ON *THE JOURNEY OF AWAKENING*

Every genuine spiritual path leads me to the same awakened realization of my Eternal Nature.

- -

OCTOBER 2   VERTICAL EVOLUTION

Life is constantly inviting me to awaken to, and embody, higher stages of consciousness.

- -

OCTOBER 3   HORIZONTAL EVOLUTION

Today I consciously deepen my relationships and connections with the people in my life.

- -

OCTOBER 4   *THE EVOLUTIONARY IMPULSE*

The Natural Intelligence that animates the Universe is the same Intelligence that animates me.

- -

OCTOBER 5   GOD AS "THE TRANSCENDENT"

Within the sanctuary of my heart, I am aware of my Oneness with the Limitless Source of Life.

- -

OCTOBER 6   CHI

I align with the Source of Limitless Power so that Life Force energy easily flows through me.

- -

III - <u>BODY AWARENESS PRACTICES</u>

OCTOBER 7   FOUNDATIONAL TRANSFORMATIVE PRACTICES

My daily transformative practices help me cultivate a life of peace and inner freedom.

- -

OCTOBER 8   THE PRACTICE OF PRAYER

I pray for the wellbeing of others through consciously co-creating with the Source of Life.

- -

OCTOBER 9   VARIOUS DIMENSIONAL FORMS OF EXERCISE

I maintain health and vitality so I may more effectively contribute my creative gifts and talents.

- -

IV - THE SONG OF EMBODIED LOVE

OCTOBER 10   THE NATURAL STATES THAT EMERGE FROM BEING

As I align my awareness with the Source of Life I attune myself to the natural state of peace.

OCTOBER 11   THE NATURAL STATE OF HARMONY

Today I feel in harmony with Life as I respond to the natural yearning within me to serve others.

OCTOBER 12   PILLARS OF AWAKENING

I am grateful for what I'm learning from every experience of my life.

OCTOBER 13   GRATITUDE

I feel grateful for the sublime gift of simply being alive.

OCTOBER 14   THE CYCLE OF ABUNDANCE

I embrace the natural "cycle of abundance and need" as an essential part of the Circle of Life.

V - BODY AWARENESS PRACTICES

OCTOBER 15   WELLBEING OF THE BODY

I consciously keep my body in a state of health and balance using daily self-care practices.

OCTOBER 16   NUTRITION

I nourish my body with energy from the Sun that has been transformed into vital nutrients.

OCTOBER 17   MOVING MEDITATION

I keep the channels within my body open so the Energy of Life may naturally flow through me.

VI - ARCHETYPES OF HIGHER KNOWLEDGE

OCTOBER 18   UNIVERSAL ARCHETYPES

Today I use my creative imagination to envision the best, most joyful future I can conceive.

OCTOBER 19   *THE GREAT CIRCLE* OF THE ARCHETYPES

My creative imagination is a powerful vehicle to help me manifest my unlimited potential.

OCTOBER 20   ARCHETYPES OF HIGHER KNOWLEDGE

I feel a natural yearning in me to seek the true, the good, and the beautiful within all of life.

OCTOBER 21   AWAKENED SCIENTIST

I live my life as an ongoing living experiment so I may cultivate greater awareness of what is true.

OCTOBER 22   FUNDAMENTAL UNIVERSAL PERSPECTIVES

As I expand my perspectives of what my life is truly about it helps me live a more meaningful life.

OCTOBER 23   DIMENSIONS OF EVOLUTION

As I embrace a more inclusive perspective of life, compassion for others blossoms within me.

OCTOBER 24   LIVING IN A STATE OF CONSCIOUS RELAXATION

Today I fully accept my life just as it is and, thus, I live in a state of conscious relaxation.

VII - BODY AWARENESS PRACTICES

OCTOBER 25   REST

Today I spend time in the sanctuary of silence so I may rest in the rejuvenative "Arms of Life".

OCTOBER 26   MAINTAINING AN AWARENESS OF WHOLENESS

Everywhere I look in the world around me I perceive Life's Perfect Wholeness.

OCTOBER 27   PHYSICAL BODY EXERCISES

I maintain a healthy body - and thus, I'm able to share more of my creative gifts and talents.

VIII - ARCHETYPES OF SPIRITUAL AWAKENING

OCTOBER 28   ARCHETYPES OF SPIRITUAL AWAKENING

I feel the limitless power of spiritual transformation that is constantly awakening in me.

OCTOBER 29   YOUNG AWAKENING SELF
I cultivate a conscious awareness of what is true so I may learn to live a life of inner freedom.

OCTOBER 30   EVOLUTION OF THE IDENTIFICATION OF SELF
My True Nature is eternal, unbounded, limitless, and one with the Source of Life.

OCTOBER 31   THE FEARFUL MIND
I am constantly guided each day to live my life within the awakened field of absolute safety.

NOVEMBER 1   SUFFERING
I relax into what is - the present moment - and accept that my life is unfolding perfectly.

NOVEMBER 2   SPHERES OF CONTROL
In this moment I have control of my choices, actions, intentions, and how I focus my attention.

IX - BODY AWARENESS PRACTICES

NOVEMBER 3   AFFIRMATIONS FOR CONSCIOUS LIVING
I consciously shape my future with new possibilities using my intentions and elevated emotions.

NOVEMBER 4   LONGEVITY
Today I choose to share my creative gifts and talents in intentional ways that serve others.

NOVEMBER 5   THE GIFTS OF CONSCIOUS BREATHING
I frequently stop to breathe deeply so I may anchor myself in the gift of the present moment.

X - THE EVOLUTIONARY PERSPECTIVE

NOVEMBER 6   GIFTS FROM AN EVOLUTIONARY PERSPECTIVE
Embracing an evolutionary perspective awakens a joy in me to develop my unlimited potential.

NOVEMBER 7   INDIVIDUAL LINES OF PERSONAL DEVELOPMENT
Today I consciously develop the areas of my life that polish "the diamond of my Soul".

NOVEMBER 8   THE FRACTAL NATURE OF EMERGENT EVOLUTION
The spiritual awakening that's unfolding in me is a natural part of the evolution of the Universe.

NOVEMBER 9   EVOLUTION OF LIFE AWAKENING
It is my sacred destiny to consciously awaken to, and fully realize, my True Eternal Nature.

NOVEMBER 10   EVOLUTION OF THE PURPOSE OF LIFE
I feel a natural yearning in me to learn, expand beyond my limits, and develop my potential.

NOVEMBER 11   EVOLUTION OF THE MEANING OF SUFFERING
I choose to perceive my experience of pain as an opportunity to cultivate inner freedom.

NOVEMBER 12   EVOLUTION OF ENLIGHTENMENT
It is my destiny, and my obligation to Life, to awaken to higher stages of spiritual awareness.

XI - ARCHETYPES OF CONSCIOUS CONTRIBUTION

NOVEMBER 13   SPHERES OF CONTRIBUTION
Today I use my creative gifts and talents to help build a more glorious world.

NOVEMBER 14   CONTRIBUTION TO THE WORLD
I use my creative imagination, together with others, to find novel ways to create a better world.

NOVEMBER 15   SPHERES OF ENLIGHTENED LEADERSHIP
Today I surrender my personal will so I may be guided by the Infinite Intelligence within me.

NOVEMBER 16   NATURAL ECONOMY OF RESOURCES
Today I cultivate a natural state of balance within myself so I may better serve the good of all.

NOVEMBER 17   SPIRITUAL PHILANTHROPIST
As I give to others I am giving to myself as well, for we're all interconnected as one global family.

NOVEMBER 18   EMPOWERING THE CHILDREN OF THE WORLD

Today I make responsible and integrous choices that empower the people in my life.

NOVEMBER 19   ARCHETYPES OF CONSCIOUS CONTRIBUTION

I consciously live my life in a way that serves, and contributes to, the wellbeing of others.

NOVEMBER 20   INTEGRAL HEALER

I surrender everything in my life to the Infinite Presence of Love, the true source of all healing.

NOVEMBER 21   GRACE

I consciously align my awareness with the Source of Life and, thus, I live in a state of grace.

NOVEMBER 22   MODES OF HEALING

A greater meaning for my life comes from offering kindness, loving fully, and serving others.

NOVEMBER 23   EMERGENCE

I feel a natural impulse in me inviting me to cultivate a life of inner freedom and service to others.

NOVEMBER 24   "HELIUM BALLOONS" (A METAPHOR FOR EMERGENT AWAKENING)

I offer compassion, loving care, and kindness to everyone I meet today.

XII - <u>BODY AWARENESS PRACTICES</u>

NOVEMBER 25   BLESSINGS

I offer simple acts of loving kindness to everyone I meet today.

NOVEMBER 26   PRAYERS FOR HEALING

Today I cultivate an open portal in my heart for the healing grace of Life to flow through me.

NOVEMBER 27   HARMONY WITH NATURE

I create balance with all the gifts I receive from Nature by what I give back in equal measure.

XIII - <u>ARCHETYPES OF LIFE MASTERY</u>

NOVEMBER 28   ARCHETYPES OF LIFE MASTERY
Today I use my creative imagination to help me become the person I desire to be.

- -

NOVEMBER 29   PEACEFUL WARRIOR
Today I embrace every experience of my life with courage, responsibility, and integrity.

- -

NOVEMBER 30   COURAGE
I am aligned with the Source of Life as I courageously walk into an unknown future.

- -

DECEMBER 1   CONSCIOUS RESPONSIBILITY
I am responsible for my peace of mind – and I consciously meet every situation with integrity.

- -

DECEMBER 2   UNLIMITED POSSIBILITY
I use my imagination joined with my joyful heart to consciously create the person I desire to be.

- -

DECEMBER 3   EXCELLENCE
I live my life as "an expression of art" – and thus, everything I do is a manifestation of beauty.

- -

DECEMBER 4   NATURAL CONFIDENCE
I experience natural confidence as I feel safe, loved, empowered, and connected to all of life.

- -

DECEMBER 5   ABSOLUTE SAFETY
Today I align with the Infinite Presence of Love and feel safe within the protective arms of Life.

- -

XIV - <u>BODY AWARENESS PRACTICES</u>

DECEMBER 6   BODY AWARENESS
I use the awareness within my body to consciously experience more aliveness and presence.

- -

DECEMBER 7   CONSCIOUS DREAMING
My evening dreams provide insight into informing my daily choices and developing my potential.

- -

DECEMBER 8   BALANCE OF DAILY ACTIVITY

I maintain a healthy balance in my life regarding my work, my play, my studies, and my prayers.

XV - <u>NAVIGATING THE JOURNEY OF *THE GREAT CIRCLE*</u>

DECEMBER 9   TRANSCENDENCE

The Source of Life is always inviting me to cultivate my next higher stage of spiritual awareness.

DECEMBER 10   TRANSCENDENT IMPULSES OF CONSCIOUSNESS

Experiencing silence is a sublime way to align my awareness with my Eternal Nature.

DECEMBER 11   *INTERIOR EVOLUTIONARY IMPULSE*

Life is always inviting me to consciously expand my awareness so I may learn to love more fully.

DECEMBER 12   MODES OF INNER DEVELOPMENT

I feel a natural yearning in me that constantly invites me to love and accept myself just as I am.

XVI - <u>THE ART OF TRANSFORMATION AND HEALING</u>

DECEMBER 13   *THE GREAT CIRCLE* OF DEVELOPMENT AND TRANSFORMATION

As I expand my awareness of what is true, I cultivate in me greater transformation and healing.

DECEMBER 14   *THE GREAT CIRCLE* OF THE SPHERES OF CONSCIOUSNESS AND FIELDS OF CREATION

As I learn what my life is truly about, my heart naturally opens to greater love and compassion.

DECEMBER 15   SPHERES OF CONSCIOUSNESS

Everything I perceive is made of universal energy that emerges from The Unified Field.

DECEMBER 16   OUTER EXPRESSIONS OF CONSCIOUSNESS

Everything in the world, as well as my body, is made of light vibrating at different frequencies.

DECEMBER 17   SPHERES OF BALANCING MODALITIES FOR THE
                     HUMAN BODY

As I align my awareness with the Infinite Presence of Love - my heart wisdom guides my life.

- -

DECEMBER 18   PROGRESSION OF HEALING AWARENESS

Learning what my life is truly about empowers me to choose inner freedom.

- -

XVII - <u>CONCLUSION — SACRED DESTINY</u>

DECEMBER 19   PRIMARY CHOICES FOR CULTIVATING INNER
                     FREEDOM

Today I choose to align with Life, be grateful, develop my potential, and be of service to others.

- -

DECEMBER 20   "THE BIG QUESTIONS"

I frequently ask the questions that help me expand my awareness of what my life is truly about.

Printed in the United States
by Baker & Taylor Publisher Services